GALLIPOLI
AND THE
DARDANELLES
1915–1916

DESPATCHES FROM THE FRONT

*The Commanding Officers' Reports from
the Field and at Sea*

GALLIPOLI AND THE DARDANELLES 1915–1916

Introduced and compiled by
John Grehan and Martin Mace

with additional research by
Sara Mitchell

Pen & Sword
MILITARY

First published in Great Britain in 2014 by
PEN & SWORD MILITARY
An imprint of
Pen & Sword Books Ltd
47 Church Street
Barnsley
South Yorkshire
S70 2AS

ISBN 978-1-78159-344-8

Typeset by Concept, Huddersfield, West Yorkshire HD4 5JL.
Printed and bound in England by CPI Group (UK) Ltd, Croydon CR0 4YY.

Pen & Sword Books Ltd incorporates the imprints of Pen & Sword Archaeology,
Atlas, Aviation, Battleground, Discovery, Family History, History, Maritime,
Military, Naval, Politics, Railways, Select, Social History, Transport, True Crime,
and Claymore Press, Frontline Books, Leo Cooper, Praetorian Press,
Remember When, Seaforth Publishing and Wharncliffe.

For a complete list of Pen & Sword titles please contact
PEN & SWORD BOOKS LIMITED
47 Church Street, Barnsley, South Yorkshire, S70 2AS, England
E-mail: enquiries@pen-and-sword.co.uk
Website: www.pen-and-sword.co.uk

Contents

List of Plates

General Sir Ian Standish Monteith Hamilton GCB, GCMG, DSO, TD.

General Sir Charles Carmichael Monro, 1st Baronet of Bearcrofts GCB, GCSI, GCMG.

A portrait of Vice-Admiral Sir John M. de Robeck by Francis Dodd, 1917.

The Allied naval bombardment of Turkish positions underway as a battleship fires its 12-inch guns in the Dardanelles Strait in 1915.

The Formidable-class pre-dreadnought battleship HMS *Irresistible* listing and sinking in the Dardanelles, 18 March 1915.

Allied troops disembarking on one of the landing beaches on the Gallipoli Peninsula, 25 April 1915. (HMP)

A contemporary artist's impression of the men of the 1st Battalion, Lancashire Fusiliers landing on 'W' Beach on 25 April 1915.

Soldiers of the Australian 1st Brigade row to the beach, whilst empty boats return from the shore to the destroyers, at about 09.45 hours on the morning of the Australians' landing at Anzac Cove, 25 April 1915.

Lancashire Fusiliers of the 125th Brigade bound for Cape Helles, Gallipoli, in May 1915.

Military supplies piled up at Anzac Cove in May 1915.

A photograph of 'V' Beach with the SS *River Clyde* beached in the background.

An artist's depiction of Captain Percy Hansen and Lance Corporal Breese, 6th Battalion, The Lincolnshire Regiment, retrieving a wounded soldier at Yilghin Burnu on 9 August 1915.

Detail from *The Taking of Lone Pine* (1921, oil-on-canvas) by the artist Fred Leist.

An Australian sniper using a periscope rifle at Gallipoli, 1915.

Members of 13th Battalion, AIF, occupying Quinn's Post on the heights above Anzac Cove.

Allied troops in a captured Turkish trench at Lone Pine on 6 August 1915.

The Gallipoli Peninsula is a spectacular place: steep valleys, deep ravines and high cliffs towering above long, narrow beaches.

'W' Beach at Cape Helles, Gallipoli, on 7 January 1916, just prior to the final evacuation of British forces.

A contemporary artist's depiction of the action for which Bombardier C.W. Cook, of the 368th Battery, Royal Field Artillery, was awarded the Distinguished Conduct Medal at Cape Helles.

The capture of the Lone Pine trenches by Australian and New Zealander troops on 7 August 1915.

The crowded beach at Anzac Cove.

Troops pictured occupying trenches at Quinn's Post, Anzac.

Troops being landed at Suvla Bay.

The busy scene at a dressing station which had been established at Suvla Bay.

The original caption to this image, which is almost certainly a staged scene, states: "A scene just before the evacuation at Anzac; Australian troops charging near a Turkish trench."

Part of the Gallipoli battlefields today: A recent view of 'V' Beach, on the other side of Cape Helles from 'W' Beach, taken from the direction of Cape Helles itself.

A reconstruction of the trenches dug by the Turkish troops on the Gallipoli Peninsula.

The Commonwealth War Graves Commission's memorial at Helles, Turkey.

Introduction

The operation against the Turkish Ottoman Empire which began in 1915 was originally intended to be nothing more than a demonstration to help relieve pressure on Britain and France's ally, Russia. Tsar Nicholas II's forces were fighting on two fronts and barely able to hold back the Germans and Austrians, leaving them severely weakened in the Caucasus. Britain's military and political leaders, Churchill, Kitchener, Fisher, Carden and Lloyd George, turned that limited objective into a major offensive which absorbed half-a-million men and vast amounts of military and naval resources. Almost half of those men became casualties.

At first the campaign against Turkey was purely naval. It was led by Vice-Admiral Sir Sackville Hamilton Carden who at the time was in command of the Royal Navy's Mediterranean Squadron. As early as November 1914, as soon as hostilities between Russia and Turkey had started, Carden with a combined Anglo-French squadron had tried to force the Dardanelles Strait, a 30-mile long strait in north-western Turkey which, linking the Sea of Marmara to the Aegean, is only between 0.75 to 3.7 miles wide.

In his first despatch, Carden reported back that the Turkish batteries opened fire as soon as the Allied ships made their run. The Allied warships' counter-fire was highly effective and it was believed that some 600 casualties had been inflicted on the Turkish gunners. When, on 19 February 1915, Carden conducted a second run past the Turkish batteries and deliberately bombarded the Turkish positions from the outset, the Turkish gunners remained under cover and did not venture out to man their guns until the afternoon.

Operations continued in February and March in which landing parties captured some of the Turkish forts. Yet it was not the land defences that ultimately proved decisive but the mine fields which had been sown across the Strait.

On 18 March, in another attempt on the Dardanelles, three battleships were sunk by mines and another damaged, and Rear Admiral John de Robeck, who had taken over from Carden just three days before, called off the attack. These were the worst losses suffered by the Royal Navy in battle since Trafalgar.

At this point, Britain and France could have scaled down their operations in this theatre. They had made the demonstration that Russia had pleaded for and if they kept a number of warships in the area, the Turks would have been compelled to maintain substantial forces on the Gallipoli Peninsula to ensure its safety. However, General Sir Ian Hamilton, who had been given command of the Allied Mediterranean Expeditionary Force, was present with the Royal Navy on 18 March and in his first despatch he wrote: 'I witnessed these stupendous events, and thereupon cabled your Lordship my reluctant deduction that the co-operation of the whole of the force under my command would be required to enable the Fleet effectively to force the Dardanelles.'

What Hamilton made clear was that 'nothing but a thorough and systematic scheme for flinging the whole of the troops under my command very rapidly ashore could be expected to meet with success; whereas, on the other hand, a tentative or piecemeal programme was bound to lead to disaster.' That, though, is exactly what happened.

The initial Allied landings took place on 25 April 1915, and in the intervening weeks the Turks had worked hard on their defences and reinforced their troops. *Generalleutnant* Otto Liman von Sanders, an adviser and military commander for the Ottoman Empire during the First World War, later noted: 'The British allowed us four good weeks of respite for all this work before their great disembarkation ... This respite just sufficed for the most indispensable measures to be taken.' Roads were constructed, small boats assembled to carry troops and equipment across the narrows, beaches were wired, makeshift mines constructed from torpedo-heads and trenches and gun emplacements were dug along the beaches.

Despite the obvious fact that a very large force indeed would be required to seize Gallipoli and achieve the new final objective of capturing Constantinople, only around 80,000 men were available to Hamilton. A month after the initial landings, little progress had been made by the Allied troops. The expeditionary force was still trapped with its back to the sea, with the Turks holding the high ground that prevented the British and Commonwealth troops from breaking inland.

The difficulties that the operation had encountered were spelt out by Hamilton in his despatch of 20 May 1915: 'The landing of an army upon the theatre of operations I have described – a theatre strongly garrisoned throughout, and prepared for any such attempt – involved difficulties for which no precedent was forthcoming in military history except possibly in the sinister legends of Xerxes. The beaches were either so well defended by works and guns, or else so restricted by nature that it did not seem possible, even by two or three simultaneous landings, to pass the troops ashore quickly enough to enable them to maintain themselves against the rapid concentration and counter-attack which the enemy was bound in such case to attempt. It became necessary, therefore, not only to land simultaneously at as many points as possible, but to threaten to land at other points as well.'

By this time these factors were only too well known. Whilst Hamilton had managed to land his forces, repeated attempts to break out of the beachheads had failed, as had Turkish counter-attacks aimed at driving the Allies from their slender toe-hold. Casualties on both sides were shocking, and conditions for the troops, continuously exposed in the heat of summer, scarcely bearable.

This is vividly described by Hamilton in his despatch of 26 August: 'The country is broken, mountainous, arid and void of supplies; the water found in the areas occupied by our forces is quite inadequate for their needs; the only practicable beaches are small, cramped breaks in impracticable lines of cliffs; with the wind in certain quarters no sort of landing is possible; the wastage, by bombardment and wreckage, of lighters and small craft has led to crisis after crisis in our carrying capacity, whilst over every single beach plays fitfully throughout each day a devastating shell fire at medium ranges.' Hamilton made 'urgent' calls for reinforcements.

August had seen a major push by Hamilton to capture the Sari Bair heights and when this had failed, further assaults were delivered, following landings at Suvla, against the notorious Hill 60. These also failed.

Whilst the despatches that follow present a clear account of the fighting at Gallipoli, they do not always illustrate the desperate conditions that the soldiers often fought under. The Battle of Hill 60 presents an opportunity to introduce a first-hand account, in this case that of a New Zealander who wrote under the name 'Digger Craven'.

After an initial bombardment, the attack at Hill 60 was delivered in the middle of the afternoon of 21 August 1915 under a blazing sun. Before being able to mount the hill, Craven and his comrades had to cross an open valley. The men ran as fast as they could with their heavy packs on their backs, bent double, dodging the bombs and the shells – and then machine-guns.

'The automatic guns opened on us before we had gone a few yards,' wrote Craven. 'We dropped, fired in a few rounds, then up again, pushing another yard or two. It is damned hard fighting in the open and in broad daylight, especially when your enemy is securely entrenched. They swept our advance line as with the swathe of some gigantic scythe. Clouds of dense smoke hung heavy on the haze of that hot afternoon. In a measure it saved a great number of us. Just the same, men were dropping like rotten sheep all over the place.

'A score of times we dashed for cover in that monstrous charge, using boulders, clumps of scrub, dead men – anything, anywhere for a breather. For as much as a minute at a time we'd stop, crouching low while officers yelled themselves hoarse.'

Some of the men responded to the futility of the situation by just jumping up and charging into the hail of bullets: 'When a fellow stood up to his full height and ran into it, we knew he was fed up with it all and wanted to go home. Hundreds did during that sunny afternoon. Hill 60 was [an] anti-climax, and every man knew it was. Of all the death-traps, this was the biggest. Men muttered and cursed in the desolation of this hopelessness.'

'In half an hour there wasn't any more left of that first wave of men who had charged Jonny's trenches. It was as if they'd never been. Every man Jack of 'em was gone from our view – killed or captured or lying wounded in front of those accursed ditches which bristled with rifles and machine-guns. There were only the smashed and the dying.'

The horror of that awful afternoon was just about to become even more terrible. The shells set fire to the low scrub and undergrowth which covered the valley and the hillside. The scorched ground was bone dry and soon the flames, 'crackling over the earth like a prairie fire', began to sweep towards where the remnants of the third wave of attackers had been forced to take cover.

'The fire licked its way over vast areas of the ground. The men in front were caught in the flames. It was spreading fan-wise over the lower slopes of the hill. It crawled over the earth like some evil thing, a holocaust come to convince us – if we needed any convincing – that we might batter ourselves for ever against these fiery mounds of Gallipoli and we should batter in vain.

'We stared in horror at that expanding carpet of fire. We saw wounded men crawling and scrambling from the flames, and as they got clear of the fire they were shot dead by jeering Turks. Those who were too badly wounded to make the attempt were burned alive. The stench of it all hung on the thick haze.

'Volumes of smoke rose until it seemed that all the world was afire ... it blazed with intense ferocity, travelling over the ground like liquid fire, so swiftly did it spread, destroying everything in its trail, leaving a vast parched blackness over which could be seen those who had failed to escape, blackened, smouldering heaps of debris, broken rifles with charred butts, tangles of rag ash that had once been uniforms with buttons and insignia of regiment industriously polished. For what? To become these little heaps of black dust.'

As Craven later conceded, coming on top of the other reverses, watching their comrades engulfed in the flames, removed utterly the last remnants of faith and confidence in their leaders, 'and brought the final touch of despair to war-sickened and weary men ... I had seen many die, but never like that.'

Now, though, Craven and those around him were faced with a terrible dilemma, one that on-one should ever have to face. 'How could we lie there, a little party adrift under a ridge, and watch those fellows burned alive? To see them squirming and struggling to get clear of the licking flames, to hear their screams – it was more than we could stand. We took aim ... even as the flames licked about them, setting fire to their clothing.' 'God forgive us!' muttered one New Zealander as they fired their rifles and killed their comrades.

The Battle of Hill 60 was the last major assault of the Gallipoli Campaign. As Craven points out, as the fighting had dragged on the Allied troops became increasingly demoralised. They could see no prospect of ever overcoming the Turkish defences. Indeed, the August offensive had never really offered any prospect of success. Hamilton, though, had to do something. Diseased and demoralised, his troops needed a quick victory. It led to a decisive defeat.

Hamilton's final despatch was compiled after he had been replaced and sent back to the United Kingdom. It forms a list of additions and corrections to his previous despatch which had been published in *The London Gazette*. His successor, General Charles Munro, took over from Hamilton in October 1915.

Munro had been instructed to report on the military situation on the Gallipoli Peninsula and to give his opinion on whether or not, on purely military grounds, the Expeditionary Force should be evacuated or that if further operations were continued how many troops would be required to take Constantinople.

In his despatch Munro explained what he found: 'The positions occupied by our troops presented a military situation unique in history. The mere fringe of the coast line had been secured. The beaches and piers upon which they depended for all requirements in personnel and materiel were exposed to registered and observed Artillery fire. Our entrenchments were dominated almost throughout by the Turks. The possible Artillery positions were insufficient and defective.

'The Force, in short, held a line possessing every possible military defect. The position was without depth, the communications were insecure and dependent on the weather. No means existed for the concealment and deployment of fresh troops destined for the offensive – whilst the Turks enjoyed full powers of observation, abundant Artillery positions, and they had been given the time to supplement the natural advantages which the position presented by all the devices at the disposal of the Field Engineer.'

Munro then listed all the difficulties experienced by the troops and the impracticality of continuing with the expedition. 'Since we could not hope to achieve any purpose by remaining on the Peninsula, the appalling cost to the nation involved in consequence of embarking on an Overseas Expedition with no base available for the rapid transit of stores, supplies and personnel, made it urgent that we should divert the troops locked up on the Peninsula to a more useful theatre ... in my opinion the evacuation of the Peninsula should be taken in hand.'

The evacuation having been agreed upon, the tricky task of withdrawing the troops became the overriding concern of Munro and Admiral de Robeck. Withdrawing from contact with the enemy is one of the most hazardous operations in warfare and Hamilton had declared that an evacuation under the guns of the Turks would result in 50 per cent casualties. He would be proved wrong, for remarkably it was achieved without the loss of a single man. De Robeck's evacuation despatch is the last of the series from Gallipoli.

Those despatches are reproduced here in the same form as when they were originally published in the UK. They have not been modified or interpreted in any way and are therefore the unedited and unique words of the commanding officers as they saw things at the time when the hopes of many nations, especially those of Australia and New Zealand, were raised only to be dashed in bitter defeat.

Abbreviations

AAD – Advanced Ammunition Depot
ACI – Army Council Instruction
ADC – *Aide-de-Camp*
ADS – Advanced Dressing Station
AF – Army Form
AG – Anti-gas
AO – Army Order
AOC – Army Ordnance Corps
AOD – Army Ordnance Depot
ARP – Ammunition Refilling Point
ARS – Advanced Regulating Station
ASC – Army Service Corps
BA – British Army
BAC – Brigade Ammunition Column
BAD – Base Ammunition Depot
Battn. – Battalion
Bde – Brigade
BGGS – Brigadier-General General Staff
BGRA – Brigadier-General Royal Artillery
BGS – Brigadier, General Staff
BM – Brigade Major
Brig – Brigade
CB – Companion of The Most Honourable Order of the Bath
CCS – Casualty Clearing Station
CDS – Corps Dressing Station
CHA – Commander Heavy Artillery
CIE – Companion of The Most Eminent Order of the Indian Empire
CMG – Companion of The Most Distinguished Order of Saint Michael and
    Saint George
CO – Commanding Officer
Co, Coy – Company
Cpl – Corporal
CQMS – Company Quartermaster Master Sergeant

CRA – Commander Royal Artillery
CPO – Chief Petty Officer
CSM – Company Sergeant Major
CT – Communication Trench
CVO – Commander of the Royal Victorian Order
DA – Divisional Artillery
DAC – Divisional Ammunition Column
DAP – Divisional Ammunition Park
DAQMG – Deputy Assistant Quartermaster General
DCM – Distinguished Conduct Medal
DD – Dishonourable Discharge
DDMS – Deputy Director Medical Services
Div – Division or Divisional
DO – Dug-out
DoW – Died of wounds
DRS – Divisional Rest Station
DSC – Distinguished Service Cross
DSO – Distinguished Service Order
FA – Field Ambulance
FDS – Field Dressing Station
FSPB – Field Service Pocket Book
GCB – Knight Grand Cross of The Most Honourable Order of the Bath
GCIE – Knight Grand Commander of The Most Eminent Order of the Indian
    Empire
GCSI – Knight Grand Commander of The Most Exalted Order of the Star of
    India
GCVO – Knight Grand Cross of The Royal Victorian Order
GHQ – General Headquarters
GOC – General Officer Commanding
GS – General Service or General Staff
GSO – General Staff Officer
GSW – Gunshot Wound
HA – Heavy Artillery
HE – High Explosive
HIRMS – His Imperial Russian Majesty's Ship
HMS – His Majesty's Ship
HQ, Hqts, HdQrs – Headquarters
Hr – Hour
HT – Horse Transport
Hy – Heavy
IB – Infantry Brigade

IC – In Charge
2/IC – Second in Charge
Inf, Infy – Infantry
Inf Bde – Infantry Brigade
Infm, Info – Information
Inf Reg, Inf Regt – Infantry Regiment
Int, Intel – Intelligence
IO – Intelligence Officer
KCB – Knight Commander of The Most Honourable Order of the Bath
KCIE – Knight Commander of The Most Eminent Order of the Indian
    Empire
KCMG – Knight Commander of The Most Distinguished Order of Saint
    Michael and Saint George
KCSI – Knight Commander of The Most Exalted Order of the Star of India
KCVO – Knight Commander of The Royal Victorian Order
KP – Knight of the Order of St Patrick
KT – Knight Companion of The Most Ancient and Most Noble Order of the
    Thistle
L.Bdr, L/Bdr – Lance Bombardier
L.Cpl, L/Cpl, L/C, Lce Cpl – Lance Corporal
L.G., L. Gun – Lewis Gun
LO – Liaison Officer
L of C, LC – Lines of Communication
L.Sgt, L/Sgt – Lance Sergeant
Lt – Lieutenant
Lt Col – Lieutenant Colonel
MC – Military Cross
MDS – Main Dressing Station
MEF – Mediterranean Expeditionary Force
Mg, MG, M.Gun – Machine-gun
MGS – Machine-Gun Section
MM – Military Medal
MO – Medical Officer
MVO – Member of The Royal Victorian Order
NCO – Non-Commissioned Officer
NTO – Naval Transport Officer
OC – Officer Commanding
OIC – Officer-in-Charge
OP – Observation Post
OR, O. Rank – Other Rank(s)
Pdr – Pounder

Pl, Plt – Platoon
Pnr – Pioneer
Pt, Pte, Prvt – Private
PW, PoW – Prisoner of War
QM, Qr.Mr. – Quarter-Master
QMG – Quartermaster General
QMS – Quarter-Master Sergeant
RA – Royal Artillery
RAMC – Royal Army Medical Corps
RAP – Regimental Aid Post
Rd – Road
RE – Royal Engineers
Rec, Recce – Reconnaissance or Reconnoitre
Recd – Received
Ref – Reference
Reg, Regt – Regimental
Res – Reserve
RFA – Royal Field Artillery
Rfn – Rifleman
Rft – Reinforcement(s)
RGA – Royal Garrison Artillery
RHQ – Regimental Headquarters
RMA – Royal Marine Artillery
RMLI – Royal Marines Light Infantry
RMO – Regimental Medical Officer
RN – Royal Navy
RNR – Royal Naval Reserve
RNVR – Royal Naval Volunteer Reserve
RO – Routine Orders
RQMS – Regimental Quarter-Master Sergeant
RSM – Regimental Sergeant-Major
RV – Rendezvous
SAA – Small Arms Ammunition
SC – Staff Captain
Sec Lt, 2/Lt – Second Lieutenant
Sgt, Sjt – Sergeant
Sig – Signal
SL – Start line
SMO – Senior Medical Officer
SO – Staff Officer
SP – Start Point, Strong Point, or support

SS – Steam Ship
ST – Support Trench
TF – Territorial Force
TM – Trench Mortar
TMB – Trench Mortar Battery
TO – Transport Officer
VC – Victoria Cross
WD – War Diary
WO – Warrant Officer

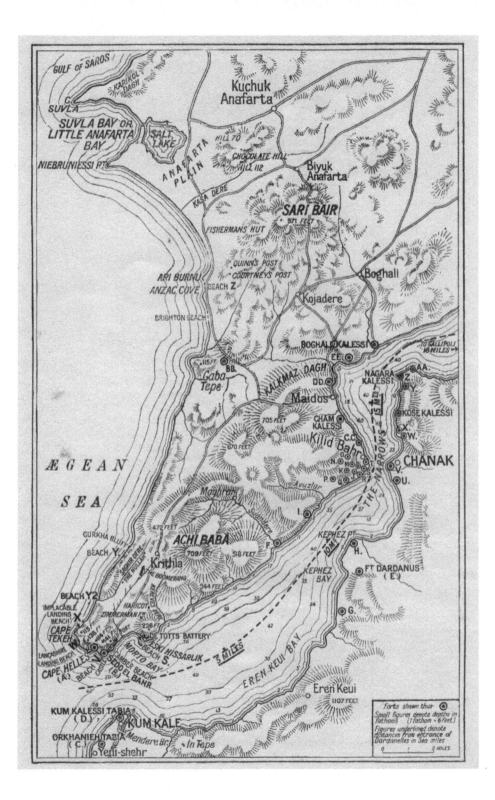

1

NAVAL ATTACK ON THE DARDANELLES, 17 MARCH 1915

FRIDAY, 2 MAY, 1919.

Admiralty, 2nd May, 1919.
LETTER FROM VICE-ADMIRAL S.H. CARDEN,
MARCH 17, 1915.

H.M.S. "Queen Elizabeth,"
March 17, 1915.

SIR,-

I have the honour to submit, for the consideration of their Lordships, the narrative of events during the operations of the Allied British and French Squadrons against the defences of the Dardanelles, from the 19th February to 16th March, 1915.

There was a marked difference in the tactics of the enemy manning the forts at the entrance when attacked on this occasion to that which they followed on the 3rd November, 1914; on that day when a short bombardment was carried out by "Indefatigable," "Indomitable," "Suffren," and "Verite," by a run past in close order, range 13,000 yards, they replied to our fire almost at once, and maintained from forts Nos. 1, 3, 4 and 6, till our squadron completed their run. The only projectiles, however, which fell close were those from the 9.4 inch guns in forts Nos. 1 and 4. Good practice was made by the Allied Squadron on forts Nos. 3 and 6, in the former of which there was a large magazine explosion. Information was received later that the casualties to personnel were high amongst the enemy, some accounts putting it at 600.

That it was considerable is, I think, shown by the fact that on the 19th February, when the present operations began, and a deliberate bombardment by our ships took place, no Turkish fort attempted to reply until late in the afternoon, when the old battleships were sent close in. They apparently kept their men in shelters until the desired moment.

Bad weather prevented a renewal until the 26th February, and then there was this difference. Fort No. 1 opened fire on "Agamemnon" at 10,000 yards as soon as that ship was in position, and hit her several times. This fort maintained its fire with great perseverance against "Queen Elizabeth," "Agamemnon," and "Gaulois," until the former ship by hitting with two consecutive

15-inch projectiles dismounted one gun and put the other out of action, and effectually silenced the fort; the surviving personnel quickly made their way down to the neighbouring village.

On the same day the accurate fire of "Irresistible" on fort No. 4 prevented its two 9.4-inch guns taking any part in the proceedings. When the ships closed in forts No. 3 and 6 fired a few ineffective rounds.

Although a heavy and prolonged fire at short range was poured into these forts, 70 per cent. of the heavy guns were found to be in a serviceable condition when the demolition parties landed.

The destruction of the guns in fort No. 3 by "Irresistible," and in Nos. 4 and 6 by "Vengeance," was most smartly and effectively carried out on the 26th February and the 1st March by demolition parties from those ships, which were ably supported by their detachments of Royal Marines.

In this service the following officers are specially and strongly recommended:-

Major G.M. Heriot, D.S.O., R.M.L.I., "Vengeance."
Lieutenant-Commander (T.) E.G. Robinson, "Vengeance."
Lieutenant (T.) F.H. Sandford, "Irresistible."

The two latter officers are further very strongly recommended for their conduct in the sweeping operations.

I was present in "Inflexible" close off Kum Kale on the 4th March, and witnessed the landing operations which were under the immediate direction of Rear-Admiral de Robeck and Brigadier-General Trotman, both of whom were on board "Irresistible'" in the entrance of the Straits. I consider the operations were correctly conducted, and that everything possible under the circumstances was done.

The skilful manner in which "Wolverine" (Commander O.J. Prentis) and "Scorpion" (Lieutenant-Commander A.B. Cunningham), ran close inshore after dark, and sent whalers ashore to bring off the remaining officers and men is highly commended.

I desire specially to endorse recommendations made by the Rear-Admiral and Brigadier-General on the conduct of Lieutenant-Colonel G.E. Matthews, R.M.L.I., and also of Major A.E. Bewes, R.M.L.I.

Four Maxim guns, which had been left on Kum Kale Pier, were recovered by volunteers from "Agamemnon" – a smart and plucky piece of work.

The sweeping operations by night between the 12th and 15th March were conducted with great gallantry under heavy fire, and though not completely successful I consider the officers and men are deserving of great praise for their efforts.

It is regretted that a complete list of those who volunteered for this dangerous duty was lost in "Ocean," but a further list is being prepared and will be submitted as soon as possible.

The attempt made on the night 13th–14th March was most determined, and I desire to bring particularly to the notice of their Lordships the following names:-

Commander W. Mellor, in charge of minesweepers.
Lieutenant-Commander J.B. Waterlow, "Blenheim."
Lieutenant-Commander J.R. Middleton, "Albion."
Lieutenant-Commander E.G. Robinson, "Vengeance."
Lieutenant-Commander G.B. Palmes, "Egmont."
Lieutenant F.H. Sandford, "Irresistible."
Lieutenant B.T. Cox, R.N.R., "Prince George."
Acting-boatswain R.G. Young, "Cornwallis."
Midshipman J.C.W. Price, "Ocean."
Captain of trawler 318.

The six officers first-mentioned carried out these duties on several nights, and I desire to submit that they may be awarded the highest decoration suitable for their rank and seniority, and that Commander Mellor and Lieutenant-Commander Waterlow be promoted now.

In connection with the operation of the night 13th–14th March I desire also to bring to their Lordships' notice the name of Commander G.J. Todd, "Amethyst."

"Amethyst" was hit several times by large projectiles, and had her steering gear and engine-room telegraphs put out of action. Arrangements were quickly made to man the hand-steering wheel, and improvise engine-room communications. Both during and after the action Commander Todd was very ably assisted by Lieutenant James C.J. Soutter, Senior Lieutenant of "Amethyst," who was indefatigable in his efforts.

The services rendered by the Destroyer Flotilla during all this period have fully maintained the high traditions of that branch of the service, their boldness in action and untiring devotion to duty are worthy of the highest praise.

I beg to call special attention to the excellent work done by the French squadron on every occasion that they have been called upon, and also to the cordial good feeling which prevails in the Allied Fleet, due so much to the personality of that dashing and courteous officer, Contre-Admiral E.P.A. Guepratte.

I consider it a special duty to call attention to the excellent work done by Malta Dockyard, under Vice-Admiral A.H. Limpus, C.B., in supplying every need of the large force off the Dardanelles in addition to the main French Fleet. Commanding officers speak most highly of the great assistance rendered to them on all occasions at Malta, and the rapidity with which work is done, which shows that the principle that the dockyard exists for the benefit of ships is fully understood and acted upon.

The conduct and ability of the commanding officers has been of a high order.

The behaviour of officers and men on all occasions has been most admirable, and in every way as could be expected.

In closing the report on this stage of the operations I wish especially to bring to the notice of their Lordships the splendid work done by Rear-Admiral J.M. de Robeck, and the great assistance I have received from him, together with the valuable services of Commodore R.J.B. Keyes, C.B., M.V.O., Flag Commander Hon. A.R.M. Ramsay and Captain W.W. Godfrey, R.M.L.I., War Staff.

I have, &c.,

S.H. CARDEN, *Vice-Admiral*,

The Secretary of the Admiralty.

Enclosure.
NARRATIVE OF EVENTS, DARDANELLES, FEBRUARY 19 TO MARCH 16, 1915.

The attack on the defences of the Dardanelles commenced on the 19th February, 1915.

Air reconnaissance on the 17th, 18th, and A.M. 19th confirmed information in our possession with regard to forts Nos. 1, 3, 4, and 6, except that an additional gun was shown in eastern bastion of fort No. 6.

Seaplanes also reported that some minor earthworks and trenches appeared to have been extensively prepared for the defence of possible landing places.

The following ships took part in the operations of the 19th February:-

SUFFREN (flag of Contre-Amiral Guepratte).
BOUVET.
TRIUMPH.
CORNWALLIS.
INFLEXIBLE (flag of Vice-Admiral).
ALBION.

The "Gaulois" acted in support of "Suffren," while "Amethyst" supported "Albion."

Seven British minesweepers were employed with "Albion."

The "Vengeance" (flag of Rear-Admiral de Robeck) was ordered to take station as convenient to observe the fire of her division.

4.30 P.M. "Queen Elizabeth" arrived with "Agamemnon," the latter taking part at the end of the day.

February 19.

9.51 A.M. "Cornwallis" fired first shot on fort No. 4.

10. "Triumph" opened fire on fort No. 1.

10.32. "Suffren" opened on fort No. 6.

10.38. Ships were ordered to anchor with a view to improving the practice.

11. The "Vengeance" and "Cornwallis" were ordered to exchange positions, "Cornwallis," owing to a defective capstan, being unable to anchor in deep water.

11.25. "Cornwallis" was ordered to spot for "Triumph" and for "Inflexible" if required.

11.45. "Inflexible" opened on fort No. 1, which was hard to distinguish, but practice appeared good.

0.14 P.M. "Vengeance" opened fire on fort No. 4 – practice was very good – her third shot appeared to hit close to northern embrasure.

0.30. "Triumph" was ordered to cease fire, as she was unable to hit fort No. 1.

"Suffren," at this time, was making excellent practice against fort No. 6, firing by indirect laying, with "Bouvet" spotting.

0.52. "Triumph,'" was ordered to open fire with light guns on men showing signs of activity in a field-work 2 miles north of Cape Tekeh.

0.55. A seaplane was ordered up to spot for "Vengeance," but, owing to wireless troubles in seaplane, no results were obtained.

1. "Inflexible" opened fire on fort No. 3, making good practice.

1.56. It was now considered that the effect produced by the bombardment at long range was great enough to allow of ships approaching nearer to the forts, and signal was made accordingly.

2.12. "Suffren" and "Triumph" were ordered to commence their operations, the "Triumph" being ordered to engage the position of the new battery of Cape Tekeh only.

3.53. "Cornwallis" was ordered to close fort No. 1 "on present line of bearing," and open fire when certain of position.

4.10. There being still no reply from the forts, "Vengeance" and "Cornwallis" were ordered to close and destroy forts. Forts Nos. 3 and 6 were heavily bombarded by "Vengeance" and "Cornwallis," assisted by "Suffren." "Vengeance" engaged fort No. 4 with her secondary armament, while "Cornwallis" did the same to fort No. 1.

4.40. "Suffren" was directed to close the forts.

4.45. At the same time "Cease fire, examine forts," was signalled to "Vengeance." Fort No. 1 opened fire on "Vengeance" and "Cornwallis," and shortly after fort No. 4 also opened fire. "Vengeance" and "Cornwallis," assisted by "Bouvet," engaged and silenced fort No. 1. Fort No. 4 being left unfired at, both inshore ships were unaware that she had opened fire.

5. "Inflexible" opened fire on fort No. 4, with the immediate effect of causing her fire to suffer in accuracy.

5.08. "Gaulois" also opened fire on this fort. "Agamemnon" was ordered to support "Vengeance."

5.09. The "General recall" was made – "Vengeance" requested permission to continue the action; this was not approved, as the light looking towards the land was becoming bad, while ships showed up well against western sky.

5.30. Cease firing was ordered and the squadron withdrew.

7. "Albion" reported "No mines or guns encountered – area has been swept."

The result of the day's action showed apparently, that the effect of long range bombardment by direct fire on modern earthwork forts is slight; forts Nos. 1 and 4 appeared to be hit, on many occasions, by 12-inch common shell well placed, but when the ships closed in all four guns in these forts opened fire.

From February 20 *to* 24.
From the 20th to 24th February, inclusive, the weather was too rough to continue operations, and no reconnaissance by seaplanes was possible.

February 25.
The weather being favourable, operations were resumed. No seaplanes took part – the sea being too rough for them to rise off the water.

The following ships took part:-

INFLEXIBLE, VENGEANCE, AGAMEMNON, QUEEN ELIZA-BETH, ALBION, CORNWALLIS, IRRESISTIBLE, TRIUMPH, SUF-FREN, GAULOIS, BOUVET, CHARLEMAGNE, and DUBLIN, with eight destroyers and two submarines.

Ships were in position to commence the long-range bombardment by 10 a.m. – the destroyers forming a screen to seaward of the battleships.

10.7 a.m. "Agamemnon" reported range obtained of fort No. 1.

10.14. "Queen Elizabeth" opened fire on fort No. 3.

10.16. Fort No. 1 opened fire on "Agamemnon," range 10,000 yards.

10.18. "Gaulois" opened fire on fort No. 6.

10.22. "Agamemnon" opened fire on fort No 1.

10.27. "Irresistible" opened fire on fort No. 4.

10.33. Fort No. 1 seemed to be getting the range of "Agamemnon," who was ordered to weigh and proceed further out – "Queen Elizabeth" being ordered to fire on fort No.1.

Between 10.34 and 10.43. "Agememnon" was hit seven times, but as the shells did not detonate it was not realised she had been struck; directly "Agamemnon" had good weigh on fort No. 1 lost the range.

10.44. Fort No. 1 opened an accurate fire on "Gaulois," who immediately replied to it from all her guns, this probably accounted for the fact that she was able to weigh and proceed further out without the fort scoring a single hit.

10.45. "Queen Elizabeth" opened fire on fort No. 1, and "Dublin" was observed firing at a gun near Yeni Shehr.

10.55. "Irresistible" reported she obtained range of fort No. 4, she was ordered to continue slow firing. She opened a very deliberate, accurate fire on the fort, which kept silent practically all day.

11.30. "Gaulois" was making excellent practice on fort 6.

11.47. Fort No. 1 was still firing at "Agamemnon" and "Gaulois," but shots were going short – its extreme range appeared to be about 11,000 yards.

Noon. "Queen Elizabeth," whose shooting had been extremely accurate, appeared to drop a shell right into fort No. 1, and at 0.02 p.m. she reported eastern gun dismounted.

0.15 p.m. "Irresistible" reported she thought her tenth round had damaged northern gun of fort No. 4.

"Vengeance" and "Cornwallis" were ordered to prepare for run 1, which was commenced at 12.45 p.m., with all covering ships firing deliberately on their allotted forts.

0.50. "Queen Elizabeth" reported she had hit the western gun of fort No. 1. "Agamemnon" also claimed to have hit this gun at 12.55 p.m. "Agamemnon" at this time was firing on fort No. 1. "Inflexible" engaging fort No. 3.

0.55. "Vengeance" and "Cornwallis" opened fire, concentrating chiefly on forts 1 and 4. Forts 3 and 6 both opened fire, but their practice was poor, and few rounds were fired. Forts 1 and 4 did not fire during the run.

By 1.22 "Vengeance" and "Cornwallis" had completed run 1, and all ships checked fire.

1.50. Rear-Admiral, "Vengeance," reported 'No. 1 battery west gun point-ing in the air, right gun not visible, battery not manned. No. 3 fired at 'Vengeance' – apparently using black powder – three guns are visible on south-west face. No. 4, both guns laid horizontal, battery not manned, one round was fired from western gun ....'

2.5. Contre-Amiral, "Suffren," was directed to commence run 2, and given the following directions: "Battery No. 1 out of action, battery No. 4 was not manned, concentrate your fire on 3, 4, and 6, especially 4."

Run 2 was carried out most deliberately, "Suffren" being about 3,000 yards ahead of "Charlemagne" – both ships made excellent practice – the only round fired at them was from fort No. 6.

The run was completed at 3 p.m. Covering ships fired very few rounds during this run; it was evident that forts were silenced.

3.5. Minesweepers were ordered to close the entrance, and carry out sweeping operations laid down.

"Albion" and "Triumph" were ordered to prepare to close forts to 2,000 yards of southern and northern shore respectively, keeping way on and carrying out destruction of guns still intact.

Rear-Admiral in "Vengeance" being directed to follow them to direct operations. While "Albion" and "Triumph" were attempting to destroy the guns of forts 1 and 6 at close range, fort No. 4 apparently fired one round from her northernmost gun. The fort was immediately engaged by "Albion" and "Irresistible." Forts 1 and 6 also appeared to fire one round each. These were the last rounds fired at the ships.

Concealed guns of apparently 6″ calibre fired from positions 1 mile north-east of Cape Tekeh, and from behind northern end of Yeni Shehr village. These guns did no damage, though "Gaulois" was struck three times on the armour.

"Albion," when off Kum Kale, reported two explosions, probably light ground mines; these occurred about 100 yards ahead of the ship, and did no damage.

By 4 p.m. the forts were reduced, and the minesweepers were ordered to enter and commence sweeping. "Vengeance," "Albion," and "Triumph," with six destroyers, covered these operations.

The remainder of the fleet returning to Tenedos during the night of the 25th/26th, minesweepers swept the entrance; they found no mines. The enemy were reported as burning the villages at entrance.

February 26.
"Albion," "Triumph," and "Majestic" entered straits between 8 a.m. and 9 a.m., and shelled forts 3 and 6 from inside entrance, also firing station below De Totts' battery. "Albion," preceded by sweepers, proceeded to a position 12,000 yards from fort 8, from which position fire was opened on that fort. "Majestic" supported "Albion," these two ships being under fire from field guns and howitzers from Asiatic shore, ships remained under weigh; enemy scored one hit on "Majestic."

"Jed" and "Chelmer" reconnoitred northern and southern shores during forenoon as far up as the line White Cliffs–Suandere, both ships being engaged with the enemy's light batteries; they sunk some large range buoys, and located several batteries.

"Vengeance," from outside straits, was engaged bombarding position on Asiatic shore near Achilles Tomb.

At 2.30 p.m., the enemy apparently having abandoned Kum Kale and Seddul Bahr, the opportunity was seized to land demolition parties on both sides – from "Vengeance" at Kum Kale, and "Irresistible" at Seddul Bahr. Parties being covered by the guns of "Vengeance," "Irresistible," "Cornwallis," "Dublin," and "Racoon," forts 3, 4, and 6 were entered and demolitions carried out, and two new 4" guns concealed near Achilles Tomb were destroyed, but owing to lateness of the landing it was impossible to verify results. Both parties encountered slight opposition, the enemy being in some force in Seddul Bahr prevented fort 1 being reached.

On night of the 26th/27th minesweepers entered straits to continue sweeping in lower area, being covered by "Colne," "Jed," and "Kennet," who engaged enemy's batteries and sunk more range buoys.

Seaplanes carried out reconnaissances inside Straits in order to locate batteries, &c.

Amongst other details they reported battery 8 now contains eight guns. Many positions for guns have been prepared on both shores.

February 27.
Weather broke, north-easterly gale, much rain with low visibility. Operations inside the Straits much impeded, small progress made.

February 28.
Heavy north-easterly gale. Operations confined to watching the Straits.

March 1.
Gale having moderated, operations inside Straits were resumed. The following battleships entered Straits to engage howitzers and field batteries:-
"Vengeance," "Ocean," "Albion," "Triumph," "Irresistible," and "Majestic."

Fort 8 and battery at White Cliffs were engaged by "Albion" and "Triumph," "Ocean" and "Majestic" meanwhile engaging guns near Aren Kioi village and on European shore. These proved extremely hard to locate, and when seen great difficulty was experienced in obtaining points of aim, the guns being well concealed.

The action was discontinued at 5 p.m. "Ocean," "Albion," and "Triumph" were each hit on several occasions by projectiles of 6-inch calibre and below without suffering any serious damage.

Demolition party from "Irresistible" landed at Seddul Bahr and completed demolition of fort 6.

The party was attacked during the operation. The fire from covering ships and destroyers in Morto Bay, however, was sufficient to disperse enemy.

During the night of lst–2nd March minesweepers entered and swept to within 3,000 yards of Kephez Point. They were covered by destroyers. When abreast of Suandere River batteries opened fire and sweepers retired, destroyers covering withdrawal.

No vessels were hit.

March 2.

"Canopus," "Swiftsure," and "Cornwallis" entered the Straits and engaged forts Nos. 8 and 7, also field guns.

Garrison of fort No. 8 were forced to withdraw, but material damage to fort could not be determined.

Howitzers and concealed field guns opened a heavy fire, which could not be silenced. All ships were hit on several occasions, suffering some material damage.

An observation mine exploded ineffectively ahead of "Canopus."

On the lst–2nd March the French squadron reconnoitred the Gulf of Xeros, bombarding the forts and earthworks of the Bulair lines and the bridge over Kavak. French minesweepers swept along the coast. They discovered no mines.

The landing-places in the Gulf of Xeros were also reported on.

Destroyers and minesweepers continued the attack on the Kephez minefield, but made no progress in the face of heavy fire.

March 3.

Weather in the morning unfavourable – foggy. In the afternoon "Albion," "Prince George," "Triumph" continued the attack on forts 7 and 8 and field batteries. These latter were not so active as on former days. Sweeping operations continued at night, covered by destroyers. Slight progress was made.

Seaplanes carried out useful reconnaissance, without, however, being able to locate batteries firing at the ships.

March 4.

It being uncertain whether forts Nos. 1 and 4 were absolutely destroyed, demolition parties were ordered to land and complete the destruction, being covered by a landing party of the Royal Marine Brigade, one company of 250 men each side.

This landing had been postponed for several days, on account of the weather. Seaplanes reconnoitred the vicinity of forts and villages near them in the morning, and reported no movement of troops.

At 10 a.m. parties landed at Seddul Bahr and Kum Kale.

Both parties met with opposition. At Seddul Bahr no progress could be made, and the party withdrew at 3 p.m.

At Kum Kale an attempt was made to reach fort No. 4, but without success, the enemy being in some force in well-concealed trenches. Great difficulty was experienced in withdrawing the advanced party, the enemy gaining possession of a cemetery near Mendere Bridge, commanding the ground over which the party had to fall back, and which could not be shelled by the ships, as our troops were between the cemetery and the ships.

Seaplanes attempted to locate the enemy's trenches without success, descending to 2,000 feet in their efforts to distinguish the positions: one seaplane was hit twenty-eight times and another eight times.

It was not till the destroyers were sent close in to shell the trenches that the retirement could be carried out.

After sunset "Scorpion" and "Wolverine" ran in and landed parties, under fire, to search the beach from Kum Kale to the cliffs below fort No. 4. The former brought off two officers and five men, who had been unable to reach the boats.

March 5.

The attack on the forts at the Narrows commenced by indirect bombardment by "Queen Elizabeth."

Three seaplanes were sent up to spot for fall of shot. One met with an accident, and the second was forced to return on account of her pilot being wounded by a rifle bullet; in consequence, they were not of assistance in the firing

"Queen Elizabeth" was under fire from field guns, being struck on many occasions, without, however, suffering any great material damage.

March 6.

Indirect attack by "Queen Elizabeth" continued.

"Vengeance," inside the Straits, spotted for "Queen Elizabeth," "Albion," "Majestic," "Prince George," and "Suffren" engaged forts No. 7, 8, and 13, with what result could not be discovered.

At night "Amethyst," with destroyers and minesweepers in company, proceeded inside Dardanelles to attack the Kephez minefield. Some progress was made, but, as on former occasions, gunfire drove the minesweepers out of the mined area.

Between the 3rd and 6th March "Sapphire" was engaged in the neighbourhood of Mitylene in destroying telegraph stations, &c.

March 7.

French squadron consisting of "Suffren," "Gaulois," "Charlemagne," and "Bouvet" entered the Straits and engaged forts Nos. 7 and 8.

Later "Agamemnon" and "Lord Nelson" attacked the forts at the Narrows by direct fire from ranges between 14,000 and 12,000 yards. After a severe engagement, during which both ships were hit by heavy projectiles, forts Nos. 13 and 19 were silenced. During this attack the French battleships kept down the fire from howitzers and field guns.

"Dublin" at Bulair was engaged with a shore battery.

During the night of the 7th–8th March destroyers attacked the searchlights at Kephez, but without result, the lights being extinguished temporarily, but invariably reappearing.

March 8.

"Queen Elizabeth" entered the Straits to continue the attack on the Narrows by direct fire. Conditions became unfavourable for spotting, and little was accomplished.

Weather was too misty for seaplanes to do any spotting.

Attack on minefield was continued at night with minesweepers and picket boats. Batteries opened fire.

March 9.

"Albion," "Prince George," and "Irresistible" entered the Straits and made a thorough search for boats, &c., and shelled look-out stations. The weather was misty throughout the day.

At night picket boats covered by destroyers attacked the Kephez minefield with explosive creeps.

March 10.

"Irresistible," "Dublin," and "Ark Royal" off Bulair. The former bombarded the enemy's positions when guns had been located. The seaplanes were unable to fly owing to the rough weather.

"Ocean" and "Albion" bombarded light gun battery in Morto Bay, also villages and positions near entrance.

After nightfall seven sweepers, attended by picket boats fitted with explosive creeps, supported by destroyers, "Amethyst" and "Canopus," entered the Straits. The latter opened fire on the batteries and searchlights protecting the minefield off Kephez Point, but was unable to extinguish the lights. The vessels were subjected to a heavy fire from guns of and below 6-inch calibre.

Sweepers and picket boats succeeded in getting above the minefield with the object of sweeping down with the current. Picket boats destroyed several cables, but only one pair of sweepers got out their sweep and little was effected. Two trawlers were hit by 6-inch projectiles.

Trawler No. 339 was sunk by a mine.

March 11.
Seaplanes carried out reconnaissance for the ships operating off Bulair. Ships inside the Straits engaged in watching both shores.

Operations against the Narrows delayed by failure to clear the minefield.

Attack on the minefield at night failed owing to the sweepers refusing to face the heavy fire opened by batteries on them and the covering destroyers.

March 12.
Daylight operations at a standstill. Weather misty.

French minesweepers attacked the minefield at night with no success, being driven off by heavy fire.

Aerial reconnaissance reported a line of mines near the surface extending from Suandere Bay in an E.S.E. direction. These were examined by a sweeper and picket boats which attacked the line with creeps and explosive sweeps. The line subsequently turned out to be an obstruction consisting of empty observation mines moored by chain cables and connected by a wire hawser. The latter apparently had a hemp netting suspended from it. It was evidently an anti-submarine obstruction.

March 13.
A determined attack on the minefield was made on the night of the 13th March, volunteer officers and men being in each trawler.

The plan of attack was similar to that on the 10th, it being very essential for the sweepers to get above the minefield before getting out their sweeps as they can make no progress against the current.

"Amethyst" and destroyers covered the operations, which commenced with a bombardment of the lights and batteries by "Cornwallis."

The defence of the minefield was well organised, and sweepers and picket boats had to pass through an area lit by six powerful searchlights, under fire from fort No. 13 and batteries Nos. 7 and 8, besides numerous light guns estimated at twenty to thirty on either shore.

The passage was accomplished, but on reaching the turning point only one pair of trawlers was able to get out the sweep owing to damage to winches and gear, and loss of personnel.

Picket boats did excellent service in blowing up cables with explosive creeps.

"Amethyst" drew the fire of the batteries at a critical period, and suffered severely.

March 14, 15 *and* 16.

Minesweepers engaged in clearing up area inside the Straits in which ships would have to manoeuvre in their combined attacks against the forts at the Narrows and the minefields at Kephez.

LETTER FROM VICE-ADMIRAL DE ROBECK, MARCH 26, 1915.
"Queen Elizabeth," March 26, 1915.

SIR,

I have the honour to enclose a detailed narrative of the operations in the Dardanelles on the 18th March, 1915.

With regard to the general results of this attack, although the principal forts remained silent for considerable intervals, only a portion of their armaments can be considered disabled. The tactics employed by the enemy when the bombardment by the fleet becomes heavy are to desert their guns and retire to bomb-proof shelters. When they consider a favourable opportunity offers they re-man the guns and open fire again.

But taking into consideration the accuracy of fire of the ships and the number of explosions which occurred in the forts, both matériel and personnel must have suffered considerably. Throughout the greater part of the day the fleet appeared to have a marked advantage as regards gunfire, so much so that the minesweepers were called in at 2 P.M. Soon after they were inside it was, however, evident from the amount of fire from howitzers and field guns that they would not be able to proceed into the minefield at Kephez Point, and beyond sweeping in the area where "Bouvet" sank the sweepers effected nothing.

Up to the time "Bouvet" was mined everything had proceeded satisfactorily, the ships receiving little damage by the enemy's gunfire, although the annoyance from concealed batteries on both sides of the Straits was very great. It was evident that some of these batteries were directing their fire on the control positions of the ships. In this way the "Inflexible" lost two very fine officers who were in her fore control, viz., Commander Rudolf H.C. Verner and Lieutenant Arthur W. Blaker.

During the period the second division battleships "Ocean," "Irresistible," "Albion," and "Vengeance" were bombarding the situation again looked satisfactory.

"Inflexible" reported shortly after 4 P.M. that she had struck a mine, and she was ordered out of the Dardanelles. I submit that it reflects great credit on Captain Phillimore and his ship's company that "Inflexible" was able to reach shoal water off Tenedos.

It was only after "Wear" had returned from "Irresistible" at 4.50 P.M. that it was realised that the latter had also struck a mine. As soon as I was informed of this I ordered "Ocean" to take her in tow. This was, however, impossible, as will be seen from the reports of "Ocean" and "Irresistible." It was also apparent that the area in which the ships were operating was too dangerous, and I therefore determined to withdraw the "B" (advance) line and break off the engagement. Whilst these orders were being carried out "Ocean" was also struck by a torpedo or mine.

Eventually the ships withdrew at dark, the destroyers having taken off the ships' companies of both "Ocean" and "Irresistible."

The conduct of all ranks was reported to be excellent and up to the best traditions of our Service. The saving of valuable lives by:

WEAR,
COLNE,
CHELMER,
JED, and
KENNET,

was a brilliant and gallant performance on their part.

I would submit the names of-

Captain Christopher P. Metcalfe, H.M.S. "Wear,"
Commander Claude Seymour, H.M.S. "Colne,"
Lieutenant Commander Hugh T. England, H.M.S. "Chelmer,"
Lieutenant Commander George F.A. Mulock, H.M.S. "Jed," and
Lieutenant Charles E.S. Farrant, H.M.S. "Kennet,"

for their Lordships' favourable consideration; and if I single out one for specially meritorious service, it is Captain Christopher P. Metcalfe, H.M.S. "Wear," of whose conduct I cannot speak too highly.

I would also bring to their Lordships' notice the excellent conduct of the officers in charge of picket boats.

These young officers, who were under fire all day, performed most valuable service.

I received every assistance from my staff.

The advice and initiative of my Chief of Staff, Commodore Roger J.B. Keyes, was of the greatest value. He left in "Wear," shortly before 5.30 P.M., to see whether it was possible to save "Ocean" or "Irresistible" but their condition made it impracticable.

Though the squadron had to retire without accomplishing its task, it was by no means a defeated force, and the withdrawal was only necessitated owing to the mine menace, all ranks being anxious to renew the attack.

As a result of this bombardment it is considered imperative for success that the area in which ships are manoeuvring shall be kept clear of mines, also that the minesweepers be manned by naval ratings, who will be prepared to work under heavy fire. In some cases their crews appear to have no objection to being blown up by mines, though they do not seem to like to work under gun-fire, which is a new element in their calling.

A reorganisation of the minesweepers' personnel is completed, and they are now manned for the most part by naval ranks and ratings.

I have, &c.
J.M. DE ROBECK,
Vice-Admiral.

The Secretary of the Admiralty.

Enclosure.
REPORT OF OPERATIONS CARRIED OUT BY THE ALLIED
BRITISH AND FRENCH FLEETS OFF THE DARDANELLES ON
MARCH 17 AND 18, 1915.
(All times are local, *i.e.*, two hours fast on G.M.T.)

The attempts to clear the minefield at Kephez Point during the dark hours having failed, it became necessary to carry this out by daylight.

The plan of operations was fully explained to captains of ships on the 16th, and issued to them on the 17th March.

Sweeping operations against Kephez minefield were suspended during the nights of the 15th–16th, 16th–17th, and 17th–18th, trawlers during this time being employed in thoroughly sweeping the area in which the ships would have to manoeuvre.

It was considered impracticable for ships to be at anchor inside the Dardanelles, owing to the heavy howitzer fire which can be brought to bear on them; subject to the necessity of occasionally moving, so as to throw off the enemy's fire, ships remained stationary on the 18th, in order that the gun-fire of the fleet might be as accurate as possible.

The morning of the 18th was fine, though it was at first doubtful whether the direction of the wind – which was from the south – would allow the operations to take place under favourable conditions for spotting; there was also a slight haze over the land; this, however, cleared, and the wind having fallen the signal was made at 8.26 a.m. that operation would be proceeded with, commencing at 10.30 a.m.

March 18.
At 8.15 a.m. the Commander of the British mine sweepers reported area between 8,000 and 10,000 yards range was traversed by sweepers on the night of the 17th–18th without result.

8.45. – Senior Officer of minesweepers reported that they had swept as far as White Cliffs, "eleven cutters showed signs of working – no mines have been caught in the sweep."

8.50. – Signal was made to French Admiral that Vice-Admiral did not wish him to approach nearer than 500 yards to the position of the reported mines situated at S.E. of Suandere Bay.

9.7. – It was reported that "Mosquito" had sunk three electric mines, none of which exploded; these were evidently empty mine-cases which were used to form a boom defence below Suandere Bay, and which had been broken up by our explosive creeps.

9.10. – Destroyers, fitted with light sweep, were ordered to sweep in ahead of the fleet.

10.30. – Ships reported – "Ready for action" – and Line "A" proceeded in the following order:-

PRINCE GEORGE (on port beam).
AGAMEMNON.
LORD NELSON.
QUEEN ELIZABETH.
INFLEXIBLE.
TRIUMPH (on starboard beam).

Destroyers with sweeps preceded Line "A" into the Dardanelles. Each battleship had one picket-boat in attendance on her to deal with floating mines, and "Wear" was also in attendance on "Queen Elizabeth."

"Dartmouth" was ordered to patrol the north coast of Gallipoli to fire on any batteries she could locate, and which were firing on the fleet inside the Straits.

"Dublin" demonstrated against Bashika Bay and watched Yeni Shehr.

11. – Ships were engaging field-guns and howitzers firing from the Asiatic shore.

11.15. – Four steamers were observed in the middle of the stream off Chanak; these made off up the Straits about fifteen minutes later.

11.25. – "Queen Elizabeth" opened fire on fort No. 19; "Agamemnon," "Lord Nelson," and "Inflexible" opening fire shortly afterwards in the order named. All line "A" were firing by 11.36 a.m.

11.40. – "Triumph" was firing at fort No. 8 at a range of 10,400 yards.

Line "A" was now being subjected to a heavy fire from howitzers and field-guns. One battery of the former, using four guns of about 6-inch calibre, which fell well together, was particularly annoying. The forts also opened fire, but the range, about 14,400 yards, was evidently too great for them, and they fired only a few shots, none of which took effect.

11.50. – A big explosion was seen in fort No. 20, on which "Queen Elizabeth" was now firing. "Agamemnon" and "Lord Nelson" were apparently making good practice against forts Nos. 13 and 17.

About this time the fire from the heavy howitzers was less intense, but there were still a large number of smaller guns firing on ships of line "A," all of whom were struck several times at this period.

0.6 p.m. – "Suffren," "Bouvet," "Gaulois," "Charlemagne" (who formed the first line "B"), were ordered to pass through line "A" and engage the forts at closer range.

The wind at this time was blowing almost straight from the ships to Chanak, making spotting difficult from aloft.

"Suffren" led the French Squadron through line "A" well ahead of "Bouvet," and by 0.32 p.m. she came under fire from, and engaged, the forts. Fort No. 13 was firing four guns, and forts Nos. 19, 7A, 9, and 8 all opened fire, and possibly 16 as well.

The action now became general, both lines "A" and "B" engaging the forts, and, at the same time, the lighter batteries.

Fort No. 7A was very persistent, and seemed hard to hit.

0.47. – "Agamemnon" was being made the target for most of the lighter guns. She turned 32 points, and the batteries lost the range.

"Inflexible'" was also under heavy fire, and a picket boat alongside her was sunk.

0.52. – Some large projectiles were falling into the water about 500 yards short of the line "B."

Forts Nos. 13, 19, 7A, and 8 were all firing: their practice was good, chiefly directed against line "B," "Prince George," and "Triumph."

0.56. – "Inflexible's" fore bridge observed to be on fire, blazing fiercely.

About this time a heavy explosion occurred in fort No. 13.

1.15. – Line "B" under a heavy fire, "Suffren" apparently hit several times, Fort No. 8 had now ceased firing.

1.25. – There was a slight lull in the firing, "Lord Nelson," however, being straddled by a 6-inch battery.

"Gaulois" and "Charlemagne" were making good practice on forts Nos. 13 and 16.

1.25. – "Inflexible" quitted line to extinguish fire and clear control top, which had been wrecked by a shell, and all personnel therein disabled.

1.38. – Seaplane reported Fort No. 16 firing; 19 hit; 17 hit but firing; new battery at Kephez Point not manned; battery south of Suandere River firing.

1.43. – There was little firing; minesweepers were ordered to close. The French Squadron were ordered out of the Straits, also "Prince George" and "Triumph," the ships relieving them being formed up just inside the Straits.

1.54. – "Suffren" leading line "B" out of Straits, with "Bouvet" immediately astern. A large explosion occurred on the starboard side of the latter, abaft the after-bridge, accompanied by dense masses of reddish-black smoke. "Bouvet" capsized to starboard and sank within two minutes of the first explosion.

From the "Queen Elizabeth" it appeared that the explosion was not due to a mine, but possibly to a large projectile; it was also considered that a magazine explosion had occurred, as she was previously observed to be on fire aft, and she sank so rapidly; there appears little doubt that her magazine blew up, but whether it was exploded by a mine, gunfire, or by an internal fire, is not clear.

British boats were quickly on the scene, but the whole episode occupied so short a time that few of the crew could have reached the upper deck; only sixty-six were picked up.

"Suffren" stood by till all the survivors were picked up, the remainder of her line proceeding out of harbour.

The enemy fired a few shells at the boats picking up survivors, without, however, obtaining any hits.

2.15. – "Queen Elizabeth" and "Lord Nelson" were practically the only ships firing, the forts being silent. About this time the enemy again opened fire with their 6-inch howitzer battery.

2.31. – Seaplane over forts at 1 p.m. reported troops at Kephez Point. Forts Nos. 13, 16, 17, and 19 all manned and firing; Saunders also firing.

2.32. – New line "B" passed through line "A" to engage forts at closer range. This line consisted of "Vengeance," "Irresistible," "Albion," and "Ocean," with "Swiftsure" and "Majestic" in support.

2.52. – Line "B" was engaged with forts of which only No. 19 was firing at all rapidly.

3.7. – Large explosion behind Fort No. 13; from the volume of smoke it appeared that an oil tank had been set on fire.

3.14. – A heavy explosion was observed alongside "Irresistible," evidently a big shell. All forts were now firing rapidly, but inaccurately.

Fort No. 19 apparently concentrating on "Irresistible," "Queen Elizabeth" in consequence opened salvo firing on it.

3.32. – "Irresistible" was observed to have slight list.

4.11. – "Inflexible" reported "struck a mine"; she proceeded out of the Straits.

4.14. – "Irresistible" apparently unable to move, and with a noticeable list. "Wear" was ordered to close her and ascertain what was the matter, signalling communication having broken down.

"Irresistible" was ordered to proceed out of the Straits, if able to do so, and "Ocean" to prepare to take "Irresistible" in tow.

"Wear" was seen to go alongside "Irresistible," and subsequently returned to "Queen Elizabeth" at 4.50 p.m. with 28 officers and 582 crew of "Irresistible" on board her. It was then ascertained for the first time that "Irresistible" had struck a mine, both engine rooms being immediately flooded.

As the ship was helpless, her commanding officer decided to remove a portion of the crew, retaining the executive officer and 10 volunteers to work wires, &c., should it be found possible to take her in tow.

The operation of removing the crew was carried out in a perfectly orderly manner, the ship being under fire the whole time from forts Nos. 7 and 8 and batteries near Aren Kioi.

4.50. – When it was learnt that "Irresistible" had also struck a mine, orders were given for line "B" to withdraw.

5.10. – "Wear" having disembarked crew of "Irresistible," was ordered to close "Ocean" and "Irresistible" and direct the former to withdraw if she was unable to take the latter in tow.

5.50. – Survivors on board "Irresistible" were removed to "Ocean," the captains of both ships being of opinion that it was impracticable to take "Irresistible" in tow, she being bows on to the Asiatic shore, listing badly, at right angles to the course for going out, and there appearing to be insufficient room to manoeuvre between her and the shore.

It was therefore determined to leave her till dark, when an attempt would be made to tow her out with destroyers and minesweepers, arrangements being meanwhile taken to torpedo and sink her in deep water should there be any chance of her grounding; this was always a possibility, as she was in the dead water off White Cliffs with a light breeze blowing up the Straits.

"Irresistible" having been abandoned, it was decided, in view of the unexpected mine menace, to abandon the mine-sweeping of the Kephez minefield, it being inadvisable to leave heavy ships inside the Straits to cover the minesweepers.

6.5. – "Ocean," while withdrawing, struck a mine and took a quick list to starboard of about 15 degrees.

At the same time a shell, striking the starboard side aft, jambed the helm nearly hard a-port.

The list becoming gradually greater, her commanding officer determined to disembark the crew; this was done in the destroyers "Colne," "Jed," and "Chelmer," under a heavy cross fire from forts Nos. 7 and 8 and batteries at Aren Kioi. "Chelmer" was twice struck while alongside "Ocean."

Destroyers "Wear," "Racoon," "Mosquito," and "Kennet" also stood by "Ocean."

When all were reported clear of the ship, the captain embarked in "Jed" and lay off till dark; he then returned to her to make absolutely certain no one was left on board and that nothing could be done to save her.

His opinion being that nothing could be done, the ship was finally abandoned in the centre of the Straits at about 7.30 p.m.

The captains of "Ocean" and "Irresistible," after reporting to the Vice-Admiral Commanding, returned to the Dardanelles to join the destroyers, which, with six minesweepers, had been ordered to enter the Straits after dark to endeavour to tow "Irresistible" into the current and prevent "Ocean" drifting out of it. No trace of either ship could be found; this was confirmed by "Jed" at 11 p.m. after an exhaustive search. "Canopus" at daylight also reconnoitred, and found no trace of either. There is no doubt both ships sank in deep water.

The squadron anchored at Tenedos for the night, "Canopus" and "Cornwallis" being on patrol with destroyers at the entrance of the Straits.

The damaged ships were dealt with as follows:-

"Inflexible" anchored north of Tenedos.

"Gaulois" grounded on north of Drepano Island – damage due to gunfire.

On the morning of the 19th instant, Contre Amiral Guépratte informed me that the "Suffren" was leaking forward; it had been necessary to flood the fore magazine on account of fire, and a heavy shell had started a leak.

"Inflexible," "Suffren," and "Gaulois" will therefore require to go to Malta for repairs.

J.M. DE ROBECK,
Vice-Admiral.

March 24, 1915.

DESTROYER OPERATIONS, MARCH 17 AND 18, 1915.
(All times are local.)

"Basilisk," "Grasshopper," "Racoon'" and "Mosquito" covered the operations of the minesweepers on the night of the 17th–18th March, being engaged during this service with shore batteries on both sides of the Straits.

At 6 a.m. on the 18th March, "Mosquito" saw and sunk three carbonite mines floating near Morto Bay – none exploded.

10 a.m. – "Colne" and "Chelmer" sweeping ahead of line "A." During this time "Colne's" whaler was struck by a 4-inch shell.

"Wear" was in attendance on "Queen Elizabeth" throughout the day, being in consequence frequently under fire. When "Bouvet" sank, "Wear" closed and lowered whaler to pick up survivors, being under fire at the time. "Basilisk," "Grasshopper," "Racoon," "Mosquito," "Ribble," "Kennet," "Colne," and "Chelmer" also closed, but were too late to pick up any survivors.

2.45 p.m. – Destroyers closed "Gaulois," who was in distress outside the Straits, "Colne," "Chelmer," "Mosquito," and "Kennet" transferring some of her crew to "Suffren," "Dartmouth" and "Lord Nelson."

4.10. – When "Irresistible" was observed to be in distress, "Wear" was ordered to close her. "Wear" went alongside and took off practically the whole crew under heavy fire, transferring them at 4.50 p.m. to "Queen Elizabeth."

She then returned and, after sounding round the "Irresistible," remained in the vicinity of the damaged ships until nightfall, when she rejoined "Queen Elizabeth" to report. "Colne," "Chelmer," "Racoon," "Mosquito," "Kennet," and "Jed" stood by "Irresistible," having come in from entrance of Straits.

6.5. – When "Ocean" struck a mine, "Racoon," "Mosquito," "Colne," "Chelmer," "Jed," "Kennet," and "Wear" stood by under heavy cross fire, "Colne," "Chelmer," "Jed," and "Kennet" going alongside to remove the crew.

7.15. – "Colne" found no signs of "Ocean"; enemy still firing on "Irresistible."

8.30 to 11.30 p.m. – "Jed" carried out a thorough search, but could find no trace of "Ocean" or "Irresistible."

Damage sustained by destroyers:-

"Chelmer," while alongside "Ocean," struck and holed by centre stokehold, which was flooded. She went alongside "Lord Nelson," where her own mat and that belonging to "Lord Nelson" were placed over the hole. She shortly afterwards proceeded to Tenedos, escorted by "Colne."

"Racoon," while standing by "Irresistible," was damaged by concussion of large shell under starboard quarter and some shrapnel bullets.

J.M. DE ROBECK,
March 24, 1915.   *Vice-Admiral.*

MINE SWEEPING OPERATIONS, MARCH 17 AND 18, 1915.
Night of March 17 *and* 18.

British and French minesweepers continued sweeping area below the line Suandere River–Kephez Light.

They reported: "No mines found."

March 18.

Minesweepers ordered to enter and commence sweeping at 2 p.m. Of these two pairs got sweeps out, when abreast of White Cliffs, about 3.30 p.m.; they were under fire. No progress was made beyond this point, as it was not considered advisable to leave heavy ships inside the Straits to cover their operations, "Inflexible" having already struck a mine.

J.M. DE ROBECK,
Vice-Admiral.

March 24, 1915.

2

SIR IAN HAMILTON'S FIRST GALLIPOLI DESPATCH, 20 MAY 1915

TUESDAY, 6 JULY, 1915.

From the General Commanding the Mediterranean Expeditionary Force.
To the Secretary of State for War, War Office, London, S.W.

General Headquarters,
Mediterranean Expeditionary Force,
MY LORD,-   *20th May,* 1915.

I have the honour to submit my report on the operations in the Gallipoli Peninsula up to and including the 5th May.

In accordance with your Lordship's instructions I left London on 13th March with my General Staff by special train to Marseilles, and thence in H.M.S. "Phaeton" to the scene of the naval operations in the Eastern Mediterranean, reaching Tenedos on the 17th March shortly after noon.

Immediately on arrival I conferred with Vice-Admiral de Robeck, Commanding the Eastern Mediterranean Fleet; General d'Amade, Commanding the French Corps Expéditionnaire; and Contre Amiral Guepratte, in command of the French Squadron. At this conference past difficulties were explained to me, and the intention to make a fresh attack on the morrow was announced. The amphibious battle between warships and land fortresses took place next day, the 18th of March. I witnessed these stupendous events, and thereupon cabled your Lordship my reluctant deduction that the co-operation of the whole of the force under my command would be required to enable the Fleet effectively to force the Dardanelles.

By that time I had already carried out a preliminary reconnaissance of the north-western shore of the Gallipoli Peninsula, from its isthmus, where it is spanned by the Bulair fortified lines, to Cape Helles, at its extremest point. From Bulair this singular feature runs in a south-westerly direction for 52 miles, attaining near its centre a breadth of 12 miles. The northern coast of the northern half of the promontory slopes downwards steeply to the Gulf of Xeros, in a chain of hills, which extend as far as Cape Sulva. The precipitous fall of these hills precludes landing, except at a few narrow gullies, far too restricted for any serious military movements. The southern half of the peninsula is shaped like a badly-worn boot. The ankle lies between Kaba Tepe and Kalkmaz Dagh; beneath the heel lie the cluster of forts at Kilid Bahr, whilst the toe is that promontory, five miles in width, stretching from Tekke Burnu to Sedd-el-Bahr.

The three dominating features in this southern section seemed to me to be:-

(1) Saribair Mountain, running up in a succession of almost perpendicular escarpments to 970 feet. The whole mountain seemed to be a network of ravines and covered with thick jungle.

(2) Kilid Bahr plateau, which rises, a natural fortification artificially forti-fied, to a height of 700 feet to cover the forts of the Narrows from an attack from the Ægean.

(3) Achi Babi, a hill 600 feet in height, dominating at long field gun range what I have described as being the toe of the peninsula.

A peculiarity to be noted as regards this last southern sector is that from Achi Babi to Cape Helles the ground is hollowed out like a spoon, presenting only its outer edges to direct fire from the sea. The inside of the spoon appears to be open and undulating, but actually it is full of spurs, nullahs and confused under-features.

Generally speaking the coast is precipitous, and good landing-places are few. Just south of Tekke Burnu is a small sandy bay (W), and half a mile north of it is another small break in the cliffs (X). Two miles further up the coast the mouth of a stream indents these same cliffs (Y 2), and yet another mile and a half up a scrub-covered gully looked as if active infantry might be able to scramble up it on to heights not altogether dissimilar to those of Abraham, by Quebec (Y). Inside Sedd-el-Bahr is a sandy beach (V), about 300 yards across, facing a semi-circle of steeply-rising ground, as the flat bottom of a half-saucer faces the rim, a rim flanked on one side by an old castle, on the other by a modern fort. By Eski Hissarlik, on the east of Morto Bay (S) was another small beach, which was however dominated by the big guns from Asia. Turning northwards again, there are two good landing places on either side of Kaba Tepe. Farther to the north of that promontory the beach was supposed to be dangerous and difficult. In most of these landing-places the trenches and lines of wire entanglements were plainly visible from on board ship. What seemed to be gun emplacements and infantry redoubts could also be made out through a telescope, but of the full extent of these defences and of the forces available to man them there was no possibility of judging except by practical test.

Altogether the result of this and subsequent reconnaissances was to con-vince me that nothing but a thorough and systematic scheme for flinging the whole of the troops under my command very rapidly ashore could be expected to meet with success; whereas, on the other hand, a tentative or piecemeal programme was bound to lead to disaster. The landing of an army upon the theatre of operations I have described – a theatre strongly garrisoned throughout, and prepared for any such attempt – involved difficulties for which no precedent was forthcoming in military history except possibly in the sinister legends of Xerxes. The beaches were either so well defended by works and guns, or else so restricted by nature that it did not seem possible, even by two or three simultaneous landings, to pass the troops ashore quickly enough to enable them to maintain themselves against the rapid concentration and counter attack which the enemy was bound in such case to attempt. It became necessary, therefore, not only to land simultaneously at as many points as possible, but to threaten to land at other points as well. The first of these necessities involved another unavoidable if awkward contingency, the separation by considerable intervals of the force.

The weather was also bound to play a vital part in my landing. Had it been British weather there would have been no alternative but instantly to give up the adventure. To land two or three thousand men, and then to have to break off and leave them exposed for a week to the attacks of 34,000 regular troops, with a hundred guns at their back, was not an eventuality to be lightly envisaged. Whatever happened the weather must always remain an incalculable factor, but at least by delay till the end of April we had a fair chance of several days of consecutive calm.

Before doing anything else I had to redistribute the troops on the transports to suit the order of their disembarkation. The bulk of the forces at my disposal had, perforce, been embarked without its having been possible to pay due attention to the operation upon which I now proposed that they should be launched.

Owing to lack of facilities at Mudros redistribution in that harbour was out of the question. With your Lordship's approval, therefore, I ordered all the transports, except those of the Australian Infantry Brigade and the details encamped at Lemnos Island, to the Egyptian ports. On the 24th March I myself, together with the General Staff, proceeded to Alexandria, where I remained until 7th April, working out the allocation of troops to transports in minutest detail as a prelude to the forthcoming disembarkation. General d'Amade did likewise.

On the 1st April the remainder of the General Headquarters, which had not been mobilised when I left England, arrived at Alexandria.

Apart from the re-arrangements of the troops, my visit to Egypt was not without profit, since it afforded me opportunities of conferring with the G.O.C. Egypt and of making myself acquainted with the troops, drawn from all parts of the French Republic and of the British Empire, which it was to be my privilege to command.

By the 7th April my preparations were sufficiently advanced to enable me to return with my General Staff to Lemnos, so as to put the finishing touches to my plan in close co-ordination with the Vice-Admiral Commanding the Eastern Mediterranean Fleet.

The covering force of the 29th Division left Mudros Harbour on the evening of 23rd April for the five beaches, S, V, W, X, and Y. Of these, V, W, and X were to be main landings, the landings at S and Y being made mainly to protect the flanks, to disseminate the forces of the enemy, and to interrupt the arrival of his reinforcements. The landings at S and Y were to take place at dawn, whilst it was planned that the first troops for V, W, and X beaches should reach the shore simultaneously at 5.30 a.m. after half an hour's bombardment from the fleet.

The transports conveying the covering force arrived off Tenedos on the morning of the 24th, and during the afternoon the troops were transferred to the warships and fleet-sweepers in which they were to approach the shore. About midnight these ships, each towing a number of cutters and other small boats, silently slipped their cables and, escorted by the 3rd Squadron of the Fleet, steamed slowly towards their final rendezvous at Cape Helles. The rendezvous was reached just before dawn on the 25th. The morning was absolutely still; there was no sign of life on the shore; a thin veil of mist hung motionless over the promontory; the surface of the sea was as smooth as glass. The four battleships and four cruisers which formed the 3rd Squadron at once took up the positions that had been allotted to them, and at 5 a.m., it being then light enough to fire, a violent bombardment of the enemy's defences was begun. Meanwhile the troops were being rapidly transferred to the small boats in which they were to be towed ashore. Not a move on the part of the enemy; except for shells thrown from the Asiatic side of the Straits the guns of the Fleet remained unanswered.

The detachment detailed for *S beach* (Eski Hissarlik Point) consisted of the 2nd South Wales Borderers (less one company) under Lieut.-Colonel Casson. Their landing was delayed by the current, but by 7.30 a.m. it had been successfully effected at the cost of some 50 casualties, and Lieut.-Colonel Casson was able to establish his small force on the high ground near De Totts Battery. Here he maintained himself until the general advance on the 27th brought him into touch with the main body.

The landing on *Y beach* was entrusted to the King's Own Scottish Borderers and the Plymouth (Marine) Battalion, Royal Naval Division, specially attached to the 29th Division for this task, the whole under command of Lieut.-Colonel Koe. The beach at this point consisted merely of a narrow strip of sand at the foot of a crumbling scrub-covered cliff some 200 feet high immediately to the west of Krithia.

A number of small gullies running down the face of the cliff facilitated the climb to the summit, and so impracticable had these precipices appeared to the Turks that no steps had been taken to defend them. Very different would it have been had we, as was at one time intended, taken Y 2 for this landing. There a large force of infantry, entrenched up to their necks, and supported by machine and Hotchkiss guns, were awaiting an attempt which could hardly have made good its footing. But at Y both battalions were able in the first instance to establish themselves on the heights, reserves of food, water and ammunition were hauled up to the top of the cliff, and, in accordance with the plan of operations, an endeavour was immediately made to gain touch with the troops landing at X beach. Unfortunately, the enemy's strong detachment from Y2 interposed, our troops landing at X were fully occupied in attacking the Turks immediately to their front, and the attempt to join hands was not persevered with.

Later in the day a large force of Turks were seen to be advancing upon the cliffs above Y beach from the direction of Krithia, and Colonel Koe was obliged to entrench. From this time onward his small force was subjected to strong and repeated attacks, supported by field artillery, and owing to the configuration of the ground, which here drops inland from the edge of the cliff, the guns of the supporting ships could render him little assistance. Throughout the afternoon and all through the night the Turks made assault after assault upon the British line. They threw bombs into the trenches, and, favoured by darkness, actually led a pony with a machine gun on its back over the defences and were proceeding to come into action in the middle of our position when they were bayonetted. The British repeatedly counter-charged with the bayonet, and always drove off the enemy for the moment, but the Turks were in a vast superiority and fresh troops took the place of those who temporarily fell back. Colonel Koe (since died of wounds) had become a casualty early in the day, and the number of officers and men killed and wounded during the incessant fighting was very heavy. By 7 a.m. on the 26th only about half of the King's Own Scottish Borderers remained to man the entrenchment made for four times their number. These brave fellows were absolutely worn out with continuous fighting; it was doubtful if rein-forcements could reach them in time, and orders were issued for them to be re-embarked. Thanks to H.M.S. "Goliath," "Dublin," "Amethyst," and "Sapphire," thanks also to the devotion of a small rearguard of the King's Own Scottish Borderers, which kept off the enemy from lining the cliff, the re-embarkation of the whole of the troops, together with the wounded, stores and ammunition, was safely accomplished, and both battalions were brought round the southern end of the peninsula. Deplorable as the heavy losses had been, and unfortunate as was the tactical failure to make good so much ground at the outset, yet, taking the operation as it stood, there can be no doubt it has contributed greatly to the success of the main attack, seeing that the plucky stand made at Y beach had detained heavy columns of the enemy from arriving at the southern end of the peninsula during what it will be seen was a very touch-and-go struggle.

The landing-place known as *X beach* consists of a strip of sand some 200 yards long by 8 yards wide at the foot of a low cliff. The troops to be landed here were the 1st Royal Fusiliers, who were to be towed ashore from H.M.S. "Implacable" in two parties, half a battalion at a time, together with a beach working party found by the Anson Battalion, Royal Naval Division. About 6 a.m. H.M.S. "Implacable," with a boldness much admired by the Army, stood quite close in to the beach, firing very rapidly with every gun she could bring to bear. Thus seconded, the Royal Fusiliers made good their landing with but little loss. The battalion then advanced to attack the Turkish trenches on the Hill 114, situated between V and W beaches, but were heavily counter-attacked and forced to give ground. Two more battalions of the 87th Brigade soon followed them, and by evening the troops had established themselves in an entrenched position extending from half a mile round the landing-place and as far south as Hill 114. Here they were in touch with the Lancashire Fusiliers, who had landed on W beach. Brigadier-General Marshall, commanding the 87th Brigade, had been wounded during the day's fighting, but continued in command of the brigade.

The landing on *V beach* was planned to take place on the following lines:-

As soon as the enemy's defences had been heavily bombarded by the fleet, three companies of the Dublin Fusiliers were to be towed ashore. They were to be closely followed by the collier "River Clyde" (Commander Unwin, R.N.), carrying between decks the balance of the Dublin Fusiliers, the Munster Fusiliers, half a battalion of the Hampshire Regiment, the West Riding Field Company, and other details.

The "River Clyde" had been specially prepared for the rapid disembarkation of her complement, and large openings for the exit of the troops had been cut in her sides, giving on to a wide gang-plank by which the men could pass rapidly into lighters which she had in tow. As soon as the first tows had reached land the "River Clyde" was to be run straight ashore. Her lighters were to be placed in position to form a gangway between the ship and the beach, and by this means it was hoped that 2,000 men could be thrown ashore with the utmost rapidity. Further, to assist in covering the landing, a battery of machine guns, protected by sandbags, had been mounted in her bows.

The remainder of the covering force detailed for this beach was then to follow in tows from the attendant battleships.

V beach is situated immediately to the west of Sedd-el-Bar. Between the bluff on which stands Sedd-el-Bahr village and that which is crowned by No. 1 Fort the ground forms a very regular amphitheatre of three or four hundred yards radius. The slopes down to the beach are slightly concave, so that the whole area contained within the limits of this natural amphitheatre, whose grassy terraces rise gently to a height of a hundred feet above the shore, can be swept by the fire of a defender. The beach itself is a sandy strip some 10 yards wide and 350 yards long, backed along almost the whole of its extent by a low sandy escarpment about 4 feet high, where the ground falls nearly sheer down to the beach. The slight shelter afforded by this escarpment played no small part in the operations of the succeeding thirty-two hours.

At the south-eastern extremity of the beach, between the shore and the village, stands the old fort of Sedd-el-Bahr, a battered ruin with wide breaches in its walls and mounds of fallen masonry within and around it. On the ridge to the north, overlooking the amphitheatre, stands a ruined barrack. Both of these buildings, as well as No. 1 Fort, had been long bombarded by the fleet, and the guns of the forts had been put out of action; but their crumbled walls and the ruined outskirts of the village afforded cover for riflemen, while from the terraced slopes already described the defenders were able to command the open beach, as a stage is overlooked from the balconies of a theatre. On the very margin of the beach a strong barbed-wire entanglement, made of heavier metal and longer barbs than I have ever seen elsewhere, ran right across from the old fort of Sedd-el-Bahr to the foot of the north-western headland. Two-thirds of the way up the ridge a second and even stronger entanglement crossed the amphitheatre, passing in front of the old barrack and ending in the outskirts of the village. A third transverse entanglement, joining these two, ran up the hill near the eastern end of the beach, and almost at right angles to it. Above the upper entanglement the ground was scored with the enemy's trenches, in one of which four pom-poms were emplaced; in others were dummy pom-poms to draw fire, while the debris of the shattered buildings on either flank afforded cover and concealment for a number of machine guns, which brought a cross-fire to bear on the ground already swept by rifle fire from the ridge.

Needless to say, the difficulties in the way of previous reconnaissance had rendered it impossible to obtain detailed information with regard either to the locality or to the enemy's preparations.

As often happens in war, the actual course of events did not quite correspond with the intentions of the Commander. The "River Clyde" came into position off Sedd-el-Bahr in advance of the tows, and, just as the latter reached the shore, Commander Unwin beached his ship also. Whilst the boats and the collier were approaching the landing place the Turks made no sign. Up to the very last moment it appeared as if the landing was to be unopposed. But the moment the first boat touched bottom the storm broke. A tornado of fire swept over the beach, the incoming boats, and the collier. The Dublin Fusiliers and the naval boats' crews suffered exceedingly heavy losses while still in the boats. Those who succeeded in landing and in crossing the strip of sand managed to gain some cover when they reached the low escarpment on the further side. None of the boats, however, were able to get off again, and they and their crews were destroyed upon the beach.

Now came the moment for the "River Clyde" to pour forth her living freight; but grievous delay was caused here by the difficulty of placing the lighters in position between the ship and the shore. A strong current hindered the work and the enemy's fire was so intense that almost every man engaged upon it was immediately shot. Owing, however, to the splendid gallantry of the naval working party, the lighters were eventually placed in position, and then the disembarkation began.

A company of the Munster Fusiliers led the way; but, short as was the distance, few of the men ever reached the farther side of the beach through the hail of bullets which poured down upon them from both flanks and the front. As the second company followed, the extemporised pier of lighters gave way in the current. The end nearest to the shore drifted into deep water, and many men who had escaped being shot were drowned by the weight of their equipment in trying to swim from the lighter to the beach. Undaunted workers were still forthcoming, the lighters were again brought into position, and the third company of the Munster Fusiliers rushed ashore, suffering heaviest loss this time from shrapnel as well as from rifle, pom-pom, and machine-gun fire.

For a space the attempt to land was discontinued. When it was resumed the lighters again drifted into deep water, with Brigadier-General Napier, Captain Costeker, his Brigade Major, and a number of men of the Hampshire Regiment on board. There was nothing for them all but to lie down on the lighters, and it was here that General Napier and Captain Costeker were killed. At this time, between 10 and 11 a.m., about 1,000 men had left the collier, and of these nearly half had been killed or wounded before they could reach the little cover afforded by the steep, sandy bank at the top of the beach. Further attempts to disembark were now given up. Had the troops all been in open boats but few of them would have lived to tell the tale. But, most fortunately, the collier was so constructed as to afford fairly efficient protection to the men who were still on board, and, so long as they made no attempt to land, they suffered comparatively little loss.

Throughout the remainder of the day there was practically no change in the position of affairs. The situation was probably saved by the machine-guns on the "River Clyde," which did valuable service in keeping down the enemy's fire and in preventing any attempt on their part to launch a counter-attack. One half-company of the Dublin Fusiliers, which had been landed at a camber just east of Sedd-el- Bahr village, was unable to work its way across to V beach, and by mid-day had only twenty-five men left. It was proposed to divert to Y beach that part of the main body which had been intended to land on V beach; but this would have involved considerable delay owing to the distance, and the main body was diverted to W beach, where the Lancashire Fusiliers had already effected a landing.

Late in the afternoon part of the Worcestershire Regiment and the Lancashire Fusiliers worked across the high ground from W beach, and seemed likely to relieve the situation by taking the defenders of V beach in flank. The pressure on their own front, however, and the numerous, barbed-wire entanglements which intervened, checked this advance, and at nightfall the Turkish garrison still held their ground. Just before dark some small parties of our men made their way along the shore to the outer walls of the Old Fort, and when night had fallen the remainder of the infantry from the collier were landed. A good force was now available for attack, but our troops were at such a cruel disadvantage as to position, and the fire of the enemy was still so accurate in the bright moonlight that all attempts to clear the fort, and the outskirts of the village during the night failed one after the other. The wounded who were able to do so without support returned to the collier under cover of darkness; but otherwise the situation at daybreak on the 26th was the same as it had been on the previous day except that the troops first landed were becoming very exhausted.

Twenty-four hours after the disembarkation began there were ashore on V beach the survivors of the Dublin and Munster Fusiliers and of two companies of the Hampshire Regiment. The Brigadier and his Brigade-Major had been killed; Lieutenant-Colonel Carrington Smith, commanding the Hampshire Regiment, had been killed and the adjutant had been wounded. The Adjutant of the Munster Fusiliers was wounded, and the great majority of the senior officers were either wounded or killed. The remnant of the landing-party still crouched on the beach beneath the shelter of the sandy escarpment which had saved so many lives. With them were two officers of my General Staff – Lieutenant-Colonel Doughty-Wylie and Lieutenant-Colonel Williams. These two officers, who had landed from the "River Clyde" had been striving, with conspicuous contempt for danger, to keep all their comrades in good heart during this day and night of ceaseless imminent peril.

Now that it was daylight once more, Lieutenant-Colonels Doughty-Wylie and Williams set to work to organise an attack on the hill above the beach. Any soldier who has endeavoured to pull scattered units together after they have been dominated for many consecutive hours by close and continuous fire will be able to take the measure of their difficulties. Fortunately, General Hunter Weston had arranged with Rear-Admiral Wemyss about this same time for a heavy bombardment to be opened by the ships upon the Old Fort, Sedd-el-Bahr Village, the Old Castle north of the village, and on the ground leading up from the beach. Under cover of this bombardment, and led by Lieutenant-Colonel Doughty-Wylie and Captain Walford, Brigade-Major R.A., the troops gained a footing in the village by 10 a.m. They encountered a most stubborn opposition and suffered heavy losses from the fire of well-concealed riflemen and machine-guns. Undeterred by the resistance, and supported by the naval gunfire, they pushed forward, and soon after midday they penetrated to the northern edge of the village, whence they were in a position to attack the Old Castle and Hill 141. During this advance Captain Walford was killed. Lieutenant-Colonel Doughty-Wylie had most gallantly led the attack all the way up from the beach through the west side of the village, under a galling fire. And now, when, owing so largely to his own inspiring example and intrepid courage, the position, had almost been gained, he was killed while leading the last assault. But the attack was pushed forward without wavering, and, fighting their way across the open with great dash, the troops gained the summit and occupied the Old Castle and Hill 141 before 2 p.m.

W beach consists of a strip of deep, powdery sand some 350 yards long and from 15 to 40 yards wide, situated immediately south of Tekke Burnu, where a small gully, running down to the sea opens out a break in the cliffs. On either flank of the beach the ground rises precipitously but, in the centre, a number of sand dunes afford a more gradual access to the ridge overlooking the sea. Much time and ingenuity had been employed by the Turks in turning this landing place into a death trap. Close to the water's edge a broad wire entanglement extended the whole length of the shore, and a supplementary barbed network lay concealed under the surface of the sea in the shallows. Land mines and sea mines had been laid. The high ground overlooking the beach was strongly fortified with trenches to which the gully afforded a natural covered approach. A number of machine guns also were cunningly tucked away into holes in the cliff so as to be immune from a naval bombardment whilst they were converging their fire on the wire entanglements. The crest of the hill overlooking the beach was in its turn commanded by high ground to the north-west and south-east, and especially by two strong infantry redoubts near point 138. Both these redoubts were protected by wire entanglements about 20 feet broad, and could be approached only by a bare glacis-like slope leading up from the high ground above W beach or from the Cape Helles lighthouse. In addition, another separate entanglement ran down from these two redoubts to the edge of the cliff near the lighthouse, making intercommunication between V and W beaches impossible until these redoubts had been captured.

So strong, in fact, were the defences of W beach that the Turks may well have considered them impregnable, and it is my firm conviction that no finer feat of arms has ever been achieved by the British soldier – or any other soldier – than the storming of these trenches from open boats on the morning of 25th April.

The landing at W had been entrusted to the 1st Battalion Lancashire Fusiliers (Major Bishop) and it was to the complete lack of the senses of danger or of fear of this daring battalion that we owed our astonishing success. As in the case of the landing at X, the disembarkation had been delayed for half an hour, but at 6 a.m. the whole battalion approached the shore together, towed by eight picket boats in line abreast, each picket boat pulling four ship's cutters. As soon as shallow water was reached, the tows were cast off and the boats were at once rowed to the shore. Three companies headed for the beach and a company on the left of the line made for a small ledge of rock immediately under the cliff at Tekke Burnu. Brigadier-General Hare, commanding the 88th Brigade, accompanied this latter party, which escaped the cross fire brought to bear upon the beach, and was also in a better position than the rest of the battalion to turn the wire entanglements.

While the troops were approaching the shore no shot had been fired from the enemy's trenches, but as soon as the first boat touched the ground a hurricane of lead swept over the battalion. Gallantly led by their officers, the Fusiliers literally hurled themselves ashore and, fired at from right, left and centre, commenced hacking their way through the wire. A long line of men was at once mown down as by a scythe, but the remainder were not to be denied. Covered by the fire of the warships, which had now closed right in to the shore, and helped by the flanking fire of the company on the extreme left, they broke through the entanglements and collected under the cliffs on either side of the beach. Here the companies were rapidly reformed, and set forth to storm the enemy's entrenchments wherever they could find them. In making these attacks the bulk of the battalion moved up towards Hill 114 whilst a small party worked down towards the trenches on the Cape Helles side of the landing-place. Several land mines were exploded by the Turks during the advance, but the determination of the troops was in no way affected. By 10 a.m. three lines of hostile trenches were in our hands, and our hold on the beach was assured.

About 9.30 a.m. more infantry had begun to disembark, and two hours later a junction was effected on Hill 114 with the troops who had landed on X beach.

On the right, owing to the strength of the redoubt on Hill 138, little progress could be made. The small party of Lancashire Fusiliers which had advanced in this direction succeeded in reaching the edge of the wire entanglements, but were not strong enough to do more, and it was here that Major Frankland, Brigade Major of the 86th Infantry Brigade, who had gone forward to make a personal reconnaissance, was unfortunately killed. Brigadier-General Hare had been wounded earlier in the day, and Colonel Woolly-Dod, General Staff 29th Division, was now sent ashore to take command at W beach and organise a further advance.

At 2 p.m., after the ground near Hill 138 had been subjected to a heavy bombardment, the Worcester Regiment advanced to the assault. Several men of this battalion rushed forward with great spirit to cut passages through the entanglement; some were killed, others persevered, and by 4 p.m. the hill and redoubt were captured.

An attempt was now made to join hands with the troops on V beach, who could make no headway at all against the dominating defences of the enemy. To help them out the 86th Brigade pushed forward in an easterly direction along the cliff. There is a limit however to the storming of barbed-wire entanglements. More of these barred the way. Again the heroic wire-cutters came out. Through glasses they could be seen quietly snipping away under a hellish fire as if they were pruning a vine-yard. Again some of them fell. The fire pouring out of No. 1 fort grew hotter and hotter, until the troops, now thoroughly exhausted by a sleepless night and by the long day's fighting under a hot sun, had to rest on their laurels for a while. When night fell, the British position in front of W beach extended from just east of Cape Helles light-house, through Hill 138, to Hill 114. Practically every man had to be thrown into the trenches to hold this line, and the only available reserves on this part of our front were the 2nd London Field Company R.E. and a platoon of the Anson Battalion, which had been landed as a beach working party.

During the night several strong and determined counter-attacks were made, all successfully repulsed without loss of ground. Meanwhile the disembarkation of the remainder of the division was proceeding on W and X beaches.

The Australian and New Zealand Army Corps sailed out of Mudros Bay on the afternoon of April 24th, escorted by the 2nd Squadron of the Fleet, under Rear-Admiral Thursby. The rendezvous was reached just after half-past one in the morning of the 25th, and there the 1,500 men who had been placed on board H.M. ships before leaving Mudros were transferred to their boats. This operation was carried out with remarkable expedition, and in absolute silence. Simultaneously the remaining 2,500 men of the covering force were transferred from their transports to six destroyers. At 2.30 a.m. H.M. ships, together with the tows and the destroyers, proceeded to within some four miles of the coast, H.M.S. "Queen" (flying Rear-Admiral Thursby's flag) directing on a point about a mile north of Kaba Tepe. At 3.30 a.m. orders to go ahead and land were given to the tows, and at 4.10 a.m. the destroyers were ordered to follow.

All these arrangements worked without a hitch, and were carried out in complete orderliness and silence. No breath of wind ruffled the surface of the sea, and every condition was favourable save for the moon, which, sinking behind the ships, may have silhouetted them against its orb, betraying them thus to watchers on the shore.

A rugged and difficult part of the coast had been selected for the landing, so difficult and rugged that I considered the Turks were not at all likely to anticipate such a descent. Indeed, owing to the tows having failed to maintain their exact direction the actual point of disembarkation was rather more than a mile north of that which I had selected, and was more closely overhung by steeper cliffs. Although this accident increased the initial difficulty of driving the enemy off the heights inland, it has since proved itself to have been a blessing in disguise, inasmuch as the actual base of the force of occupation has been much better defiladed from shell fire.

The beach on which the landing was actually effected is a very narrow strip of sand, about 1,000 yards in length, bounded on the north and the south by two small promontories. At its southern extremity a deep ravine, with exceedingly steep, scrub-clad sides, runs inland in a north-easterly direction. Near the northern end of the beach a small but steep gully runs up into the hills at right angles to the shore. Between the ravine and the gully the whole of the beach is backed by the seaward face of the spur which forms the north-western side of the ravine. From the top of the spur the ground falls almost sheer, except near the southern limit of the beach, where gentler slopes give access to the mouth of the ravine behind. Further inland lie in a tangled knot the under-features of Saribair, separated by deep ravines, which take a most confusing diversity of direction. Sharp spurs, covered with dense scrub, and falling away in many places in precipitous sandy cliffs, radiate from the principal mass of the mountain, from which they run north-west, west, south-west, and south to the coast.

The boats approached the land in the silence and the darkness, and they were close to the shore before the enemy stirred. Then about one battalion of Turks was seen running along the beach to intercept the lines of boats. At this so critical a moment the conduct of all ranks was most praiseworthy. Not a word was spoken – everyone remained perfectly orderly and quiet awaiting the enemy's fire, which sure enough opened, causing many casualties. The moment the boats touched land the Australians' turn had come. Like lightning they leapt ashore, and each man as he did so went straight as his bayonet at the enemy. So vigorous was the onslaught that the Turks made no attempt to withstand it and fled from ridge to ridge pursued by the Australian infantry.

This attack was carried out by the 3rd Australian Brigade, under Major (temporary Colonel) Sinclair Maclagan, D.S.O. The 1st and 2nd Brigades followed promptly, and were all disembarked by 2 p.m., by which time 12,000 men and two batteries of Indian Mountain Artillery had been landed. The disembarkation of further artillery was delayed owing to the fact that the enemy's heavy guns opened on the anchorage and forced the transports, which had been subjected to continuous shelling from his field guns, to stand further out to sea.

The broken ground, the thick scrub, the necessity for sending any formed detachments post haste as they landed to the critical point of the moment, the headlong valour of scattered groups of the men who had pressed far further into the peninsula than had been intended – all these led to confusion and mixing up of units. Eventually the mixed crowd of fighting men, some advancing from the beach, others falling back before the oncoming Turkish supports, solidified into a semi-circular position with its right about a mile north of Kaba Tepe and its left on the high ground over Fisherman's Hut. During this period parties of the 9th and 10th Battalions charged and put out of action three of the enemy's Krupp guns. During this period also the disembarkation of the Australian Division was being followed by that of the New Zealand and Australian Division (two brigades only).

From 11 a.m. to 3 p.m. the enemy, now reinforced to a strength of 20,000 men, attacked the whole line, making a specially strong effort against the 3rd Brigade and the left of the 2nd Brigade. This counter-attack was, however, handsomely repulsed with the help of the guns of H.M. ships. Between 5 and 6.30 p.m. a third most determined counter-attack was made against the 3rd Brigade, who held their ground with more than equivalent stubbornness. During the night again the Turks made constant attacks, and the 8th Battalion repelled a bayonet charge; but in spite of all the line held firm. The troops had had practically no rest on the night of the 24/25th; they had been fighting hard all day over most difficult country, and they had been subjected to heavy shrapnel fire in the open. Their casualties had been deplorably heavy. But, despite their losses and in spite of their fatigue, the morning of the 26th found them still in good heart and as full of fight as ever.

It is a consolation to know that the Turks suffered still more seriously. Several times our machine guns got on to them in close formation, and the whole surrounding country is still strewn with their dead of this date.

The reorganisation of units and formations was impossible during the 26th and 27th owing to persistent attacks. An advance was impossible until a re-organisation could be effected, and it only remained to entrench the position gained and to perfect the arrangements for bringing up ammunition, water, and supplies to the ridges – in itself a most difficult undertaking. Four battalions of the Royal Naval Division were sent up to reinforce the Army Corps on the 28th and 29th April.

On the night of May 2nd a bold effort was made to seize a commanding knoll in front of the centre of the line. The enemy's enfilading machine guns were too scientifically posted, and 800 men were lost without advantage beyond the infliction of a corresponding loss to the enemy. On May 4th an attempt to seize Kaba Tepe was also unsuccessful, the barbed-wire here being something beyond belief. But a number of minor operations have been carried out, such as the taking of a Turkish observing station; the strength-ening of entrenchments; the reorganisation of units; and the perfecting of communication with the landing place. Also a constant strain has been placed upon some of the best troops of the enemy who, to the number of 24,000, are constantly kept fighting and being killed and wounded freely, as the Turkish sniper is no match for the Kangaroo shooter, even at his own game.

The assistance of the Royal Navy, here as elsewhere, has been invaluable. The whole of the arrangements have been in Admiral Thursby's hands, and I trust I may be permitted to say what a trusty and powerful friend he has proved himself to be to the Australian and New Zealand Army Corps.

Concurrently with the British landings a regiment of the French Corps was successfully disembarked at Kum Kale under the guns of the French fleet, and remained ashore till the morning of the 26th, when they were re-embarked. 500 prisoners were captured by the French on this day.

This operation drew the fire of the Asiatic guns from Morto Bay and V beach on to Kum Kale, and contributed largely to the success of the British landings.

On the evening of the 26th the main disembarkation of the French Corps was begun, V beach being allotted to our Allies for this purpose, and it was arranged that the French should hold the portion of the front between the telegraph wire and the sea.

The following day I ordered a general advance to a line stretching from Hill 236 near Eski Hissarlik Point to the mouth of the stream two miles north of Tekke Burnu. This advance, which was commenced at midday, was com-pleted without opposition, and the troops at once consolidated their new line.

The forward movement relieved the growing congestion on the beaches, and by giving us possession of several new wells afforded a temporary solution to the water problem, which had hitherto been causing me much anxiety.

By the evening of the 27th the Allied forces had established themselves on a line some three miles long, which stretched from the mouth of the nullah, 3,200 yards north-east of Tekke Burnu, to Eski Hissarlik Point, the three brigades of the 29th Division less two battalions on the left and in the centre, with four French battalions on the right, and beyond them again the South Wales Borderers on the extreme right.

Owing to casualties this line was somewhat thinly held. Still, it was so vital to make what headway we could before the enemy recovered himself and received fresh reinforcements that it was decided to push on as quickly as possible. Orders were therefore issued for a general advance to commence at 8 a.m. next day.

The 29th Division were to march on Krithia, with their left brigade leading, the French were directed to extend their left in conformity with the British movements and to retain their right on the coast-line south of the Kereves Dere.

The advance commenced at 8 a.m. on the 28th, and was carried out with commendable vigour, despite the fact that from the moment of landing the troops had been unable to obtain any proper rest.

The 87th Brigade, with which had been incorporated the Drake Battalion, Royal Naval Division, in the place of the King's Own Scottish Borderers and South Wales Borderers, pushed on rapidly, and by 10 a.m. had advanced some two miles. Here the further progress of the Border regiment was barred by a strong work on the left flank. They halted to concentrate and make dispositions to attack it, and at that moment had to withstand a determined counter-attack by the Turks. Aided by heavy gun fire from H.M.S. "Queen Elizabeth," they succeeded in beating off the attack, but they made no further progress that day, and when night fell entrenched themselves on the ground they had gained in the morning.

The Inniskilling Fusiliers, who advanced with their right on the Krithia ravine, reached a point about three-quarters of a mile southwest of Krithia. This was, however, the farthest limit attained, and later on in the day they fell back into line with other corps.

The 88th Brigade on the right of the 87th progressed steadily until about 11.30 a.m., when the stubbornness of the opposition, coupled with a dearth of ammunition, brought their advance to a standstill. The 86th Brigade, under Lieutenant-Colonel Casson, which had been held in reserve, were thereupon ordered to push forward through the 88th Brigade in the direction of Krithia.

The movement commenced at about 1 p.m., but though small reconnoitring parties got to within a few hundred yards of Krithia, the main body of the brigade did not get beyond the line held by the 88th Brigade. Meanwhile, the French had also pushed on in the face of strong opposition along the spurs on the western bank of the Kereves Dere, and had got to within a mile of Krithia with their right thrown back and their left in touch with the 88th Brigade. Here they were unable to make further progress; gradually the strength of the resistance made itself felt, and our Allies were forced during the afternoon to give ground.

By 2 p.m. the whole of the troops with the exception of the Drake Battalion had been absorbed into the firing line. The men were exhausted, and the few guns landed at the time were unable to afford them adequate artillery support. The small amount of transport available did not suffice to maintain the supply of munitions, and cartridges were running short despite all efforts to push them up from the landing-places.

Hopes of getting a footing on Achi Babi had now perforce to be abandoned – at least for this occasion. The best that could be expected was that we should be able to maintain what we had won, and when at 3 p.m. the Turks made a determined counter-attack with the bayonet against the centre and right of our line, even this seemed exceedingly doubtful. Actually a partial retirement did take place. The French were also forced back, and at 6 p.m. orders were issued for our troops to entrench themselves as best they could in the positions they then held, with their right flank thrown back so as to maintain connection with our Allies. In this retirement the right flank of the 88th Brigade was temporarily uncovered, and the Worcester Regiment suffered severely.

Had it been possible to push in reinforcements in men, artillery and munitions during the day, Krithia should have fallen, and much subsequent fighting for its capture would have been avoided.

Two days later this would have been feasible, but I had to reckon with the certainty that the enemy would, in that same time, have received proportionately greater support. I was faced by the usual choice of evils, and although the result was not what I had hoped, I have no reason to believe that hesitation and delay would better have answered my purpose.

For, after all, we had pushed forward quite appreciably on the whole. The line eventually held by our troops on the night of the 28th ran from a point on the coast three miles north-west of Tekke Burnu to a point one mile north of Eski Hissarlik, whence it was continued by the French south-east to the coast.

Much inevitable mixing of units of the 86th and 88th Brigades had occurred during the day's fighting, and there was a dangerous re-entrant in the line at the junction of the 87th and 88th Brigades near the Krithia nullah.

The French had lost heavily, especially in officers, and required time to re-organise.

The 29th April was consequently spent in straightening the line, and in consolidating and strengthening the positions gained. There was a certain amount of artillery and musketry fire, but nothing serious.

Similarly, on the 30th, no advance was made, nor was any attack delivered by the enemy. The landing of the bulk of the artillery was completed, and a readjustment of the line took place, the portion held by the French being somewhat increased.

Two more battalions of the Royal Naval Division had been disembarked, and these, together with three battalions of the 88th Brigade withdrawn from the line, were formed into a reserve. This reserve was increased on the 1st May by the addition of the 29th Indian Infantry Brigade, which released the three battalions of the 88th Brigade to return to the trenches. The Corps Expéditionnaire d'Orient had disembarked the whole of their infantry and all but two of their batteries by the same evening.

At 10 p.m. the Turks opened a hot shell fire upon our position, and half an hour later, just before the rise of the moon, they delivered a series of desperate attacks. Their formation was in three solid lines, the men in the front rank being deprived of ammunition to make them rely only upon the bayonet. The officers were served out with coloured Bengal lights to fire from their pistols, red indicating to the Turkish guns that they were to lengthen their range; white that our front trenches had been stormed; green that our main position had been carried. The Turkish attack was to crawl on hands and knees until the time came for the final rush to be made. An eloquent hortative was signed Von Zowenstern and addressed to the Turkish rank and file who were called upon, by one mighty effort, to fling us all back into the sea:

"Attack the enemy with the bayonet and utterly destroy him!

"We shall not retire one step; for, if we do, our religion, our country and our nation will perish!

"Soldiers! The world is looking at you! Your only hope of salvation is to bring this battle to a successful issue or gloriously to give up your life in the attempt!"

The first momentum of this ponderous onslaught fell upon the right of the 86th Brigade, an unlucky spot, seeing all the officers thereabouts had already been killed or wounded. So when the Turks came right on without firing and charged into the trenches with the bayonet they made an ugly gap in the line. This gap was instantly filled by the 5th Royal Scots (Territorials), who faced to their flank and executed a brilliant bayonet charge against the enemy, and by the Essex Regiment detached for the purpose by the Officer Commanding

88th Brigade. The rest of the British line held its own with comparative ease, and it was not found necessary to employ any portion of the reserve. The storm next broke in fullest violence against the French left, which was held by the Senegalese. Behind them were two British Field Artillery Brigades and a Howitzer Battery. After several charges and counter-charges the Senegalese began to give ground and a company of the Worcester Regiment and some gunners were sent forward to hold the gap. Later, a second company of the Worcester Regiment was also sent up, and the position was then maintained for the remainder of the night, although, about 2 a.m., it was found necessary to despatch one battalion Royal Naval Division to strengthen the extreme right of the French.

About 5 a.m. a counter-offensive was ordered, and the whole line began to advance. By 7.30 a.m. the British left had gained some 500 yards, and the centre had pushed the enemy back and inflicted heavy losses. The right also had gained some ground in conjunction with the French left, but the remainder of the French line was unable to progress. As the British centre and left were now subjected to heavy cross fire from concealed machine guns, it was found impossible to maintain the ground gained, and therefore, about 11 a.m., the whole line withdrew to its former trenches.

The net result of the operations was the repulse of the Turks and the infliction upon them of very heavy losses. At first we had them fairly on the run, and had it not been for those inventions of the devil – machine guns and barbed wire – which suit the Turkish character and tactics to perfection, we should not have stopped short of the crest of Achi Babi. As it was, all brigades reported great numbers of dead Turks in front of their lines, and 350 prisoners were left in our hands.

On the 2nd, during the day, the enemy remained quiet, burying his dead under a red crescent flag, a work with which we did not interfere. Shortly after 9 p.m., however, they made another attack against the whole allied line, their chief effort being made against the French front, where the ground favoured their approach. The attack was repulsed with loss.

During the night 3rd/4th the French front was again subjected to a heavy attack, which they were able to repulse without assistance from my general reserve.

The day of the 4th was spent in reorganisation, and a portion of the line held by the French, who had lost heavily during the previous night's fighting, was taken over by the 2nd Naval Brigade. The night passed quietly.

During the 5th the Lancashire Fusilier Brigade of the East Lancashire Division was disembarked and placed in reserve behind the British left.

Orders were issued for an advance to be carried out next day, and these and the three days' battle which ensued, will be dealt with in my next despatch.

The losses, exclusive of the French, during the period covered by this despatch were, I regret to say, very severe, numbering:-

177 Officers and 1,990 other ranks killed,
412 Officers and 7,807 other ranks wounded,
13 Officers and 3,580 other ranks missing.

From a technical point of view it is interesting to note that my Administrative Staff had not reached Mudros by the time when the landings were finally arranged. All the highly elaborate work involved by these landings was put through by my General Staff working in collaboration with Commodore Roger Keyes, C.B., M.V.O., and the Naval Transport Officers allotted for the purpose by Vice-Admiral de Robeck. Navy and Army carried out these combined duties with that perfect harmony which was indeed absolutely essential to success.

Throughout the events I have chronicled the Royal Navy has been father and mother to the Army. Not one of us but realises how much he owes to Vice-Admiral de Robeck; to the warships, French and British; to the destroyers, minesweepers, picket boats, and to all their dauntless crews, who took no thought of themselves, but risked everything to give their soldier comrades a fair run in at the enemy.

Throughout these preparations and operations Monsieur le Général d'Amade has given me the benefit of his wide experiences of war, and has afforded me, always, the most loyal and energetic support. The landing of Kum Kale planned by me as a mere diversion to distract the attention of the enemy was transformed by the Commander of the Corps Expéditionnaire de l'Orient into a brilliant operation, which secured some substantial results. During the fighting which followed the landing of the French Division at Sedd-el-Bahr no troops could have acquitted themselves more creditably under very trying circumstances, and under very heavy losses, than those working under the orders of Monsieur le Général d'Amade.

Lieutenant-General Sir W.R. Birdwood, K.C.S.I., C.B., C.I.E., D.S.O., was in command of the detached landing of the Australian and New Zealand Army Corps above Kaba Tepe, as well as during the subsequent fighting. The fact of his having been responsible for the execution of these difficult and hazardous operations – operations which were crowned with a very remarkable success – speaks, I think, for itself.

Major-General A.G. Hunter-Weston, C.B., D.S.O., was tried very highly, not only during the landings, but more especially in the day and night attacks and counter attacks which ensued. Untiring, resourceful and ever more cheerful as the outlook (on occasion) grew darker, he possesses, in my opinion, very special qualifications as a Commander of troops in the field. Major-General

W.P. Braithwaite, C.B., is the best Chief of the General Staff it has ever been my fortune to encounter in war. I will not pile epithets upon him. I can say no more than what I have said, and I can certainly say no less.

I have many other names to bring to notice for the period under review, and these will form the subject of a separate report at an early date.

I have the honour to be
Your Lordship's most obedient Servant,
IAN HAMILTON, General,
Commanding Mediterranean Expeditionary Force.

3

DE ROBECK'S GALLIPOLI LANDINGS DESPATCH, 1 JULY 1915

MONDAY, 16 AUGUST, 1915.

Admiralty, 16th August, 1915.

The following despatch has been received from Vice-Admiral John M. de Robeck, reporting the landing of the Army on the Gallipoli Peninsula, 25th–26th April, 1915:-

"Triad,"

SIR,-   *July* 1, 1915.

I have the honour to forward herewith an account of the operations carried out on the 25th and 26th April, 1915, during which period the Mediterranean Expeditionary Force was landed and firmly established in the Gallipoli peninsula.

The landing commenced at 4.20 a.m. on 25th. The general scheme was as follows:-

Two main landings were to take place, the first at a point just north of Gaba Tepe, the second on the southern end of the peninsula. In addition, a landing was to be made at Kum Kale, and a demonstration in force to be carried out in the Gulf of Xeros near Bulair.

The night of the 24th–25th was calm and very clear, with a brilliant moon, which set at 3 a.m.

The first landing, north of Gaba Tepe, was carried out under the orders of Rear-Admiral C.F. Thursby, C.M.G. His squadron consisted of the following ships:-

Battleships.	Cruiser.	Destroyers.	Seaplane Carrier.	Balloon Ship.	Trawlers.
Queen.	Bacchante.	Beagle.	Ark Royal.	Manica.	15
London.		Bulldog.			
Prince of Wales.		Foxhound.			
Triumph.		Scourge.			
Majestic.		Colne.			
		Usk.			
		Chelmer.			
		Ribble.			

To "Queen," "London," and "Prince of Wales" was delegated the duty of actually landing the troops. To "Triumph," "Majestic," and "Bacchante" the duty of covering the landing by gunfire.

In this landing a surprise was attempted. The first troops to be landed were embarked in the battleships "Queen," "London," and "Prince of Wales."

The squadron then approached the land at 2.58 a.m. at a speed of 5 knots. When within a short distance of the beach selected for landing the boats were sent ahead. At 4.20 a.m. the boats reached the beach and a landing was effected.

The remainder of the infantry of the covering force were embarked at 10 p.m., 24th. The troops were landed in two trips, the operation occupying about half an hour, this in spite of the fact that the landing was vigorously opposed, the surprise being only partially effected.

The disembarkation of the main body was at once proceeded with. The operations were somewhat delayed owing to the transports having to remain a considerable distance from the shore in order to avoid the howitzer and field guns' fire brought to bear on them and also the fire from warships stationed in the Narrows, Chanak.

The beach here was very narrow and continuously under shell fire. The difficulties of disembarkation were accentuated by the necessity of evacuating the wounded; both operations proceeded simultaneously. The service was one which called for great determination and coolness under fire, and the success achieved indicates the spirit animating all concerned. In this respect I would specially mention the extraordinary gallantry and dash shown by the 3rd Australian Infantry Brigade (Colonel E.G. Sinclair Maclagan, D.S.O.), who formed the covering force. Many individual acts of devotion to duty were performed by the personnel of the Navy; these are dealt with below. Here I should like to place on record the good service performed by the vessels employed in landing the second part of the covering force; the seamanship displayed and the rapidity with which so large a force was thrown on the beach is deserving of the highest praise.

On the 26th the landing of troops, guns and stores continued throughout the day; this was a most trying service, as the enemy kept up an incessant shrapnel fire, and it was extremely difficult to locate the well-concealed guns of the enemy. Occasional bursts of fire from the ships in the Narrows delayed operations somewhat, but these bursts of fire did not last long, and the fire from our ships always drove the enemy's ships away.

The enemy heavily counter-attacked, and though supported by a very heavy shrapnel fire he could make no impression on our line, which was every minute becoming stronger. By nightfall on the 26th April our position north of Gaba Tepe was secure. The landing at the southern extremity of the

Gallipoli Peninsula was carried out under the orders of Rear-Admiral R.E. Wemyss, C.M.G., M.V.O., his squadron consisting of the following ships:-

Battleships.	Cruisers.	Fleet Sweepers.	Trawlers.
Swiftsure.	Euryalus.	6	14
Implacable.	Talbot.		
Cornwallis.	Minerva.		
Albion.	Dublin.		
Vengeance.			
Lord Nelson.			
Prince George.			

Landings in this area were to be attempted at five different places; the conditions at each landing varied considerably. The position of beaches is given below.

Position of Beach. – "Y" beach, a point about 7,000 yards north-east of Cape Tekeh. "X" beach, 1,000 yards north-east of Cape Tekeh. "W" beach, Cape Tekeh – Cape Helles. "V" beach, Cape Helles – Seddul Bahr. Camber, Seddul Bahr. "S" beach, Eski-Hissarlik Point.

Taking these landings in the above order:-

Landing at "T" Beach. – The troops to be first landed, the King's Own Scottish Borderers, embarked on the 24th in the "Amethyst'" and "Sapphire'" and proceeded with the transports "Southland" and "Braemar Castle" to a position off Cape Tekeh. At 4.0 a.m. the boats proceeded to "Y" beach, timing their arrival there at 5.0 a.m., and pulled ashore covered by fire from H.M.S. "Goliath." The landing was most successfully and expeditiously carried out, the troops gaining the top of the high cliffs overlooking this beach without being opposed; this result I consider due to the rapidity with which the disembarkation was carried out and the well-placed covering fire from ships.

The Scottish Borderers were landed in two trips, followed at once by the Plymouth Battalion Royal Marines. These troops met with severe opposition on the top of the cliffs, where fire from covering ships was of little assistance and, after heavy fighting, were forced to re-embark on the 26th. The re-embarkation was carried out by the following ships: "Goliath," "Talbot," "Dublin," "Sapphire," and "Amethyst." It was most ably conducted by the beach personnel and covered by the fire of the warships, who prevented the enemy reaching the edge of the cliff, except for a few snipers.

Landing at "X" Beach. – The 2nd Battalion Royal Fusiliers (two companies and M.G. Section) embarked in "Implacable" on 24th, which ship proceeded to a position off the landing-place, where the disembarkation of the troops commenced at 4.30 a.m., and was completed at 5.15 a.m.

A heavy fire was opened on the cliffs on both sides. The "Implacable" approached the beach, and the troops were ordered to land, fire being continued until the boats were close into the beach. The troops on board the "Implacable" were all landed by 7 a.m. without any casualties. The nature of the beach was very favourable for the covering fire from ships, but the manner in which this landing was carried out might well serve as a model.

Landing at "W" Beach. – The 1st Battalion Lancashire Fusiliers embarked in "Euryalus" and "Implacable" on the 24th, who proceeded to positions off the landing-place, where the troops embarked in the boats at about 4 a.m. Shortly after 5 a.m. "Euryalus" approached "W" beach and "Implacable" "X" beach. At 5 a.m. the covering ships opened a heavy fire on the beach, which was continued up to the last moment before landing. Unfortunately this fire did not have the effect on the extensive wire entanglements and trenches that had been hoped for, and the troops, on landing at 6 a.m., were met with a very heavy fire from rifles, machine guns, and pom-poms, and found the obstructions on the beach undamaged. The formation of this beach lends itself admirably to the defence, the landing-place being commanded by sloping cliffs offering ideal positions for trenches and giving a perfect field of fire.

The only weakness in the enemy's position was on the flanks, where it was just possible to land on the rocks and thus enfilade the more important defences. This landing on the rocks was effected with great skill, and some maxims, cleverly concealed in the cliffs and which completely enfiladed the main beach, were rushed with the bayonet. This assisted to a great extent in the success of the landing, the troops, though losing very heavily, were not to be denied and the beach and the approaches to it were soon in our possession

The importance of this success cannot be overestimated; "W" and "V" beaches were the only two of any size in this area, on which troops, other than infantry, could be disembarked, and failure to capture this one might have had serious consequences as the landing at "V" was held up. The beach was being continuously sniped and a fierce infantry battle was carried on round it throughout the entire day and the following night. It is impossible to exalt too highly the service rendered by the 1st Battalion Lancashire Fusiliers in the storming of the beach; the dash and gallantry displayed were superb. Not one whit behind in devotion to duty was the work of the beach personnel, who worked untiringly throughout the day and night, landing troops and stores under continual sniping. The losses due to rifle and machine-gun fire sustained by the boats' crews, to which they had not the satisfaction of being able to reply, bear testimony to the arduous nature of the service.

During the night of the 25th–26th enemy attacked continuously, and it was not till 1 p.m. on the 26th, when "V" beach was captured, that our position might be said to be secure.

The work of landing troops, guns, and stores continued throughout this period and the conduct of all concerned left nothing to be desired.

Landing at. "V" Beach. – This beach, it was anticipated, would be the most difficult to capture; it possessed all the advantages for defence which "W" beach had, and in addition the flanks were strongly guarded by the old castle and village of Seddul Bahr on the east and perpendicular cliffs on the west; the whole foreshore was covered with barbed wire entanglements which extended in places under the sea. The position formed a natural amphitheatre with the beach as stage.

The first landing here, as at all other places, was made in boats, but the experiment was tried of landing the remainder of the covering force by means of a collier, the "River Clyde." This steamer had been specially prepared for the occasion under the directions of Commander Edward Unwin; large ports had been cut in her sides and gangways built whereby the troops could reach the lighters which were to form a bridge on to the beach.

"V" beach was subjected to a heavy bombardment similarly to "W" beach, with the same result, *i.e.*, when the first trip attempted to land they were met with a murderous fire from rifle, pom-pom and machine gun, which was not opened till the boats had cast off from the steamboats.

A landing on the flanks here was impossible and practically all the first trip were either killed or wounded, a few managing to find some slight shelter under a bank on the beach; in several boats all were either killed or wounded; one boat entirely disappeared, and in another there were only two survivors. Immediately after the boats had reached the beach the "River Clyde" was run ashore under a heavy fire rather towards the eastern end of the beach, where she could form a convenient breakwater during future landing of stores, &c.

As the "River Clyde" grounded, the lighters which were to form the bridge to the shore were run out ahead of the collier, but unfortunately they failed to reach their proper stations and a gap was left between two lighters over which it was impossible for men to cross; some attempted to land by jumping from the lighter which was in position into the sea and wading ashore; this method proved too costly, the lighter being soon heaped with dead and the disembarkation was ordered to cease.

The troops in the "River Clyde" were protected from rifle and machine-gun fire and were in comparative safety.

Commander Unwin, seeing how things were going left the "River Clyde" and, standing up to his waist in water under a very heavy fire, got the lighters into position; he was assisted in this work by Midshipman G.L. Drewry, R.N.R., of H.M.S. "Hussar"; Midshipman W. St. A. Malleson, R.N., of H.M.S. "Cornwallis": Able Seaman W.C. Williams, O.N. 186774 (R.F.R. B.3766), and Seaman R.N.R. George McKenzie Samson, O.N. 2408A, both of H.M.S. "Hussar."

The bridge to the shore, though now passable, could not be used by the troops, anyone appearing on it being instantly shot down, and the men in "River Clyde" remained in her till nightfall.

At 9.50 a.m. "Albion" sent in launch and pinnace manned by volunteer crews to assist in completing bridge, which did not quite reach beach; these boats, however, could not be got into position until dark owing to heavy fire.

It had already been decided not to continue to disembark on "V" Beach, and all other troops intended for this beach were diverted to "W."

The position remained unchanged on "V" beach throughout the day, men of war and the maxims mounted in "River Clyde" doing their utmost to keep down the fire directed on the men under partial shelter on the beach.

During this period many heroic deeds were performed in rescuing wounded men in the water.

During the night of the 25th–26th the troops in "River Clyde" were able to disembark under cover of darkness and obtain some shelter on the beach and in the village of Seddul Bahr, for possession of which now commenced a most stubborn fight.

The fight continued, supported ably by gunfire from H.M.S. "Albion," until 1.24 p.m., when our troops had gained a position from which they assaulted hill 141, which dominated the situation. "Albion" then ceased fire, and the hill, with old fort on top, was most gallantly stormed by the troops, led by Lieutenant-Colonel C.H.H. Doughty-Wylie, General Staff, who fell as the position was won. The taking of this hill effectively cleared the enemy from the neighbourhood of the "V" Beach, which could now be used for the disembarkation of the allied armies. The capture of this beach called for a display of the utmost gallantry and perseverance from the officers and men of both services – that they successfully accomplished their task bordered on the miraculous.

Landing on the Camber, Seddul Bahr.- One half company Royal Dublin Fusiliers landed here, without opposition, the Camber being "dead ground." The advance from the Camber, however, was only possible on a narrow front, and after several attempts to enter the village of Seddul Bahr this half company had to withdraw after suffering heavy losses.

Landing at "De Totts" "S" Beach.- The 2nd South Wales Borderers (less one company) and a detachment 2nd London Field Company R.E. were landed in boats, convoyed by "Cornwallis," and covered by that ship and "Lord Nelson."

Little opposition was encountered, and the hill was soon in the possession of the South Wales Borderers. The enemy attacked this position on the evening of the 25th and during the 26th, but our troops were firmly established, and with the assistance of the covering ships all attacks were easily beaten off.

Landing at Kum Kale.- The landing here was undertaken by the French.

It was most important to prevent the enemy occupying positions in this neighbourhood, whence he could bring gun fire to bear on the transports off Cape Helles. It was also hoped that by holding this position it would be possible to deal effectively with the enemy's guns on the Asiatic shore immediately east of Kum Kale, which could fire into Seddul Bahr and De Totts.

The French, after a heavy preliminary bombardment, commenced to land at about 10 a.m., and by the afternoon the whole of their force had been landed at Kum Kale. When they attempted to advance to Yeni Shehr, their immediate objective, they were met by heavy fire from well-concealed trenches, and were held up just south of Kum Kale village.

During the night of the 25th–26th the enemy made several counter-attacks, all of which were easily driven off; during one of these 400 Turks were captured, their retreat being cut off by the fire from the battleships.

On the 26th, when it became apparent that no advance was possible without entailing severe losses and the landing of large reinforcements, the order was given for the French to withdraw and re-embark, which operation was carried out without serious opposition.

I now propose to make the following more general remarks on the conduct of the operations:-

From the very first the co-operation between army and navy was most happy; difficulties which arose were quickly surmounted, and nothing could have succeeded the tactfulness and forethought of Sir Ian Hamilton and his staff.

The loyal support which I received from Contre-Amiral E.P.A. Guepratte simplified the task of landing the Allied armies simultaneously.

The Russian fleet was represented by H.I.R.M.S. "Askold," which ship was attached to the French squadron. Contre-Amiral Guepratte bears testimony to the value of the support he received from Captain Ivanoff, especially during the landing and re-embarkation of the French troops at Kum Kale.

The detailed organisation of the landing could not be commenced until the Army Headquarters returned from Egypt on the 10th April. The work to be done was very great, and the naval personnel and material available small.

Immediately on the arrival of the Army Staff at Mudros, committees, composed of officers of both services, commenced to work out the details of the landing operations, and it was due to these officers' indefatigable efforts that the expedition was ready to land on the 22nd April. The keenness displayed by the officers and men resulted in a good standard of efficiency, especially in the case of the Australian and New Zealand Corps, who appear to be natural boatmen.

Such actions as the storming of the Seddul Bahr position by the 29th Division must live in history for ever; innumerable deeds of heroism and daring were performed; the gallantry and absolute contempt for death displayed alone made the operations possible.

At Gaba Tepe the landing and the dash of the Australian Brigade for the cliffs was magnificent – nothing could stop such men. The Australian and New Zealand Army Corps in this, their first battle, set a standard as high as that of any army in history, and one of which their countrymen have every reason to be proud.

In closing this despatch I beg to bring to their Lordships' notice the names of certain officers and men who have performed meritorious service. The great traditions of His Majesty's Navy were well maintained, and the list of names submitted of necessity lacks those of many officers and men who performed gallant deeds unobserved and therefore unnoted. This standard was high, and if I specially mention one particular Action it is that of Commander Unwin and the two young officers and two seamen who assisted him in the work of establishing communication between "River Clyde" and the beach. Rear-Admirals R.E Wemyss, C.M.G., M.V.O., C.F. Thursby, C.M.G., and Stuart Nicholson, M.V.O., have rendered invaluable service. Throughout they have been indefatigable in their efforts to further the success of the operations, and their loyal support has much lightened my duties and responsibilities.

I have at all times received the most loyal support from the Commanding Officers of His Majesty's ships during an operation which called for the display of great initiative and seamanship.

Captain R.F. Phillimore, C.B., M.V.O., A.D.C., as principal Beach Master, and Captain D.L. Dent, as principal Naval Transport Officer, performed most valuable service.

SPECIAL RECOMMENDATIONS.

Commander Edward Unwin, R.N.

While in "River Clyde," observing that the lighters which were to form the bridge to the shore had broken adrift, Commander Unwin left the ship and under a murderous fire attempted to get the lighters into position. He worked on until, suffering from the effects of cold and immersion, he was obliged to return to the ship, where he was wrapped up in blankets. Having in some degree recovered, he returned to his work against the doctor's order and completed it. He was later again attended by the doctor for three abrasions caused by bullets, after which he once more left the ship, this time in a lifeboat, to save some wounded men who were lying in shallow water near the beach. He continued at this heroic labour under continuous fire, until forced to stop through pure physical exhaustion.

Midshipman George L. Drewry, R.N.R.

Assisted Commander Unwin at the work of securing the lighters under heavy rifle and maxim fire. He was wounded in the head, but continued his work and twice subsequently attempted to swim from lighter to lighter with a line.

Midshipman Wilfred St. A. Malleson, R.N.

Also assisted Commander Unwin, and after Midshipman Drewry had failed from exhaustion to get a line from lighter to lighter, he swam with it himself and succeeded. The line subsequently broke, and he afterwards made two further but unsuccessful attempts at his self-imposed task.

Able Seaman William Chas. Williams, O.N. 186774 (R.F.R. B.3766).

Held on to a line in the water for over an hour under heavy fire, until killed.

Seaman R.N.R. George McKenzie Samson, O.N. 2408A.

Worked on a lighter all day under fire, attending wounded and getting out lines; he was eventually dangerously wounded by maxim fire.

Lieutenant-Commander Ralph B. Janvrin, R.N.

Conducted the trawlers into Morto Bay, for the landing at "De Totts," with much skill.

This officer showed great judgment and coolness under fire, and carried out a difficult task with great success.

Lieutenant John A.V. Morse, R.N.

Assisted to secure the lighters at the bows, of the "River Clyde" under a heavy fire, and was very active throughout the 25th and 26th at "V" beach.

Surgeon P.B. Kelly, R.N., attached to R.N.A.S.

Was wounded in the foot on the morning of the 25th in "River Clyde." He remained in "River Clyde" until morning of the 27th, during which time he attended 750 wounded men, although in great pain and unable to walk during the last twenty-four hours.

Lieutenant-Commander Adrian St. V. Keyes, R.N.

General Sir Ian Hamilton reports as follows:-

"Lieutenant-Commander Keyes showed great coolness, gallantry, and ability. The success of the landing on 'Y' beach was largely due to his good services. When circumstances compelled the force landed there to re-embark, this officer showed exceptional resource and leadership in successfully conducting that difficult operation."

I entirely concur in General Hamilton's, opinion of this officer's services on the 25th–26th April.

Commander William H. Cottrell, R.N.V.R.

This officer has organised the entire system of land communication; has laid and repaired cables several times under fire; and on all occasions shown zeal, tact, and coolness beyond praise.

Mr. John Murphy, Boatswain, H.M.S. "Cornwallis."

Midshipman John Saville Metcalf, R.N.R., H.M.S. "Triumph."

Midshipman Rupert E.M. Bethune, H.M.S. "Inflexible."

Midshipman Eric Oloff de Wet, H.M.S. "London."

Midshipman Charles W. Croxford, R.N.R., H.M.S. "Queen."

Midshipman C.A.L. Mansergh, H.M.S. "Queen."

Midshipman Alfred M. Williams, H.M.S. "Euryalus."

Midshipman Hubert M. Wilson, H.M.S. "Euryalus."

Midshipman G.F.D. Freer, H.M.S, "Lord Nelson."

Midshipman R.V. Symonds-Taylor, H.M.S. "Agamemnon."

Midshipman C.H.C. Matthey, H.M.S. "Queen Elizabeth."

Lieutenant Massy Goolden, H.M.S. "Prince of Wales."

Recommended for accelerated promotion:-

Mr. Charles Edward Bounton, Gunner, R.N., H.M.S. "Queen Elizabeth."

The following officers are "Commended for service in action":-

Captain H.A.S. Fyler, H.M.S. "Agamemnon," Senior Officer inside the Straits.

Captain A.W. Heneage, M.V.O., who organised and trained the mine-sweepers.

Captain E.K. Loring, Naval Transport Officer, Gaba Tepe.

Captain H.C. Lockyer, H.M.S. "Implacable."

Captain C. Maxwell-Lefroy, H.M.S. "Swiftsure."

Captain The Hon. A.D.E.H. Boyle, M.V.O., H.M.S. "Bacchante."

Captain A.V. Vyvyan, Beach Master, "Z" beach.

Captain C.S. Townsend, Beach Master, "W" beach.

Captain R.C.K. Lambert, Beach Master, "V" beach.

Commander The Hon. L.J.O. Lambart, H.M.S. "Queen."

Commander (now Captain) B. St. G. Collard, Assistant Beach Master "W" beach.

Commander C.C. Dix, Assistant Beach Master, "Z" beach.

Commander N.W. Diggle, Assistant Beach Master, "V" beach.
Commander H.L. Watts-Jones, H.M.S. "Albion" (acting Captain).
Commander I.W. Gibson, M.V.O., H.M.S. "Albion."
Lieutenant-Commander (now Commander) J.B. Waterlow,
    H.M.S. "Blenheim."
Lieutenant-Commander H.V. Coates, H.M.S. "Implacable."
Lieutenant-Commander E.H. Cater, H.M.S. "Queen Elizabeth."
Lieutenant-Commander G.H. Pownall, H.M.S. "Adamant" (killed in action).
Lieutenant A.W. Bromley, R.N.R., H.M.S. "Euryalus."
Lieutenant H.R.W. Turnor, H.M.S. "Implacable."
Lieutenant H.F. Minchin, H.M.S. "Cornwallis."
Lieutenant Oscar Henderson, H.M.S. "Ribble."
Lieutenant Kenneth Edwards, H.M.S. "Lord Nelson."
Major W.T.C. Jones, D.S.O., R.M.L.I. Beach Master, "X" beach.
Major W.W. Frankis, R.M.L.I., H.M.S. "Cornwallis."
Temporary Surgeon W.D. Galloway, H.M.S. "Cornwallis."
Mr. Alfred M. Mallett, Gunner T., H.M.S. "Ribble."
Mr. John Pippard, Boatswain, H.M.S. "Sapphire."
Midshipman Eric Wheler Bush, H.M.S. "Bacchante."
Midshipman Charles D.H.H. Dixon, H.M.S. "Bacchante."
Midshipman Donald H. Barton, H.M.S. "London."
Midshipman A.W. Clarke, H.M.S. "Implacable."
Probationary Midshipman William D.R. Hargreaves, R.N.R.,
    H.M.S. "Sapphire."
Midshipman F.E. Garner, R.N.R., H.M.S. "Triumph."
Midshipman George H. Morris, R.N.R., H.M.S. "Lord Nelson."
Midshipman The Honourable G.H.E. Russell, H.M.S. "Implacable."
Midshipman D.S.E. Thompson, H.M.S. "Implacable."
Midshipman W.D. Brown, H.M.S. "Implacable."

The work accomplished by the destroyer flotillas fully maintained the high standard they have established in these waters.

On the 25th and 26th "Wolverine" (Commander O.J. Prentis) (killed in action), "Scorpion" (Lieutenant-Commander (now Commander) A.B. Cunningham), "Renard" (Lieutenant-Commander L.G.B.A. Campbell), "Grampus" (Lieutenant-Commander R. Bacchus), "Pincher" (Lieutenant-Commander H.W. Wyld), and "Rattlesnake" (Lieutenant-Commander P.G. Wodehouse) carried out minesweeping operations under Captain Heneage inside the Dardanelles in a most satisfactory manner, being frequently under heavy fire. On the 26th the French sweepers "Henriette" (Lieutenant de Vaisseau Auverny), "Marius Chambon" (Lieutenant de Vaisseau Blanc), and

"Camargue" (Lieutenant de Vaisseau Bergeon) assisted them, "Henriette" doing particularly well.

"Beagle" (Commander (now Captain) H.R. Godfrey), "Bulldog" (Lieutenant-Commander W.B. Mackenzie), "Scourge" (Lieutenant-Commander H. de B. Tupper), "Foxhound" (Commander W.G. Howard), "Colne" (Commander C. Seymour), "Chelmer" (Lieutenant-Commander (now Commander) H.T. England), "Usk" (Lieutenant-Commander W.G.C. Maxwell), and "Ribble" (Lieutenant-Commander R.W. Wilkinson) assisted in the disembarkation at Gaba Tepe.

Rear-Admiral Thursby reports as follows on the work accomplished by these boats:-

"The destroyers under Captain C.P.R. Coode (Captain 'D') landed the second part of the covering force with great gallantry and expedition, and it is in my opinion entirely due to the rapidity with which so large a force was thrown on the beach that we were able to establish ourselves there."

I entirely concur in Admiral Thursby's remarks on the good work performed by this division.

PETTY OFFICERS AND MEN: SPECIAL RECOMMENDATIONS.

Petty Officer John Hepburn Russell, O.N. F.839, of the Royal Naval Air Service, was wounded in gallantly going to Commander Unwin's assistance.

Petty Officer Mechanic Geoffrey Charlton Paine Rummings, O.N. F.813, Royal Naval Air Service, assisted Commander Unwin in rescuing wounded men.

Petty Officer, Second Class, Frederick Gibson, O.N. 191025, R.F.R. B.3829, H.M.S. "Albion," jumped overboard with a line and got his boat beached to complete bridge from "River Clyde" to shore. He then took wounded to "River Clyde" under heavy fire.

Ordinary Seaman Jesse Lovelock, H.M.S. "Albion," J.28798, assisted in getting pontoon in position; also helped wounded on beach and in boats to reach "River Clyde," displaying great gallantry and coolness under fire.

Able Seaman Lewis Jacobs, O.N. J.4081, H.M.S. "Lord Nelson." Took his boat into "V" beach unaided, after all the remainder of the crew and the troops were killed or wounded. When last seen Jacobs was standing up and endeavouring to pole the cutter to the shore. While thus employed he was killed.

Herbert J.G. Morrin, Leading Seaman, O.N. 236225, H.M.S. "Bacchante."

Alfred J. Chatwin, Chief Yeoman Signals, O.N. 156109,
    H.M.S. "Cornwallis."

Albert Playford, Petty Officer, O.N. 202189, H.M.S. "Cornwallis."

Arthur Roake, Able Seaman, O.N. S.S. 1940 (R.F.R. B.8843),
  H.M.S. "Cornwallis."
Henry Thomas Morrison, Seaman, R.N.R., O.N. 1495D., H.M.S. "Albion."
Daniel Roach, Seaman, R.N.R., 1685D, H.M.S. "Albion."
David S. Kerr, Able Seaman, O.N. 239816, H.M.S. "Ribble."
Albert Balson, Petty Officer, O.N. 211943, H.M.S. "Prince of Wales."
William Morgan, Petty Officer, O.N. 193834, H.M.S. "Prince of Wales."
James Getson, Stoker, Petty Officer, O.N. 295438, H.M.S. "London."
Edward L. Barons, Able Seaman, O.N. J.7775, H.M.S. "London."
William Putman, Petty Officer, O.N. 236783, H.M.S. "Queen."
Robert Fletcher, Leading Seaman, O.N. 213297, H.M.S. "Queen."
Samuel Forsey, Able Seaman, S.S. 2359, (R.F.R. B.4597), H.M.S. "Albion."
Henry J. Anstead, Acting C.P.O. 179989, H.M.S. "Implacable."
Kenneth Muskett, Leading Seaman, J.1325, H.M.S. "Implacable."
Thomas P. Roche, Chief Petty Officer (Pensioner), O.N. 165533,
  H.M.S. "Prince George."
John Maple, Leading Seaman, O.N. 171890, (R.F.R. Chat., B.2658),
  H.M.S. "Euryalus."
Henry Williams, Leading Seaman, O.N. 176765 (R.F.R. Chat., B.1326),
  H.M.S. "Euryalus."
William F. Hoffman, Able Seaman, O.N. 195940 (R.F.R. Chat., B.2650),
  H.M.S. "Euryalus."
Henry G. Law, Able Seaman, O.N. 195366, (R.F.R. Chat., B.8261),
  H.M.S. "Euryalus."
Henry Ridsdale, Stoker, R.N.R., O.N. 1136U, H.M.S. "Euryalus."
Colin McKechnie, Leading Seaman, O.N. 157509, H.M.S. "Lord Nelson"
  (killed).
Stanley E. Cullum, Leading Seaman, O.N. 225791, H.M.S. "Lord Nelson"
  (killed).
Frederick T.M. Hyde, Able Seaman, O.N. J.21153, H.M.S. "Lord Nelson"
  (killed).
William E. Rowland, Able Seaman, O.N. J.17029, H.M.S. "Lord Nelson"
  (wounded).
Albert E. Bex, Able Seaman, O.N. J.17223, H.M.S. "Lord Nelson"
  (wounded).
The above men from "Lord Nelson" were part of boats' crews landing troops
on "V" beach, a service from which few returned.

Commended for service in action:-
Harry E. Pallant, Petty Officer, O.N. 186521, H.M.S. "Implacable."
Jesse Bontoft, Petty Officer, O.N. 193398, H.M.S. "Implacable."

Thomas J. Twells, Leading Seaman, O.N. 232269, H.M.S. "Implacable."
Richard Mullis, Leading Seaman, O.N. 220072, H.M.S. "Implacable."
Matthew B. Knight, Leading Seaman, O.N. 230546, H.M.S. "Implacable."
John E. Mayes, Leading Seaman, O.N. 196849 (R.F.R. B.8581),
    H.M.S. "Implacable."
William J. White, P.O.I., O.N. 142848, H.M.S. "Albion."
Frederick G. Barnes, P.O., O.N. 209085, H.M.S. "Swiftsure."
Henry Minter, P.O., O.N. 163128, H.M.S. "Queen Elizabeth."
Harry R. Jeffcoate, Serjeant, R.M.L.I., Ch.10526, H.M.S. "Cornwallis."
Frank E. Trollope, Private, R.M.L.I., Ch. 19239, H.M.S. "Cornwallis."
George Brown, Chief P.O., 276085, H.M.S. "Sapphire."
Bertie Sole, Leading Seaman, 208019 (R.F.R. B.10738), H.M.S. "Sapphire."
Charles H. Soper, Signalman, J.9709, H.M.S. "Sapphire."
Frank Dawe, Able Seaman, 231502, H.M.S. "Albion."
Samuel Quick, Seaman, R.N.R., 3109 B, H.M.S. "Albion."
James Rice, Seaman, R.N.R., 519 D, H.M.S. "Albion."
William Thomas, Seaman, R.N.R., 2208 B, H.M.S. "Albion."
William H. Kitchen, Seaman, R.N.R., 4330 A, H.M.S. "Albion."
Francis A. Sanders, Able Seaman, 221315 (R.F.R. Chat., B.8199),
    H.M.S. "Euryalus."
William F. Hicks, Able Seaman, S.S. 4795, H.M.S. "Euryalus."
William F. Hayward, Able Seaman, 235109, H.M.S. "London."
George Gilbertson, Able Seaman, 207941 (R.F.R. B.4910),
    H.M.S. "London."
Andrew Hope, Able Seaman, S.S. 2837 (R.F.R. B.5847), H.M.S. "London."
Charles A. Smith, Able Seaman, J.27753, H.M.S. "Lord Nelson" (wounded).
Basil Brazier, Able Seaman, J.6116, H.M.S. "Lord Nelson" (wounded).
Charles H. Smith, Able Seaman, J.28377, H.M.S., "Lord Nelson."
Henry A.B. Green, Able Seaman, 238024, H.M.S. "Lord Nelson" (wounded).

No officer could have been better served by his staff than I have been during these operations. The energy and resource of my Chief of Staff, Commodore R.J.B. Keyes, was invaluable, and, in combination with Major-General Braithwaite – Chief of the General Staff – he established a most excellent working agreement between the two services.

Captain George P.W. Hope, of "Queen Elizabeth," acted as my flag captain. His gift of organisation was of the greatest assistance in dealing with the mass of details inseparable from an operation of such magnitude.

Commander the Hon. A.R.M. Ramsay has used his sound practical knowledge of gunnery to great advantage in working out, in connection with the military, the details of gunfire from the covering ships.

Captain William W. Godfrey, R.M., a staff officer of great ability, has given me invaluable assistance throughout the operations.

I would also mention my secretary, Mr. Basil F. Hood, Acting Paymaster, and secretarial staff, whose good services under the direction and example of Mr. Edward W. Whittington-Ince, Assistant Paymaster, will form the subject of a later separate report. Also Lieutenant-Commander James F. Sommerville (Fleet Wireless Telegraph Officer), and Flag Lieutenants L.S. Ormsby-Johnson, Hugh S. Bowlby, and Richard H.L. Bevan, who have performed good service in organising with the military the intercommunication between the allied fleets and armies.

I have, &c.,

J.M. DE ROBECK, *Vice-Admiral.*

The Secretary of the Admiralty.

Admiralty, 16th August, 1915.

The KING has been graciously pleased to approve of the grant of the Victoria Cross to the undermentioned Officers and men for the conspicuous acts of bravery mentioned in the foregoing despatch:-

Commander Edward Unwin, R.N.
Midshipman Wilfred St. Aubyn Malleson, R.N.
Midshipman George Leslie Drewry, R.N.R.
Able Seaman William Chas. Williams, O.N. 186774 (R.F.R. B.3766) (since killed).
Seaman R.N.R. George McKenzie Samson, O.N. 2408A

The KING has been graciously pleased to give orders for the following appointments to the Distinguished Service Order and for the award of the Distinguished Service Cross to the undermentioned Officers, in recognition of their services as mentioned in the foregoing despatch:-

To be Companions of the Distinguished Service Order.

Lieutenant-Commander Ralph Benest Janvrin, R.N.
Lieutenant-Commander Adrian St. Vincent Keyes, R.N.
Lieutenant John Anthony Vere Morse, R.N.
Surgeon Peter Burrows Kelly, R.N.

To receive the Distinguished Service Cross.

Lieutenant Mass, Goolden, R.N.
Boatswain John Murphy, R.N.
Midshipman Rupert Edward Maximilian Bethune, R.N.
Midshipman Eric Oloff de Wet, R.N.
Midshipman Charles Wilfred Croxford, R.N.R.

Midshipman Cecil Aubrey Lawson Mansergh, R.N.
Midshipman Alfred Martyn Williams, R.N.
Midshipman Hubert Malcolm Wilson, R.N.
Midshipman George Francis Dudley Freer, R.N.
Midshipman Richard Victor Symonds-Taylor, R.N.
Midshipman Cecil Hugh Clinton Matthey, R.N.
Midshipman John Saville Metcalf, R.N.R.

The following awards have also been made:-

To receive the Conspicuous Gallantry Medal.

Petty Officer Mechanic John Hepburn Russell, R.N. Air Service O.N. F.839.
Petty Officer Mechanic Geoffrey Charlton Paine Rumming, R.N. Air Service O.N. F.813.
Petty Officer 2nd Class Frederick Gibson, O.N. 191025 (R.F.R. B.3829).
Ordinary Seaman Jesse Lovelock, O.N. J28798.

To receive the Distinguished Service Medal.

Chief Petty Officer Thomas P. Roche, O.N. 165533 (since promoted Acting Gunner).
Acting Chief Petty Officer Henry J. Anstead, O.N. 179989.
Petty Officer Albert Balson, O.N. 211943.
Petty Officer, 1st Class, William Morgan, O.N. 193834.
Petty Officer Albert Playford, O.N. 202189.
Petty Officer William Putman, O.N. 236783.
Leading Seaman Robert Fletcher, O.N. 213297.
Leading Seaman John Maple, O.N. 171890 (R.F.R. Chat., B.2658).
Leading Seaman Herbert J.G. Merrin, O.N. 236225.
Leading Seaman Kenneth S. Muskett, J.1325.
Leading Seaman Henry Williams, O.N. 176765 (R.F.R. Chat., B.1326).
Able Seaman Edward L. Barons, O.N. J.7775.
Able Seaman Albert E. Bex, O.N. J.17223.
Able Seaman Samuel Forsey, O.N. S.S. 2059 (R.F.R. B.4597).
Able Seaman William F. Hoffman, O.N. 195940 (R.F.R. Chat., B.2650).
Able Seaman David S. Kerr, O.N. 239816.
Able Seaman Henry G. Law, O.N. 195366 (R.F.R. Chat., B.8261).
Able Seaman Arthur Roake, O.N. S.S. 1940 (R.F.R. B.8843).
Able Seaman William E. Rowland, O.N. J.17029.
Seaman R.N.R., Henry Thomas Morrison, O.N. 1495D.
Chief Yeoman of Signals Alfred J. Chatwin, O.N. 156IU9.
Seaman R.N.R., Daniel Roach, 1685D.

Stoker Petty Officer James Getson, O.N. 295438.
Stoker R.N.R., Henry Ridsdale, O.N. 1136U.

Admiralty, 16th August, 1915.

The following awards have been made in recognition of services during the operations in the vicinity of the Dardanelles prior to 25th–26th April:-

The KING has been graciously pleased to approve of the grant of the Victoria Cross to Lieutenant-Commander (now Commander) Eric Gascoigne Robinson, R.N., for the conspicuous act of bravery specified below.

> Lieutenant-Commander Robinson on the 26th February advanced alone, under heavy fire, into an enemy's gun position, which might well have been occupied, and destroying a four-inch gun, returned to his party for another charge with which the second gun was destroyed. Lieutenant-Commander Robinson would not allow members of his demolition party to accompany him, as their white uniforms rendered them very conspicuous. Lieutenant-Commander Robinson took part in four attacks on the mine fields – always under heavy fire.

The KING has been graciously pleased to give orders for the following appointments to the Distinguished Service Order and for the award of the Distinguished Service Cross to the undermentioned Officers in recognition of their services as mentioned:-

To be Companions of the Distinguished Service Order.

Commander William Mellor, R.N.

> Commander Mellor was in charge of the trawler minesweepers, and took part in all the mine-sweeping operations under fire prior to and including the 18th March; he displayed conspicuous gallantry, always being to the fore in a picket boat, in the most exposed positions, encouraging his sweepers and setting a fine example.

Lieutenant-Commander (now Commander) John Rickards Middleton, R.N.

> Lieutenant-Commander Middleton on three occasions entered the minefields under heavy fire, where he organised and successfully carried out attacks – by means of explosive creeps – on the cables and jack stays.

Lieutenant Francis Hugh Sandford, R.N.

> Lieutenant Sandford was specially recommended for his good work in connection with the attacks on the minefields, which he entered on several occasions, including night of 13th–14th March. He invariably displayed great determination when under fire. Lieutenant Sandford also rendered good service in the demolition of Fort Seddul Bahr.

Acting Lieutenant Bernard Thomas Cox, R.N.R.

Lieutenant Cox behaved in a most gallant manner when a volunteer in trawler No. 318 during the attack on the minefield on 13th–14th March. Though severely wounded he refused to quit his bridge until out of action. His vessel suffered serious damage and severe casualties.

Captain Christopher Powell Metcalfe, R.N.

On the 18th March, after H.M.S. "Irresistible" struck a mine, Captain Metcalfe took H.M.S. "Wear" alongside her, and rescued nearly the whole of her crew under a very heavy fire, which caused several casualties – a very fine display of seamanship.

Lieutenant-Commander (now Commander) the Hon. Patrick George Edward Cavendish Aeheson, M.V.O., R.N.

Acting Sub-Lieutenant (now Sub-Lieutenant) Alfred Edward Boscawen Giles, R.N.

Lieutenant-Commander Acheson, with Acting Sub-Lieutenant Alfred E.B. Giles, Chief E.R.A. 2nd Class Robert Snowdon, O.N. 270654, and Stoker 1st Class Thomas Davidson, O.N.K. 14753, went down into the fore magazine and shell room of H.M.S. "Inflexible" when the parties working in these places had been driven out by fumes, caused by the explosion of a mine under the ship; they closed valves and water-tight doors, lights being out, the shell room having two feet of water in it, rising quickly, and the magazine flooding slowly.

The fumes were beginning to take effect on Acting Sub-Lieutenant Giles, but neither he nor the others left until ordered to do so by Lieutenant-Commander Acheson, who was the last to leave the shell room.

Engineer-Commander Harry Lashmore, C.B., R.N.

Engineer-Lieutenant-Commander Arthur Ellis Lester, R.N.

Engineer Lieutenant Rey. Griffith Parry, R.N.

Surgeon Martyn Henry Langford, R.N.

During the time H.M.S. "Inflexible" was steaming to Tenedos – after having struck a mine – the engine-room being in semi-darkness and great heat, the ship in possible danger of sinking on passage, a high standard of discipline was called for in the Engineer Department, a call which was more than met. Engineer-Commander Harry Lashmore, responsible for the discipline of the engine-room department, was in the starboard engine-room throughout the passage, and set a fine example to his men.

Engineer-Lieutenant-Commander Lester was in the port engine-room carrying out the same duties as Engineer-Commander Lashmore did in the starboard engine-room.

Engineer-Lieutenant Parry went twice through the thick fumes to the refrigerator flat to see if the doors and valves were closed; he also closed the escape hatch from the submerged flat, fumes and vapour coming up the trunk at the time.

Surgeon Langford brought up the wounded from the fore distributing station in the dark. Fumes permeated the place rendering five men unconscious. Surgeon Langford, though partially overcome by the fumes, continued his work.

Lieutenant Claud Herbert Godwin, R.N.

Lieutenant Godwin commanded H.M.S. "Majestic's" picket boat, and was responsible for the successful shot by which the submarine E. 15 was destroyed after running aground.

To receive the Distinguished Service Cross.

Sub-Lieutenant (now Acting Lieutenant) Stephen Augustus Bayford, R.N.R., H.M.S. "Majestic."

Midshipman James Charles Woolmer Price. H.M.S. "Ocean."

These officers were both in command of picket boats on night of 13th–14th March.

When "Ocean's" boat lay helpless, having been struck in the boiler-room by a shell, "Majestic's" took her in tow, under heavy fire, the conduct of these two young officers being altogether admirable, as was their handling of their boats.

Gunner (T) John William Alexander Chubb, R.N.

Mr. Chubb, when a volunteer in trawler No. 488, on the night of 13th–14th March, brought his vessel out of action in a sinking condition, his commanding officer and three of the small crew being killed.

Gunner (T) William Walter Thorrowgood, R.N.

Mr. Thorrowgood was in command of an armed whaler which, on night of 4th–5th March, twice went into the shore between Kum Kale and Yeni Shehr, bringing off two officers and five men, two of them wounded, exposed to rifle fire on both occasions.

Midshipman Hugh Dixon, R.N.

Midshipman Dixon was in command of "Queen Elizabeth's" picket boat, and was responsible for saving several officers and men from "Irresistible" while under heavy fire, on the 18th March.

Acting Sub-Lieutenant (now Sub-Lieutenant) George Tothill Philip, R.N.

Acting Sub-Lieutenant Philip, H.M.S. "Inflexible," was in charge of his picket boat on the 18th March to deal with floating mines.

The picket-boat was struck by a heavy shell. Acting Sub-Lieutenant Philip got her alongside "Inflexible," ordered his crew inboard, and, though his knee was injured, got into the engine-room, shut off steam and closed scuttle to stokehold before leaving his boat.

Lieutenant Arthur Cyril Brooke-Webb, R.N.R.

Midshipman John Blaxland Woolley, R.N.

These officers took part in the picket-boat attack on the 18th April.

Lieutenant Colin George MacArthur, R.N.

Lieutenant MacArthur (commanding submarine B 6) carried out two most enterprising reconnaissances of E lo, both under fire. During the latter reconnaissance his skilful handling saved his ship.

The following Officers are *Commended for service in Action:-*
Between 19th February and 24th April.

Captain Charles Penrose Rushton Coode, R.N.

Captain Richard Fortescue Phillimore, C.B., M.V.O., A.D.C., R.N.

Commander Osmond James Prentis, R.N. (since killed).

Commander Claude Seymour, R.N.

Commander (now Captain) George James Todd, R.N.

Commander (now Captain) Ernest Wigram, R.N.

Acting Commander Michael Barne, R.N.

Lieutenant-Commander Charles Gordon Brodie, R.N.

Lieutenant-Commander (now Commander) Andrew Browne Cunningham, R.N.

Lieutenant-Commander (now Commander) Hugh Turnour England, R.N.

Lieutenant-Commander George Francis Arthur Mulock, R.N.

Lieutenant-Commander George Bryan Palmes, D.S.O., R.N.

Lieutenant-Commander Richard St. John, R.N.

Lieutenant-Commander James Cantrell Johnstone Soutter, R.N.

Lieutenant John Foster Barham Carslake, R.N.

Lieutenant Charles Eric Seaburne Farrant, R.N.

Lieutenant Harold Richard George Kinahan, R.N.

Lieutenant Ernald Lushington Morant, R.N.

Lieutenant Robert Don Oliver, R.N.

Acting Lieutenant Robert Don Oliver, R.N.

Flight-Lieutenant (now Flight-Commander), Geoffrey Rhodes Bromet.

Flight-Lieutenant (now Flight-Commander). Ronald Hargrave Kershaw.

Sub-Lieutenant (now Lieutenant) Charles Vincent Jack, R.N.

Sub-Lieutenant Humphrey Robert Sandwith, R.N.

Sub-Lieutenant William Bagot Walker, R.N.

Mate Thomas Edward Lane, R.N.

Acting Mate John Taylor, R.N.

Midshipman Sir John Stuart Page Wood, Bt. R.N.

Midshipman John Blaxland Woolley, R.N.

Fleet Surgeon Edward Henry Meaden, R.N.

Surgeon John Harding Baynes Martin, R.N.
Major Arthur Edward Bewes, R.M.L.I.
Major (now Brevet Lieutenant-Colonel) Granville Mackay Heriot, D.S.O., R.M.L.I.
Gunner George William Charles Goss, R.N.
Gunner (T) Francis Jeremiah Thomas, R.N.
Acting Gunner Charles Frederick Paul, R.N.
Acting Boatswain Robert George Young, R.N.
Acting Boatswain William Henry Young, R.N.
Acting Boatswain Francis John Buckingham, R.N.
Lieutenant Stephen Percy Elliott, R.N.R.
Lieutenant John Henry Pitts, R.N.R.
Acting Lieutenant Angus George Brown, R.N.R.
Skipper William Henry Collins, R.N.R.
Skipper Albert Edward Olley, R.N.R.

The Vice-Admiral commanding the Eastern Mediterranean Squadron also notices specially the good work done by the following Officers:-

Commander (now Acting Captain) Percy Pitts, R.N.

Lieutenant-Commander (now Commander) John Beauchamp Waterlow, R.N.

Engineer Commander William Anderson Wilson, R.N.

The following awards have also been made:-

To receive the Conspicuous Gallantry Medal.

For services when H.M.S. "Inflexible" was damaged by a mine on 18th March:-

Chief Engine Room Artificer, 2nd Class, Robert Snowdon, O.N. 270654.
Stoker, 1st Class, Thomas Davidson, D.S.M., O.N. K14753.
Able Seaman Walter Samuel Smedley, O.N. J.13729.
Engine Room Artificer, 2nd Class, Joseph J. Fielding Runalls, O.N. 272059.
Chief Sick Berth Steward Henry A. Hamlin, O.N. 150438.

The services of Snowdon and Davidson are mentioned above.

Able Seaman Smedley. Though wounded himself carried a wounded Petty Officer down from the fore top after it had been struck by a shell; he subsequently went aloft twice more, and started for a third attempt.

Engine Room Artificer Runalls. Escaped up the trunk from the fore air compressor room with difficulty, helped up his stoker and closed the W.T. door of the trunk before he fell insensible.

Chief Sick Berth Steward Hamlin, though partially overcome by fumes, assisted Surgeon Langford while the "Inflexible" was proceeding to Tenedos.

To receive the Distinguished Service Medal.

For services on the night of 4th–5th March, as crew of armed whaler H.M.S. "Scorpion":-
Petty Officer Samuel G. Newell, O.N. 224817.
Leading Seaman Charles Balls, O.N. 228520.
Able Seaman George A. Shaw, O.N. 219819.
Able Seaman Albert E. Holbrook, O.N. J.297.
Able Seaman George Ong, O.N. J.2888.
Able Seaman Henry John Floyd, O.N. J.8819.
Able Seaman Leonard Pettis, O.N. 234659.
Signalman Michael T. Hughes, O.N. 230108.

For services as volunteers in H.M. Trawlers on night of 13th–14th March:-
Petty Officer, 1st Class, Andrew B. Rennie, O.N. 138878 (R.F.R. A.2994).
Petty Officer, 1st Class, William F. Clode, Pensioner, 125800 (R.F.R. A.3308).
Petty Officer Charles Hochen, O.N. 148252 (R.F.R. A.3963).
Petty Officer Montague H. Botley, O.N. 209682.
Petty Officer Ernest F. Marsh, O.N. 195116.
Petty Officer, 1st Class, Alfred C. Beacham, O.N. 151064.
Signalman Ernest W. Sendall, O.N. 236137 (R.F.R. B.5081).
Signalman Alfred Edward Herbert, R.N.V.R., O.N. Bristol 3/922.
Signalman Walter Dawson, O.N. J.8746.
Signalman R.T. Hyslop, O.N. J.15800.
Signalman Alfred Edwards, O.N. J.8632.
Signalman Alfred E. Coles, O.N. J.8664.
Signalman Charles W. Jeffery, O.N. 197627 (R.F.R. B.4140).

For services on board H.M.S. "Amethyst" on the night of 13th–14th March:-
Petty Officer 2nd Class George T. Lumb, O.N. 159139.
Chief Stoker Robert G. Verey, O.N. 284974.

For services during the attack on minefields under fire:-
Chief Petty Officer William Harbon, O.N. 120947 (Pensioner).
Chief Petty Officer Thomas Scamaton, O.N. 130358 (R.F.R. A.2565).
Chief Petty Officer W.H. Minards, O.N. 136554 (R.F.R. A.2250).
Petty Officer William Snow, O.N. 97167 (Pensioner).
Second Hand, R.N.R. (Trawler Section), Charles M. Chisholm, 524, D.A.
Second Hand, R.N.R. (Trawler Section), Joseph Booz Burgon, O.N. 739, S.A.
Second Hand, R.N.R. (Trawler Section), Arthur Fenwick George, O.N. 63, S.A.

Second Hand, R.N.R. (Trawler Section), Thomas William Reynolds, O.N. 8, S.A.

Deckhand, R.N.R. (Trawler Section), John Thomas Brown, O.N. 95, D.A.

Leading Signalman Richard May, R.N.V.R., O.N. Mersey, 6/71.

Signalman J.J. Gavan, O.N. J.I9901.

Engineman, R.N.R. (Trawler Section), John Keiller Anderson, O.N. 129, E.S.

Engineman, R.N.R. (Trawler Section), Francis Brown Bridge Robinson, O.N. 813, E.S.

Engineman, R.N.R. (Trawler Section), Wm. Richard Kemp, O.N. 846, E.S.

Engineman, R.N.R. (Trawler Section), Wm. Mathers, O.N. 135, E.S.

Engineman, R.N.R. (Trawler Section), Benjamin Germaney, O.N. 1134, E.S.

Engineman, R.N.R. (Trawler Section), James Cheyne, O.N. 17, E.S.

For services on 18th March:-

Petty Officer 1st Class Thomas W. Kemp, O.N. 171663.

Petty Officer, 1st Class, Frederick Nash, O.N. 181003.

Signalman Isaac Overton, O.N. 225837.

Able Seaman Charles R. Hooper, O.N. J. 5912.

For services in picket boats of H.M.S. "Majestic" and "Triumph" 18th April:-

H.M.S. "Triumph."

Petty Officer William Bradbury, O.N. 199926.

Able Seaman Leonard E. Beresford, O.N. J.20546.

Leading Seaman Daniel McCarthy, O.N. J.1868.

Petty Officer Joseph J. Martin, O.N. 214321.

Able Seaman John G. Morley, O.N. 219291.

Able Seaman Jack Robinson, O.N. 223124.

Able Seaman John Symons, O.N. 218505.

Leading Stoker Frederick C. Fisher, O.N. 310629.

Stoker, 1st Class, Valliant Mackenzie, O.N. S.S. 112172.

Stoker, 1st Class, Matthew Rowel, O.N. K.12718.

H.M.S. "Majestic."

Leading Seaman James McEligott, O.N. 148265.

Able Seaman David Collins, O.N. 212148 (R.F.R. B.5415).

Able Seaman Robert Cocks, O.N. S.S. 1501 (R.F.R. B.3835).

Able Seaman William Longworth, O.N. 205543 (R.F.R. B.5103).

Able Seaman Arthur Maddy, O.N. 201782.

Seaman, R.N.R., Frederick Armstrong, O.N. 5139A.

Ordinary Signalman Edward A.W. Hill, O.N. J.28122.

Engine Room Artificer, R.N.R., Rothwell Randal Patterson, O.N. 1614, E.A.

Stoker Petty Officer Robert J. Foster, O.N. 153254 (R.F.R. A.3430).

Stoker Percy J. Edwards, O.N. 307004.

For services in Submarine B.6:-

Petty Officer E.W. Heasman, O.N. 233663.

Leading Seaman A.W. Roe, O.N. 238262.

The following Petty Officers and Men are *Commended for service in Action* between 19th February and 24th April:-

Petty Officer, 1st Class, Harry Ives, O.N. 185920 (since killed).

Petty Officer Henry Minter, O.N. 163128.

Petty Officer, 1st Class, Edwin Breen, O.N. 184172.

Petty Officer William Saffhill, O.N. 219209.

Petty Officer Ernest R.F. Castle, O.N. 179279.

Petty Officer Frederick G. Barnes, O.N. 209085.

Petty Officer, 1st Class (Pensioner), Henry G. Dumsday, O.N. 125998 (R.F.R. A.1784).

Petty Officer Alfred P. Marchant, O.N. 232250.

Petty Officer Frederick R. Porter, O.N. 171745.

Petty Officer Robert Dempsey, O.N. 190898.

Leading Seaman Benjamin Randall, O.N. 220183.

Leading Boatman (C.G.) Thomas H. Lindupp, O.N. 170491.

Leading Signalman Thomas O. Pyne, O.N. 225593.

Able Seaman Francis H. Verge, O.N. J. 10816.

Able Seaman Walter T. Birtwhistle, O.N. J.5180.

Able Seaman Alfred Gibson, O.N. J.10284.

Able Seaman Frank Lewis, O.N. J.19463.

Able Seaman Alfred T. Smith, O.N. J.5158.

Able Seaman George Benton, O.N. J.10765.

Able Seaman Harry Saunders, O.N. J.3745.

Able Seaman George Hannah, O.N. 164612.

Able Seaman Robert K. Perrie, O.N. J.19094.

Able Seaman Thomas Lane, O.N. 195028.

Acting E.R.A. 4th Class William Scrimgour, O.N. M.1504.

Stoker Petty Officer Robert J. Ellen, O.N. 293785.

Stoker Petty Officer John W. Payne, O.N. K. 1052.

Stoker Petty Officer William G. Luckhurst, O.N. 304438.

Stoker Petty Officer William T. Collins, O.N. 308278.

Stoker Petty Officer John E.D. Williams, O.N. 154530 (R.F.R. A.3601).

Stoker Petty Officer Arthur Whittington, O.N. 288477.
Stoker Petty Officer William H. Moody, O.N. 308628.
Stoker, 1st Class, Fred M. Bond, O.N. 311570.
Stoker, 1st Class, Alfred Barrett, O.N. S.S. 100096 (R.F.R. B.2347).
Stoker, 1st Class, Albert E. Barter, O.N. 278767.
Chief Shipwright Arthur Woolley, O.N. 346887.
Armourer Thomas Hooper, O.N. 156567 (since died of wounds).
Second Sick Berth Steward William H. Young, O.N. M.1232.

4

SIR IAN HAMILTON'S
SECOND GALLIPOLI DESPATCH,
26 AUGUST 1915

MONDAY, 20 SEPTEMBER, 1915.
From the General Commanding the Mediterranean Expeditionary Force.
To the Secretary of State for War, War Office, London, S.W.

General Headquarters,
Mediterranean Expeditionary Force,
MY LORD,-   *26th August, 1915.*

At the close of the ten days and ten nights described in my first despatch our troops had forced their way forward for some 5,000 yards from the landing places at the point of the peninsula. Opposite them lay the Turks, who since their last repulse had fallen back about half a mile upon previously prepared redoubts and entrenchments. Both sides had drawn heavily upon their stock of energy and munitions, but it seemed clear that whichever could first summon up spirit to make another push must secure at least several hundreds of yards of the debatable ground between the two fronts. And several hundred yards, whatever it might mean to the enemy, was a matter of life or death to a force crowded together under gun fire on so narrow a tongue of land. Such was the situation on the 5th of May, the date last mentioned in my despatch of the 20th of that month.

On that day I determined to continue my advance, feeling certain that even if my tired troops could not carry the formidable opposing lines they would at least secure the use of the intervening ground. Orders were forthwith issued for an attack.

The many urgent calls for reinforcements made during the previous critical fighting had forced me to disorganise and mix together several of the formations in the southern group, to the extent even of the French on our right having a British battalion holding their own extremest right. For the purposes of the impending fight it became therefore necessary to create temporarily a Composite Division, consisting of the 2nd Australian and New Zealand Infantry Brigades (withdrawn for the purpose from the northern section), together with a Naval Brigade formed of the Plymouth and Drake battalions. The 29th Division was reconstituted into four brigades, *i.e.*, the 88th and 87th Brigades, the Lancashire Fusilier Brigade (T.F.), and the 29th Indian Infantry

Brigade. The French Corps Expeditionnaire was reinforced by the 2nd Naval Brigade, and the new Composite Division formed my General Reserve. The 29th Division, whose left rested on the coast about three miles north-east of Cape Tekke, was ordered to direct, its right moving on the south-east edge of Krithia, while the Corps Expeditionnaire with the 2nd Naval Brigade had assigned to them for their first point of attack the commanding ridge running from north to south above the Kereves Dere. A foothold upon this ridge was essential, as its capture would ensure a safe pivot on which the 29th Division could swing in making any further advance. Communication between these two sections of the attack was to be maintained by the Plymouth and Drake battalions.

During the three days (6th–8th May) our troops were destined to be very severely tried. They were about to attack a series of positions scientifically selected in advance which, although not yet joined up into one line of entrenchment, were already strengthened by works on their more important tactical features.

The 29th Division led off at 11 a.m., the French Corps followed suit at 11.30 a.m.; every yard was stubbornly contested; some Brigades were able to advance, others could do no more than maintain themselves. Positions were carried and held, other positions were carried and lost; but, broadly, our gunners kept lengthening the fuzes of their shrapnel, and by 1.30 p.m. the line had been pushed forward two to three hundred yards. Here and there this advance included a Turkish trench, but generally speaking the main enemy position still lay some distance ahead of our leading companies.

By 4.30 p.m. it became clear that we should make no more progress that day. The French Corps were held up by a strong field work. They had made good a point upon the crest line of the lower slope of the Kereves Dere ridge, but there they had come under a fire so galling that they were unable, as it turned out, to entrench until nightfall. The 88th Brigade could not carry a clump of fir trees to their front: company after company made the perilous essay, but the wood swept by hidden machine-guns proved a veritable death-trap. The Lancashire Fusiliers Brigade also were only just barely holding on and were suffering heavy losses from these same concealed machine-guns. The troops were ordered to entrench themselves in line and link up their flanks on either side.

At night, save for rifle fire, there was quiet along the whole British line. On the right a determined bayonet charge was made upon the French, who gave ground for the moment, but recovered it again at dawn.

Next morning (the 7th May) we opened with shrapnel upon the enemy's trenches opposite our extreme left, and at 10 a.m. the Lancashire Fusiliers Brigade began the attack. But our artillery had not been able to locate the cleverly sited German machine-gun batteries, whose fire rendered it physically impossible to cross that smooth glacis. Next to the right the 88th Brigade swept forward, and the 1/5th Royal Scots, well supported by artillery fire, carried the fir trees with a rush. This time it was discovered that not only the enfilading machine-guns had made the wood so difficult to hold. Amongst the branches of the trees Turkish snipers were perched, sometimes upon small wooden platforms. When these were brought down the surroundings became much healthier. The Royal Inniskilling Fusiliers, of the 87th Brigade, were pushed up to support the left of the 88th, and all seemed well, when, at 1.20 p.m., a strong Turkish counter-attack drove us back out of the fir clump. As an offset to this check the Royal Inniskilling Fusiliers captured three Turkish trenches and a second battalion of the 87th Brigade, The King's Own Scottish Borderers, was sent forward on the left to make these good.

At 3 p.m. the Lancashire Fusiliers Brigade again reported they were definitely held up by the accurate cross-fire of batteries of machine-guns concealed in the scrub on the ridge between the ravine and the sea, batteries which also enfiladed the left flank of the 88th Brigade as it endeavoured to advance in the centre. Unless we were to acquiesce in a stalemate the moment for our effort had arrived, and a general attack was ordered for 4.45 p.m., the whole of the 87th Brigade to reinforce the 88th Brigade, and the New Zealand Brigade to support it. Despite their exhaustion and their losses the men responded with a will. The whole force, French and British, rose simultaneously and made a rush forward. All along the front we made good a certain amount of ground, excepting only on our extreme left. For the third time British bayonets carried the fir clump in our centre, and when darkness fell the whole line (excepting always the left) had gained from 200 to 300 yards, and had occupied or passed over the first line of Turkish trenches.

The troops were now worn out; the new lines needed consolidating, and it was certain that fresh reinforcements were reaching the Turks. Balancing the actual state of my own troops against the probable condition of the Turks, I decided to call upon the men to make one more push before the new enemy forces could get into touch with their surroundings.

Orders were therefore issued to dig in at sundown on the line gained; to maintain that line against counter-attack, and to prepare to advance again next morning. The Lancashire Fusiliers Brigade was withdrawn into reserve, and its place on the left was taken by the Brigade of New Zealanders.

General Headquarters were shifted to an entrenchment on a hill in rear of the left of our line. Under my plan for the fresh attack the New Zealand Brigade was to advance through the line held during the night by the 88th Brigade and press on towards Krithia. Simultaneously, the 87th Brigade was to threaten the works on the west of the ravine, whilst endeavouring, by means of parties of scouts and volunteers, to steal patches of ground from the areas dominated by the German machine-guns.

At 10.15 a.m. heavy fire from ships and batteries was opened on the whole front, and at 10.30 a.m. the New Zealand Brigade began to move, meeting with strenuous opposition from the enemy, who had received his reinforcements. Supported by the fire of the batteries and the machine-guns of the 88th Brigade, they pushed forward on the right and advanced their centre beyond the fir trees, but could make little further progress. By 1.30 p.m. about 200 yards had been gained beyond the previously most advanced trenches of the 88th Brigade.

At this hour the French Corps reported they could not advance up the crest of the spur west of Kereves Dere till further progress was made by the British.

At 4 p.m. I gave orders that the whole line, reinforced by the 2nd Australian Brigade, would fix bayonets, slope arms, and move on Krithia precisely at 5.30 p.m.

At 5.15 p.m. the ships' guns and our heavy artillery bombarded the enemy's position for a quarter of an hour, and at 5.30 p.m. the field guns opened a hot shrapnel fire to cover the infantry advance.

The co-operation of artillery and infantry in this attack was perfect, the timing of the movement being carried out with great precision. Some of the companies of the New Zealand regiments did not get their orders in time, but acting on their own initiative they pushed on as soon as the heavy howitzers ceased firing, thus making the whole advance simultaneous.

The steady advance of the British could be followed by the sparkle of their bayonets until the long lines entered the smoke clouds. The French at first made no move, then, their drums beating and bugles sounding the charge, they suddenly darted forward in a swarm of skirmishers, which seemed in one moment to cover the whole southern face of the ridge of the Kereves Dere. Against these the Turkish gunners now turned their heaviest pieces, and as the leading groups stormed the first Turkish redoubt the ink-black bursts of high-explosive shells blotted out both assailants and assailed. The trial was too severe for the Senegalese tirailleurs. They recoiled. They were rallied. Another rush forward, another repulse, and then a small supporting column of French soldiers was seen silhouetted against the sky as they charged upwards along the crest of the ridge of the Kereves Dere, whilst elsewhere it grew so dark that the whole of the battlefield became a blank.

Not until next morning did any reliable detail come to hand of what had happened. The New Zealanders' firing line had marched over the cunningly concealed enemy's machine-guns without seeing them, and these, re-opening on our supports as they came up, caused them heavy losses. But the first line pressed on and arrived within a few yards of the Turkish trenches which had been holding up our advance beyond the fir wood. There they dug themselves in.

The Australian Brigade had advanced through the Composite Brigade, and, in spite of heavy losses from shrapnel, machine-gun, and rifle fire, had progressed from 300 to 400 yards.

The determined valour shown by these two brigades, the New Zealand Brigade, under Brigadier-General F.E. Johnston, and the 2nd Australian Infantry Brigade, under Brigadier-General the Hon. J.W. McCay, are worthy of particular praise. Their losses were correspondingly heavy, but in spite of fierce counter-attacks by numerous fresh troops they stuck to what they had won with admirable tenacity.

On the extreme left the 87th Brigade, under Major-General W.R. Marshall, made a final and especially gallant effort to advance across the smooth, bullet-swept area between the ravine and the sea, but once more the enemy machine-guns thinned the ranks of the leading companies of the South Wales Borderers, and again there was nothing for it but to give ground. But when night closed in the men of the 87th Brigade of their own accord asked to be led forward, and achieved progress to the extent of just about 200 yards. During the darkness the British troops everywhere entrenched themselves on the line gained.

On the right the French column, last seen as it grew dark, had stormed and still held the redoubt round which the fighting had centred until then. Both General d'Amade and General Simonin had been present in person with this detachment and had rallied the Senegalese and encouraged the white troops in their exploit. With their bayonets these brave fellows of the 8th Colonials had inflicted exceedingly heavy losses upon the enemy.

The French troops whose actions have hitherto been followed belonged, all of them, to the 2nd Division. But beyond the crest of the ridge the valley of the Kereves Dere lies dead to anyone occupying my post of command. And in this area the newly arrived Brigade of the French 1st Division had been also fighting hard. Here they had advanced simultaneously with the 2nd Division and achieved a fine success in their first rush, which was jeopardised when a battalion of Zouaves was forced to give way under a heavy bombardment. But, as in the case of the 2nd Division, the other battalions of the 1st Regiment de Marche d'Afrique, under Lieutenant-Colonel Nieger, restored the situation, and in the end the Division carried and held two complete lines of Turkish redoubts and trenches.

The net result of the three days' fighting had been a gain of 600 yards on the right of the British line and 400 yards on the left and centre. The French had captured all the ground in front of the Farm Zjimmerman, as well as a redoubt, for the possession of which there had been obstinate fighting during the whole of the past three days.

This may not seem very much, but actually more had been won that at first meets the eye. The German leaders of the Turks were quick to realise the fact. From nightfall till dawn on the 9th–10th efforts were made everywhere to push us back. A specially heavy attack was made upon the French, supported by a hot cannonade and culminating in a violent hand-to-hand conflict in front of the Brigade Simonin. Everywhere the assailants were repulsed, and now for the first time I felt that we had planted a fairly firm foothold upon the point of the Gallipoli Peninsula.

Meanwhile in the Northern Zone also, the Australian and New Zealand Army Corps had strengthened their grip on Turkish soil. Whilst in the south we had been attacking and advancing they had been defending and digging themselves more and more firmly into those cliffs on which it had seemed at first that their foothold was so precarious.

On the 11th May, the first time for eighteen days and nights, it was found possible to withdraw the 29th Division from the actual firing line and to replace it by the 29th Indian Infantry Brigade and by the 42nd Division, which had completed its disembarkation two days previously. The withdrawal gave no respite from shells, but at least the men were, most nights, enabled to sleep.

The moment lent itself to reflection, and during this breathing space I was able to realise we had now nearly reached the limit of what could be attained by mingling initiative with surprise. The enemy was as much in possession of my numbers and dispositions as I was in possession of their first line of defence; the opposing fortified fronts stretched parallel from sea to straits; there was little scope left now, either at Achi Baba or at Kaba Tepe, for tactics which would fling flesh and blood battalions against lines of unbroken barbed wire. Advances must more and more tend to take the shape of concentrated attacks on small sections of the enemy's line after full artillery preparation. Siege warfare was soon bound to supersede manoeuvre battles in the open. Consolidation and fortification of our front, improvement of approaches, selection of machine-gun emplacements and scientific grouping of our artillery under a centralised control must ere long form the tactical basis of our plans. So soon, then, as the troops had enjoyed a day or two of comparative rest I divided my front into four sections. On the left was the 29th Division, to which the 29th Indian Infantry Brigade was attached. In the left centre came the 42nd (East Lancashire) Division, on the right centre stood the Royal Naval Division, and at my right was the Corps Expeditionnaire. Thus I secured organisation in depth as well as front, enabling each division to arrange for its own reliefs, supports, and reserves, and giving strength for defence as well as attack. Hitherto the piecemeal arrival of reinforcements had forced a hand-to-mouth procedure upon headquarters; now the control became more decentralised.

Already, before the new system of local efforts had come into working order, the 29th Indian Brigade had led the way towards it by a brilliant little affair on the night of the 10th/11th May. The Turkish right rested upon the steep cliff north-east of Y beach, where the King's Own Scottish Borderers and the Plymouth Battalion, Royal Naval Division, had made their first landing. Since those days the enemy had converted the bluff into a powerful bastion, from which the fire of machine-guns had held up the left of our attacks. Two gallant attempts by the Royal Munster Fusiliers and the Royal Dublin Fusiliers to establish a footing on this cliff on the 8th and 9th May had both of them failed.

During the night of the 10th/11th May the 6th Gurkhas started off to seize this bluff. Their scouts descended to the sea, worked their way for some distance through the broken ground along the shore, and crawled hands and knees up the precipitous face of the cliff. On reaching the top they were heavily fired on. As a surprise the enterprise had failed, but as a reconnaissance it proved very useful. On the following day Major-General H.V. Cox, commanding 29th Indian Infantry Brigade, submitted proposals for a concerted attack on this bluff (now called Gurkha Bluff), and arrangements were made with the Navy for co-operation. These arrangements were completed on 12th May; they included a demonstration by the Manchester Brigade of the 42nd Division and by our artillery and the support of the attack from the sea by the guns of H.M.S. "Dublin" and H.M.S. "Talbot." At 6.30 p.m. on the 12th May the Manchester Brigade and the 29th Divisional artillery opened fire on the Turkish trenches, and under cover of this fire a double company of the 1/6th Gurkhas once more crept along the shore and assembled below the bluff. Then, the attention of the Turks being taken up with the bombardment, they swiftly scaled the cliffs and carried the work with a rush. The machine-gun section of the Gurkhas was hurried forward, and at 4.30 a.m. a second double company was pushed up to join the first.

An hour later these two double companies extended and began to entrench to join up their new advanced left diagonally with the right of the trenches previously held by their battalion. At 6 a.m. a third double company advanced across the open from their former front line of trenches under a heavy rifle and machine-gun fire, and established themselves on this diagonal line between the main ravine on their right and the newly captured redoubt. The 4th double company moved up as a support, and held the former firing line.

(*Above left*) General Sir Ian Standish Monteith Hamilton GCB, GCMG, DSO, TD. Prior to the First World War, Hamilton had seen much military service. He was wounded in the wrist in the First Boer War leaving his left hand almost useless. Also, his left leg was shorter than the right as a result of a serious injury suffered when he fell from a horse. During his career, Hamilton had twice been recommended for the Victoria Cross, but on the first occasion was considered too young, and on the second too senior. (*US Library of Congress*)

(*Above right*) General Sir Charles Carmichael Monro, 1st Baronet of Bearcrofts GCB, GCSI, GCMG. Following his involvement in the Gallipoli Campaign, in 1916 Monro briefly commanded the British First Army in France before becoming Commander-in-Chief in India later the same year. Whilst in this post, Monro had responsibility for the Mesopotamian Campaign. (*US Library of Congress*)

(*Right*) A portrait of Vice-Admiral Sir John M. de Robeck by Francis Dodd, 1917. De Robeck was on half pay when the war began and was recalled to command the 9th Cruiser Squadron, a force of elderly cruisers taken up from the reserve. In January 1915 he was transferred to second in command of the eastern Mediterranean squadron. The squadron was commanded by Vice-Admiral Sir Sackville Carden, whom he would ultimately succeed when Carden's health broke down under the strain, forcing him to relinquish his command. (*HMP*)

The Allied naval bombardment of Turkish positions underway as a battleship fires its 12-inch guns in the Dardanelles Strait in 1915. The naval operations in the Dardanelles Campaign were predominantly carried out by the Royal Navy with substantial support from the French and minor contributions from Russia and Australia. (*HMP*)

The Formidable-class pre-dreadnought battleship HMS *Irresistible* listing and sinking in the Dardanelles, 18 March 1915 – an image taken from the battleship HMS *Lord Nelson*. Having struck a mine at 16.16 hours, the badly-damaged *Irresistible* was left without power, causing her to drift within range of Turkish guns which laid down a heavy barrage on her. HMS *Irresistible* finally sank at about 19.30 hours, her crew suffering about 150 casualties. (*HMP*)

Allied troops disembarking on one of the landing beaches on the Gallipoli Peninsula, 25 April 1915. (*HMP*)

A contemporary artist's impression of the men of the 1st Battalion, Lancashire Fusiliers landing on 'W' Beach on 25 April 1915. Note the presence of the barbed wire defences which caused the Allied troops difficulties. (*HMP*)

Soldiers of the Australian 1st Brigade row to the beach, whilst empty boats return from the shore to the destroyers, at about 09.45 hours on the morning of the Australians' landing at Anzac Cove, 25 April 1915. The men who were landed in the morning first rushed the small plateau nearby, afterwards called Plugge's Plateau, and then went over the skyline into Shrapnel Valley. (*Courtesy of the Australian War Memorial*)

Lancashire Fusiliers of the 125th Brigade bound for Cape Helles, Gallipoli, in May 1915. The soldiers have just disembarked aboard Trawler 318 from the transport SS *Nile*, from the deck of which this picture was taken. (*US Library of Congress*)

Military supplies piled up at Anzac Cove in May 1915. The cove is a mere 600 yards long and is bounded by the headlands of Ari Burnu to the north and Little Ari Burnu, known as 'Hell Spit', to the south. Following the landing at Anzac Cove, the beach became the main base for the Australian and New Zealand troops for the eight months of the campaign on the Gallipoli Peninsula. (*HMP*)

A photograph of 'V' Beach with the SS *River Clyde* beached in the background. The ship was purposely run aground in order to facilitate rapid disembarkation of the soldiers through spacious doors cut in her side. (*HMP*)

An artist's depiction of Captain Percy Hansen and Lance Corporal Breese, 6th Battalion, The Lincolnshire Regiment, retrieving a wounded soldier at Yilghin Bumu on 9 August 1915. Hansen would be awarded the Victoria Cross for his actions; Breese the Distinguished Conduct Medal. Hansen's citation states: 'Captain Hansen's battalion was forced to retire leaving some wounded behind, owing to the intense heat from the scrub which had been set on fire. After the retirement, Captain Hansen, with three or four volunteers, dashed forward several times over 300–400 yards of open scrub, under a terrific fire and succeeded in rescuing six wounded men from inevitable death by burning.' A total of thirty-nine VCs were awarded for actions during the Gallipoli Campaign, among them the first Australian VC, first New Zealand VC and first Royal Marine VC. The total represented the highest number of VCs won in a theatre of war other than the Western Front. (*HMP*)

Detail from *The Taking of Lone Pine* (1921, oil-on-canvas) by the artist Fred Leist. It depicts the attack by the Australian 1st Brigade on covered Turkish trenches at Lone Pine, 6 August 1915. Leist was one of ten official Australian war artists appointed during the First World War.

An Australian sniper using a periscope rifle at Gallipoli, 1915 – he is aided by a spotter who is also using a trench periscope. The men are believed to belong to the Australian 2nd Light Horse Regiment and the location is probably Quinn's Post. (*HMP*)

Members of 13th Battalion, AIF, occupying Quinn's Post on the heights above Anzac Cove. Quinn's Post was established on the afternoon of the 25 April 1915, by a New Zealand machine-gun crew. In the coming months, the post was held by a number of different ANZAC and was the subject of incessant attacks and continual hand-to-hand fighting with the Turkish post opposite, who knew it as 'Bomba Sirt' (Bomb Ridge). The post was named after Major Hugh Quinn of the 15th Battalion, Australian Infantry, who was killed there during a fierce attack on 29 May.

Allied troops in a captured Turkish trench at Lone Pine on 6 August 1915. Made famous by the fighting here in August 1915, Plateau 400, or Lone Pine as it is more usually known, drew its name from the fact that the Turkish defenders had cut down all but one of the trees that clothed the ridge to cover their trenches. In so doing, the view of the ridge became dominated by the single pine tree. (*HMP*)

The Gallipoli Peninsula is a spectacular place: steep valleys, deep ravines and high cliffs towering above long, narrow beaches. It can be searingly hot in summer and bone chillingly cold in winter. For most of 1915, this impressive and unforgiving landscape was home to many thousands of Allied troops, all of whom had to make the most of the space available to them – as this typical view of the dug-outs they occupied reveals. *(HMP)*

'W' Beach at Cape Helles, Gallipoli, on 7 January 1916, just prior to the final evacuation of British forces. The explosion of a Turkish shell in the water, fired from the Asian side of the Dardanelles, can be seen. (*HMP*)

A contemporary artist's depiction of the action for which Bombardier C.W. Cook, of the 368th Battery, Royal Field Artillery, was awarded the Distinguished Conduct Medal at Cape Helles. On 28 June 1915, the position of his battery was discovered by Turkish observers on the Asiatic shore and was subjected to a severe bombardment. One lucky shot hit the gun on which Cook was working and killed or wounded the whole detachment. A little later the ammunition wagon was set on fire. Bombardier Cook immediately rushed forward to save the ammunition. No one could have blamed him for retiring to a safe distance in such an emergency, but far from retiring he saved most of the shells from the wagon and also the ammunition stored in the pits beneath. (*HMP*)

The capture of the Lone Pine trenches by Australian and New Zealander troops on 7 August 1915, stands out as one of the most memorable feats of the Gallipoli campaign. During the fighting, Private Leonard Keysor saved the lives of his comrades by hurling out two Turkish bombs that had been thrown into his sap. Though he was then wounded, Keysor continued to throw bombs in order to hold a vital position. All that day and the next he went on throwing bombs, even after being wounded a second time, and was not relieved for fifty hours. He was subsequently awarded the Victoria Cross. (*HMP*)

The crowded beach at Anzac Cove. (*HMP*)

Troops pictured occupying trenches at Quinn's Post, Anzac. (*HMP*)

Troops being landed at Suvla Bay. (*HMP*)

The busy scene at a dressing station which had been established at Suvla Bay. (*HMP*)

The original caption to this image, which is almost certainly a staged scene, states: 'A scene just before the evacuation at Anzac; Australian troops charging near a Turkish trench.' (*IIMP*)

Part of the Gallipoli battlefields today: A recent view of 'V' Beach, on the other side of Cape Helles from 'W' Beach, taken from the direction of Cape Helles itself. Sedd-el-Bahr is in the background with Sedd-el-Bahr fort behind it. The Commonwealth War Graves Commission's V Beach Cemetery can be seen in the middle of the picture.

A reconstruction of the trenches dug by the Turkish troops on the Gallipoli Peninsula – this example can be seen by visitors at Chunuk Bair. (Courtesy of Paul Reed, www.battlefields1418.com)

The Commonwealth War Graves Commission's memorial at Helles, Turkey. The United Kingdom and Indian forces named on the memorial died in operations throughout the peninsula, the Australians just at Helles. There are also panels for those who died or were buried at sea in the waters off Gallipoli. The memorial bears more than 21,000 names. (*Courtesy of the CWGC*)

Our left flank, which had been firmly held up against all attempts on the 6th–8th was now, by stratagem, advanced nearly 500 yards. Purchased as it was with comparatively slight losses (21 killed, 92 wounded) this success was due to careful preparation and organisation by Major-General H.V. Cox, commanding 29th Indian Infantry Brigade, Lieutenant-Colonel Hon. C.G. Bruce, commanding 1/6th Gurkhas, and Major (temporary Lieutenant-Colonel) F.A. Wynter, R.G.A., commanding the Artillery Group supporting the attack. The co-operation of the two cruisers was excellent, and affords another instance of the admirable support by the Navy to our troops.

On May 14th General Gouraud arrived and took over from General d'Amade the command of the Corps Expeditionnaire. As General d'Amade quitted the shores of the peninsula he received a spontaneous ovation from the British soldiers at work upon the beaches.

The second division of the Corps Expeditionnaire, commanded by General Bailloud, had now completed disembarkation.

From the time of the small local push forward made by the 6th Gurkhas on the night of the 10th/11th May until the 4th of June the troops under my command pressed against the enemy continuously by sapping, reconnaissance and local advances, whilst, to do them justice, they (the enemy) did what they could to repay us in like coin. I have given the escalade of Gurkha Bluff as a sample; no 48 hours passed without something of the sort being attempted or achieved either by the French or ourselves.

Turning now to where the Australian and New Zealand Army Corps were perched upon the cliffs of Sari Bair, I must begin by explaining that their *rôle* at this stage of the operations was – first, to keep open a door leading to the vitals of the Turkish position; secondly, to hold up as large a body as possible of the enemy in front of them, so as to lessen the strain at Cape Helles. Anzac, in fact, was cast to play second fiddle to Cape Helles, a part out of harmony with the dare-devil spirit animating those warriors from the South, and so it has come about that, as your Lordship will now see, the defensive of the Australians and New Zealanders has always tended to take on the character of an attack.

The line held during the period under review by the Australian and New Zealand Army Corps formed a rough semi-circle inland from the beach of Anzac Cove, with a diameter of about 1,100 yards. The firing line is every-where close to the enemy's trenches, and in all sections of the position sapping, counter-sapping and bomb attacks have been incessant. The shelling both of the trenches and beaches has been impartial and liberal. As many as 1,400 shells have fallen on Anzac within the hour, and these of all calibres, from 11 inches to field shrapnel. Around Quinn's Post, both above and below ground, the contest has been particularly severe. This section of the line is situated on the circumference of the Anzac semi-circle at the furthest point from its diameter. Here our fire trenches are mere ledges on the brink of a sheer precipice falling 200 feet into the valley below. The enemy's trenches are only a few feet distant. On 9th May a night assault, supported by enfilade fire, was delivered on the enemy's trenches in front of Quinn's Post. The trenches were carried at the point of the bayonet, troops established in them, and reinforcements sent up.

At dawn on the 10th May a strong counter attack forced our troops to evacuate the trenches and fall back on Quinn's Post. In opposing this counter-attack our guns did great execution, as we discovered later from a Turkish officer's diary that two Turkish regiments on this date lost 600 killed and 2,000 wounded.

On the night of 14th–15th May a sortie was made from Quinn's Post with the object of filling in Turkish trenches in which bomb-throwers were active. The sortie, which cost us some seventy casualties, was not successful.

On 14th May Lieutenant-General Sir W.R. Birdwood was slightly wounded, but, I am glad to say, he was not obliged to relinquish the command of his Corps.

On 15th May I deeply regret to say Major-General W.T. Bridges, commanding the Australian Division, received a severe wound, which proved fatal a few days later. Sincere and single-minded in his devotion to Australia and to duty, his loss still stands out even amidst the hundreds of other brave officers who have gone.

On the 18th May Anzac was subjected to a heavy bombardment from large calibre guns and howitzers. At midnight of the 18th–19th the most violent rifle and machine-gun fire yet experienced broke out along the front. Slackening from 3 a.m. to 4 a.m. it then broke out again, and a heavy Turkish column assaulted the left of No. 2 Section. This assault was beaten off with loss. Another attack was delivered before daylight on the centre of this section; it was repeated four times and repulsed each time with very serious losses to the enemy. Simultaneously a heavy attack was delivered on the north-east salient of No. 4 section, which was repulsed and followed up, but the pressing of the counter-attack was prevented by shrapnel. Attacks were also delivered on Quinn's Post, Courtney's Post, and along the front of our right section. At about 5 a.m. the battle was fairly joined, and a furious cannonade was begun by a large number of enemy guns, including 12 inch and 9.2 inch, and other artillery that had not till then opened. By 9.30 a.m. the Turks were pressing hard against the left of Courtney's and the right of Quinn's Post. At 10 a.m. this attack, unable to face fire from the right, swung round to the left, where it was severely handled by our guns and the machine-guns of our left section. By 11 a.m. the enemy, who were crowded together in the trenches beyond Quinn's Post, were giving way under their heavy losses.

According to prisoners' reports 30,000 troops, including five fresh regiments, were used against us. General Liman Von Sanders was himself in command.

The enemy's casualties were heavy, as may be judged from the fact that over 3,000 dead were lying in the open in view of our trenches. A large proportion of these losses were due to our artillery fire. Our casualties amounted to about 100 killed and 500 wounded, including 9 officers wounded.

The next four days were chiefly remarkable for the carrying through of the negotiations for the suspension of arms, which actually took place on 24th May. About 5 p.m. on 20th May white flags and Red Crescents began to appear all along the line. In No. 2 section a Turkish staff officer, two medical officers, and a company commander came out and were met by Major-General H.B. Walker, commanding the Australian Division, half-way between the trenches. The staff officer explained that he was instructed to arrange a suspension of arms for the removal of dead and wounded. He had no written credentials, and he was informed that neither he nor the General Officer Commanding Australian Division had the power to arrange such a suspension of arms, but that at 8 p.m. an opportunity would be given of exchanging letters on the subject, and that meanwhile hostilities would recommence after 10 minutes' grace. At this time some stretcher parties on both sides were collecting wounded, and the Turkish trenches opposite ours were packed with men standing shoulder to shoulder two deep. Matters were less regular in front of other sections, where men with white flags came out to collect wounded. Meanwhile it was observed that columns were on the march in the valley up which the Turks were accustomed to bring up their reinforcements.

On hearing the report of these movements, General Sir W.R. Birdwood, commanding Australian and New Zealand Army Corps, ordered his trenches to be manned against a possible attack. As the evening drew in the enemy's concentration continued, and everything pointed to their intention of making use of the last of the daylight to get their troops into position without being shelled by our artillery. A message was therefore sent across to say that no clearing of dead or wounded could be allowed during the night, and that any negotiations for such a purpose should be opened through the proper channel and initiated before noon on the following day.

Stretcher and other parties fell back, and immediately fire broke out. In front of our right section masses of men advanced behind lines of unarmed men holding up their hands. Firing became general all along the line, accompanied by a heavy bombardment of the whole position, so that evidently this attack must have been prearranged. Musketry and machine-gun fire continued without interruption till after dark, and from then up to about 4 a.m. next day.

Except for a half-hearted attack in front of Courtney's Post, no assault was made till 1.20 a.m., when the enemy left their trenches and advanced on Quinn's Post. Our guns drove the Turks back to their trenches, and beat back all other attempts to assault. By 4.30 a.m. on 21st May musketry fire had died down to normal dimensions.

As the Turks seemed anxious to bury their dead, and as human sentiment and medical science were both of one accord in favour of such a course, I sent Major-General W.P. Braithwaite, my Chief of the General Staff, on 22nd May to assist Lieutenant-General Sir W.R. Birdwood, commanding the Army Corps, in coming to some suitable arrangements with the representative sent by Essad Pasha. The negotiations resulted in a suspension of arms from 7.30 a.m. to 4.30 p.m. on 24th May. The procedure laid down for this suspension of arms was, I am glad to inform your Lordship, correctly observed on both sides.

The burial of the dead was finished about 3 p.m. Some 3,000 Turkish dead were removed or buried in the area between the opposing lines. The whole of these were killed on or since the 18th of May. Many bodies of men killed earlier were also buried.

On the 25th May, with the assistance of two destroyers of the Royal Navy, a raid was carried out on Nibrunesi Point. A fresh telephone line was destroyed and an observing station demolished. On 28th May, at 9 p.m., a raid was made on a Turkish post overlooking the beach 1,200 yards north of Kaba Tepe, H.M.S. "Rattlesnake" co-operating. A party of 50 rifles rushed the post, killing or capturing the occupants. A similar raid was made against an enemy trench to the left of our line which cost the Turks 200 casualties, as was afterwards ascertained.

From 28th May till 5th June the fighting seemed to concentrate itself around Quinn's Post. Three enemy galleries had been detected there, and work on them stopped by counter-mines, which killed 20 Turks and injured 30. One gallery had, however, been overlooked, and at 3.30 a.m. on 29th May a mine was sprung in or near the centre of Quinn's Post. The explosion was followed by a very heavy bomb attack, before which our left centre subsection fell back, letting in a storming party of Turks. This isolated one subsection on the left from the two other subsections on the right.

At 5.30 a.m. our counter-attack was launched, and by 6 a.m. the position had been retaken with the bayonet by the 15th Australian Infantry Battalion, led by Major Quinn, who was unfortunately killed. All the enemy in the trench were killed or captured, and the work of restoration was begun.

At 6.30 a.m. the Turks again attacked, supported by artillery, rifle and machine-gun fire and by showers of bombs from the trenches. The fine shooting of our guns and the steadiness of the Infantry enabled us to inflict upon the enemy a bloody repulse, demoralising them to such an extent that the bomb throwers of their second line flung the missiles into the middle of their own first line.

At 8.15 a.m. the attack slackened, and by 8.45 a.m. the enemy's attacks had practically ceased.

Our casualties in this affair amounted to 2 officers, 31 other ranks killed, 12 officers and 176 other ranks wounded. The enemy's losses must have been serious, and were probably equal to those sustained on 9th/10th May. Except for the first withdrawal in the confusion of the mine explosion, all ranks fought with the greatest tenacity and courage.

On 30th May preparations were made in Quinn's Post to attack and destroy two enemy saps, the heads of which had reached within 5 yards of our fire trench. Two storming parties of 35 men went forward at 1 p.m., cleared the sap heads and penetrated into the trenches beyond, but they were gradually driven back by Turkish counter-attacks, in spite of our heavy supporting fire, our casualties being chiefly caused by bombs, of which the enemy seem to have an unlimited supply.

During 31st May close fighting continued in front of Quinn's Post.

On 1st June, an hour after dark, two sappers of the New Zealand Engineers courageously crept out and laid a charge of guncotton against a timber and sandbag bomb-proof. The structure was completely demolished.

After sunset on the 4th of June three separate enterprises were carried out by the Australian and New Zealand Army Corps. These were undertaken in compliance with an order which I had issued that the enemy's attention should be distracted during an attack I was about to deliver in the southern zone.

(1) A demonstration in the direction of Kaba Tepe the Navy co-operating by bombarding the Turkish trenches.

(2) A sortie at 11 p.m. towards a trench 200 yards from Quinn's Post. This failed, but a second sortie by 100 men took place at 2.55 a.m. on 5th June and penetrated to the Turkish trench; demolished a machine-gun emplacement which enfiladed Quinn's Post, and withdrew in good order.

(3) At Quinn's Post an assault was delivered at 11 p.m. A party of 60 men, accompanied by a bomb-throwing party on either flank, stormed the enemy's trench. In the assault many Turks were bayonetted and 28 captured. A working party followed up the attack and at once set to work. Meanwhile the Turkish trenches on the left of the post were heavily assailed with machine-gun fire and grenades, which drew from them a very heavy fire. After daybreak

a strong bomb attack developed on the captured trench, the enemy using a heavier type of bomb than hitherto.

At 6.30 a.m. the trench had to be abandoned, and it was found necessary to retire to the original fire trench of the post and the bombproof in front of its left. Our casualties were 80; those of the enemy considerably greater.

On 5th June a sortie was made from Quinn's Post by 2 officers and 100 men of the 1st Australian Infantry, the objective being the destruction of a machine-gun in a trench known as German Officer's Trench. A special party of 10 men with the officer commanding the party (Lieutenant E.E.L. Lloyd, 1st Battalion (New South Wales) Australian Imperial Force) made a dash for the machine-gun; one of the 10 men managed to fire three rounds into the gun at a range of five feet and another three at the same range through a loophole. The darkness of the trench and its overhead cover prevented the use of the bayonet, but some damage was done by shooting down over the parapet. As much of the trench as possible was dismantled. The party suffered some casualties from bombs, and was enfiladed all the time by machine-guns from either flank. The aim of this gallant assault being attained the party withdrew in good order with their wounded. Casualties in all were 36.

I now return to the Southern Zone and to the battle of the 4th of June.

From 25th May onwards the troops had been trying to work up within rushing distance of the enemy's front trenches. On the 25th May the Royal Naval and 42nd Divisions crept 100 yards nearer to the Turks, and on the night of 28th/29th May the whole of the British line made a further small advance. On that same night the French Corps Expeditionnaire was successful in capturing a small redoubt on the extreme Turkish left west of the Kereves Dere. All Turkish counter-attacks during 29th May were repulsed. On the night of 30th May two of their many assaults effected temporary lodgment. But on both occasions they were driven out again with the bayonet.

On every subsequent night up to that of the 3rd/4th June assaults were made upon the redoubt and upon our line, but at the end of that period our position remained intact.

This brings the narrative up to the day of the general attack upon the enemy's front line of trenches which ran from the west of the Kereves Dere in a northerly direction to the sea. Taking our line of battle from right to left the troops were deployed in the following order:- The Corps Expeditionnaire, the Royal Naval Division, the 42nd (East Lancs) Division and the 29th Division.

The length of the front, so far as the British troops were concerned, was rather over 4,000 yards, and the total infantry available amounted to 24,000 men, which permitted the General Officer Commanding 8th Army Corps to form a corps reserve of 7,000 men.

My General Headquarters for the day were at the command post on the peninsula.

At 8 a.m. on 4th June our heavy artillery opened with a deliberate bombardment which continued till 10.30 a.m. At 11 a.m. the bombardment recommenced and continued till 11.20 a.m., when a feint attack was made which successfully drew heavy fire from the enemy's guns and rifles. At 11.30 a.m. all our guns opened fire and continued with increasing intensity till noon.

On the stroke of noon the artillery increased their range and along the whole line the infantry fixed bayonets and advanced.

The assault was immediately successful. On the extreme right the French 1st Division carried a line of trench, whilst the French 2nd Division, with the greatest dash and gallantry captured a strong redoubt called the "Haricot," for which they had already had three desperate contests. Only the extreme left of the French was unable to gain any ground, a feature destined to have an unfortunate effect upon the final issue.

The 2nd Naval Brigade of the Royal Naval Division rushed forward with great dash; the "Anson" Battalion captured the southern face of a Turkish redoubt which formed a salient in the enemy's line, the "Howe" and "Hood" Battalions captured trenches fronting them, and by 12.15 p.m. the whole Turkish line forming their first objective was in their hands. Their consolidating party went forward at 12.25 p.m.

The Manchester Brigade of the 42nd Division advanced magnificently. In five minutes the first line of Turkish trenches were captured, and by 12.30 p.m. the Brigade had carried with a rush the line forming their second objective, having made an advance of 600 yards in all. The working parties got to work without incident, and the position here could not possibly have been better.

On the left the 29th Division met with more difficulty. All along the section of the 88th Brigade the troops jumped out of their trenches at noon and charged across the open at the nearest Turkish trench. In most places the enemy crossed bayonets with our men and inflicted severe loss upon us. But the 88th Brigade was not to be denied. The Worcester Regiment was the first to capture trenches, and the remainder of the 88th Brigade, though at first held up by flanking as well as fronting fire, also pushed on doggedly until they had fairly made good the whole of the Turkish first line.

Only on the extreme left did we sustain a check. Here the Turkish front trench was so sited as to have escaped damage from our artillery bombardment, and the barbed wire obstacle was intact. The result was that, though the 14th Sikhs on the right flank pushed on despite losses amounting to three-fourths of their effectives, the centre of the Brigade could make no headway.

A company of the 6th Gurkhas on the left, skilfully led along the cliffs by its commander, actually forced its way into a Turkish work, but the failure of the rest of the Brigade threatened isolation, and it was as skilfully withdrawn under fire. Reinforcements were therefore sent to the left so that, if possible, a fresh attack might be organised. Meanwhile, on the right of the line, the gains of the morning were being compromised. A very heavy counter-attack had developed against the "Haricot." The Turks poured in masses of men through prepared communication trenches, and, under cover of accurate shell fire, were able to recapture that redoubt. The French, forced to fall back, uncovered in doing so the right flank of the Royal Naval Division. Shortly before 1 p.m. the right of the 2nd Naval Brigade had to retire with very heavy loss from the redoubt they had captured, thus exposing in their turn the "Howe" and "Hood" Battalions to enfilade, so that they, too, had nothing for it but to retreat across the open under exceedingly heavy machine gun and musketry fire.

By 1.30 p.m. the whole of the captured trenches in this section had been lost again, and the Brigade was back in its original position, the "Collingwood" Battalion, which had gone forward in support, having been practically destroyed.

The question was now whether this rolling up of the newly captured line from the right would continue until the whole of our gains were wiped out. It looked very like it, for now the enfilade fire of the Turks began to fall upon the Manchester Brigade of the 42nd Division, which was firmly consolidating the furthest distant line of trenches it had so brilliantly won. After 1.30 p.m. it became increasingly difficult for this gallant Brigade to hold its ground. Heavy casualties occurred; the Brigadier and many other officers were wounded or killed; yet it continued to hold out with the greatest tenacity and grit. Every effort was made to sustain the Brigade in its position. Its right flank was thrown back to make face against the enfilade fire and reinforcements were sent to try to fill the diagonal gap between it and the Royal Naval Division. But, ere long, it became clear that unless the right of our line could advance again it would be impossible for the Manchesters to maintain the very pronounced salient in which they now found themselves.

Orders were issued, therefore, that the Royal Naval Division should co-operate with the French Corps in a fresh attack, and reinforcements were despatched to this end. The attack, timed for 3 p.m., was twice postponed at the request of General Gouraud, who finally reported that he would be unable to advance again that day with any prospect of success. By 6.30 p.m., therefore, the 42nd Division had to be extricated with loss from the second line Turkish trenches, and had to content themselves with consolidating on the first line which they had captured within five minutes of commencing the attack. Such was the spirit displayed by this Brigade that there was great difficulty in persuading the men to fall back. Had their flanks been covered nothing would have made them loosen their grip.

No further progress had been found possible in front of the 88th Brigade and Indian Brigade. Attempts were made by their reserve battalions to advance on the right and left flanks respectively, but in both cases heavy fire drove them back.

At 4 p.m. under support of our artillery the Royal Fusiliers were able to advance beyond the first line of captured trenches, but the fact that the left flank was held back made the attempt to hold any isolated position in advance inadvisable.

As the reserves had been largely depleted by the despatch of reinforcements to various parts of the line, and information was to hand of the approach of strong reinforcements of fresh troops to the enemy, orders were issued for the consolidation of the line then held.

Although we had been forced to abandon so much of the ground gained in the first rush, the net result of the day's operations was considerable – namely, an advance of 200 to 400 yards along the whole of our centre, a front of nearly 3 miles. That the enemy suffered severely was indicated, not only by subsequent information, but by the fact of his attempting no counter-attack during the night, except upon the trench captured by the French 1st Division on the extreme right. Here two counter-attacks were repulsed with loss.

The prisoners taken during the day amounted to 400, including 11 officers: amongst these were 5 Germans, the remains of a volunteer machine-gun detachment from the *Goeben*. Their commanding officer was killed and the machine-gun destroyed. The majority of these captures were made by the 42nd Division under Major-General W. Douglas.

From the date of this battle to the end of the month of June the incessant attacks and counter-attacks which have so grievously swelled our lists of casualties have been caused by the determination of the Turks to regain ground they had lost, a determination clashing against our firm resolve to continue to increase our holding. Several of these daily encounters would have been the subject of a separate despatch in the campaigns of my youth and middle age, but, with due regard to proportion, they cannot even be so much as mentioned here. Only one example each from the French, British and Australian and New Zealand spheres of action will be most briefly set down so that Your Lordship may understand the nature of the demands made upon the energies and fortitude of the troops.

(1) At 4.30 a.m. on June the 21st the French Corps Expeditionnaire attacked the formidable works that flank the Kereves Dere. By noon their 2nd Division had stormed all the Turkish first and second line trenches to

their front, and had captured the Haricot redoubt. On their right the 1st Division took the first line of trenches, but were counter-attacked and driven out. Fresh troops were brought up and launched upon another assault, but the Turks were just as obstinate and drove out the second party before they had time to consolidate. At 2.45 p.m. General Gouraud issued an order that full use must be made of the remaining five hours of daylight, and that, before dark, these trenches must be taken and held, otherwise the gains of the 2nd Division would be sacrificed. At 6 p.m. the third assault succeeded: 600 yards of trenches remained in our hands, despite all the heavy counter-attacks made through the night by the enemy. In this attack the striplings belonging to the latest French drafts specially distinguished themselves by their forwardness and contempt of danger. Fifty prisoners were taken, and the enemy's casualties (mostly incurred during counter-attacks) were estimated at 7,000. The losses of the Corps Expeditionnaire were 2,500.

(2) The Turkish right had hitherto rooted itself with special tenacity into the coast. In the scheme of attack submitted by Lieutenant- General A.G. Hunter Weston, commanding VIIIth Army Corps, our left, pivoting upon a point in our line about one mile from the sea, was to push forward until its outer flank advanced about 1,000 yards. If the operation was successful then, at its close, we should have driven the enemy back for a thousand yards along the coast, and the trenches of this left section of our line would be facing east instead of, as previously, north-east. Obviously the ground to be gained lessened as our line drew back from the sea towards its fixed or pivotal right. Five Turkish trenches must be carried in the section nearest the sea: only two Turkish trenches in the section furthest from the sea. At 10.20 a.m. on the 28th June our bombardment began. At 10.45 a.m. a small redoubt known as the Boomerang was rushed by the Border Regiment. At 11 a.m. the 87th Brigade, under Major-General W.R. Marshall, captured three lines of Turkish trenches. On their right the 4th and 7th Royal Scots captured the two Turkish trenches allotted to them, but further to the east; near the pivotal point the remainder of the 156th Brigade were unable to get on. Precisely at 11.30 a.m. the second attack took place. The 86th Brigade, led by the 2nd Royal Fusiliers, dashed over the trenches already captured by their comrades of the 87th Brigade, and, pushing on with great steadiness, took two more lines of trenches, thus achieving the five successive lines along the coast. This success was further improved upon by the Indian Brigade, who managed to secure, and to place into a state of defence, a spur running from the west of the furthest captured Turkish trench to the sea. Our casualties were small; 1,750 in all. The enemy suffered heavily, especially in the repeated counter-attacks, which for many days and nights afterwards they launched against the trenches they had lost.

(3) On the night of the 29th/30th June the Turks, acting, as we afterwards ascertained, under the direct personal order of Enver Pasha, to drive us all into the sea, made a big attack on the Australian and New Zealand Army Corps, principally on that portion of the line which was under the command of Major-General Sir A.J. Godley. From midnight till 1.30 a.m. a fire of musketry and guns of greatest intensity was poured upon our trenches. A heavy column then advanced to the assault, and was completely crumpled up by the musketry and machine-guns of the 7th and 8th Light Horse. An hour later another grand attack took place against our left and left centre, and was equally cut to pieces by our artillery and rifle fire. The enemy's casualties may be judged by the fact that in areas directly exposed to view between 400 and 500 were actually seen to fall.

On the evening of this day, the 30th of June, the Mediterranean Expeditionary Force suffered grevious loss owing to the wounding of General Gouraud by a shell. This calamity, for I count it nothing less, brings us down to the beginning of the month of July.

The command of the Corps Expeditionnaire francais d'Orient was then taken over by General Bailloud, at which point I shall close my despatch.

During the whole period under review the efforts and expedients whereby a great army has had its wants supplied upon a wilderness have, I believe, been breaking world records.

Upon such a situation appeared quite suddenly the enemy submarines. On 22nd May all transports had to be despatched to Mudros for safety. Thenceforth men, stores, guns, horses, etc., etc., had to be brought from Mudros – a distance of 40 miles – in fleet sweepers and other small and shallow craft less vulnerable to submarine attack. Every danger and every difficulty was doubled.

But the Navy and the Royal Engineers were not to be thwarted in their landing operations either by nature or by the enemy, whilst the Army Service Corps, under Brigadier-General F.W.B. Koe, and the Army Ordnance Corps, under Brigadier-General R.W.M. Jackson, have made it a point of honour to feed men, animals, guns and rifles in the fighting line as regularly as if they were only out for manoeuvres on Salisbury Plain.

I desire, therefore, to record my admiration for the cool courage and unfailing efficiency with which the Royal Navy, the beach personnel, the engineers and the administrative services have carried out these arduous duties.

In addition to its normal duties the Signal Service, under the direction of Lieutenant-Colonel M.G.E. Bowman-Manifold, Director of Army Signals, has provided the connecting link between the Royal Navy and the Army in their combined operations, and has rapidly readjusted itself to amphibious methods. All demands made on it by sudden expansion of the fighting forces or by the movements of General Headquarters have been rapidly and effectively met. The working of the telegraphs, telephones and repair of lines, often under heavy fire, has been beyond praise. Casualties have been unusually high, but the best traditions of the Corps of Royal Engineers have inspired the whole of their work. As an instance, the central telegraph office at Cape Helles (a dug-out) was recently struck by a high explosive shell. The officer on duty and twelve other ranks were killed or wounded and the office entirely demolished. But No. 72003 Corporal G.A. Walker, Royal Engineers, although much shaken, repaired the damage, collected men, and within 39 minutes reopened communication by apologising for the incident and by saying he required no assistance.

The Royal Army Medical Service have had to face unusual and very trying conditions. There are no roads, and the wounded who are unable to walk must be carried from the firing line to the shore. They and their attendants may be shelled on their way to the beaches, at the beaches, on the jetties, and again, though I believe by inadvertence, on their way out in lighters to the hospital ships. Under shell fire it is not as easy as some of the critically disposed seem to imagine to keep all arrangements in apple-pie order. Here I can only express my own opinion that efficiency, method and even a certain quiet heroism have characterised the evacuations of the many thousands of our wounded.

In my three Commanders of Corps I have indeed been thrice fortunate.

General Gouraud brought a great reputation to our help from the battlefields of the Argonne, and in so doing he has added to its lustre. A happy mixture of daring in danger and of calm in crisis, full of energy and resource, he has worked hand in glove with his British comrades in arms, and has earned their affection and respect.

Lieutenant-General Sir W.R. Birdwood has been the soul of Anzac. Not for one single day has he ever quitted his post. Cheery and full of human sympathy, he has spent many hours of each twenty-four inspiring the defenders of the front trenches, and if he does not know every soldier in his force, at least every soldier in the force believes he is known to his Chief. Lieutenant-General A.G. Hunter Weston possesses a genius for war. I know no more resolute Commander. Calls for reinforcements, appeals based on exhaustion or upon imminent counter-attack are powerless to divert him from his aim. And this aim, in so far as he may be responsible for it, is worked out with insight, accuracy, and that wisdom which comes from close study in peace combined with long experience in the field.

In my first despatch I tried to express my indebtedness to Major-General W.P. Braithwaite, and I must now again, however inadequately, place on record the untiring, loyal assistance he has continued to render me ever since.

The thanks of every one serving in the Peninsula are due to Lieutenant-General Sir John Maxwell. All the resources of Egypt and all of his own remarkable administrative abilities have been ungrudgingly placed at our disposal.

Finally, if my despatch is in any way to reflect the feelings of the force, I must refer to the shadow cast over the whole of our adventure by the loss of so many of our gallant and true-hearted comrades. Some of them we shall never see again; some have had the mark of the Dardanelles set upon them for life, but others, and, thank God, by far the greater proportion, will be back in due course at the front.

I have the honour to be
Your Lordship's most obedient Servant,
IAN HAMILTON,
General, Commanding Mediterranean
Expeditionary Force.

5

SIR IAN HAMILTON'S THIRD GALLIPOLI DESPATCH, 11 DECEMBER 1915

THURSDAY, 6 JANUARY, 1916.

War Office, 6th January, 1916.

The following despatch has been received by the Secretary of State for War from General Sir Ian Hamilton, G.C.B.

1, *Hyde Park Gardens,*
London, W.

MY LORD,-   11*th December*, 1915.

For the understanding of the operations about to be described I must first set forth the situation as it appeared to me early in July.

The three days' battle of the 6th–8th May had shown that neither of my forces, northern or southern, were strong enough to fight their way to the Narrows. On the 10th of May I had cabled asking that two fresh divisions might be sent me to enable me to press on and so prevent my attack degenerating into trench warfare. On the 17th of May I again cabled, saying that if we were going to be left to face Turkey on our own resources we should require two Army Corps additional to my existing forces at the Dardanelles. The 52nd (Lowland) Division had been sent me, but between their dates of despatch and arrival Russia had given up the idea of co-operating from the coast of the Black Sea. Thereby several Turkish divisions were set free for the Dardanelles, and the battle of the 4th June, locally successful as it was, found us just as weak, relatively, as we had been a month earlier.

During June Your Lordship became persuaded of the bearing of these facts, and I was promised three regular divisions plus the infantry of two Territorial divisions. The advance guard of these troops was due to reach Mudros by the 10th of July; by the 10th of August their concentration was to be complete.

Eliminating the impracticable, I had already narrowed down the methods of employing these fresh forces to one of the following four:-

(*a*) Every man to be thrown on to the southern sector of the Peninsula to force a way forward to the Narrows.

(*b*) Disembarkation on the Asiatic side of the Straits, followed by a march on Chanak.

(c) A landing at Enos or Ebrije for the purpose of seizing the neck of the isthmus at Bulair.

(d) Reinforcement of the Australian and New Zealand Army Corps, combined with a landing in Suvla Bay. Then with one strong push to capture Hill 305, and, working from that dominating point, to grip the waist of the Peninsula.

As to (a) I rejected that course-

(1) Because there were limits to the numbers which could be landed and deployed in one confined area.

(2) Because the capture of Krithia could no longer be counted upon to give us Achi Baba, an entirely new system of works having lately appeared upon the slopes of that mountain – works so planned that even if the enemy's western flank was turned and driven back from the coast the central and eastern portions of the mountain could still be maintained as a bastion to Kilid Bahr.

(3) Because, if I tried to disengage myself both from Krithia and Achi Baba by landing due west of Kilid Bahr, my troops would be exposed to artillery fire from Achi Baba, the Olive Grove, and Kilid Bahr itself; the enemy's large reserves were too handy; there were not fair chances of success.

As to (b), although much of the Asiatic coast had now been wired and entrenched, the project was still attractive. Thereby the Turkish forces on the peninsula would be weakened; our beaches at Cape Helles would be freed from Asiatic shells; the threat to the enemy's sea communications was obvious. But when I descended into detail I found that the expected reinforcements would not run to a double operation. I mean that, unless I could make a thorough, whole-hearted attack on the enemy in the peninsula I should reap no advantage in that theatre from the transference of the Turkish peninsula troops to reinforce Asia, whereas, if the British forces landed in Asia were not strong enough in themselves seriously to threaten Chanak, the Turks for their part would not seriously relax their grip upon the peninsula.

To cut the land communications of the whole of the Turkish peninsular army, as in (c), was a better scheme on paper than on the spot. The naval objections appeared to my coadjutor, Vice-Admiral de Robeck, well-nigh insurmountable. Already, owing to submarine dangers, all reinforcements, ammunition and supplies had to be brought up from Mudros to Helles or Anzac by night in fleet-sweepers and trawlers. A new landing near Bulair would have added another 50 miles to the course such small craft must cover, thus placing too severe a strain upon the capacities of the flotilla. The landing promised special hazards owing to the difficulty of securing the transports and covering ships from submarine attack. Ibrije has a bad beach, and the distance to Enos, the only point suitable to a disembarkation on a large scale, was so great that the enemy would have had time to organise a formidable opposition from his garrisons in Thrace. Four divisions at least would be required to overcome such opposition. These might now be found; but, even so, and presupposing every other obstacle overcome, it was by no manner of means certain that the Turkish army on the peninsula would thereby be brought to sue for terms, or that the Narrows would thereby be opened to the Fleet. The enemy would still be able to work supplies across the Straits from Chanak. The swiftness of the current, the shallow draft of the Turkish lighters, the guns of the forts, made it too difficult even for our dauntless submarine commanders to paralyse movement across these land-locked waters. To achieve that purpose I must bring my artillery fire to bear both on the land and water communications of the enemy.

This brings me to (*d*), the storming of that dominating height, Hill 305, with the capture of Maidos and Gaba Tepe as its sequel.

From the very first I had hoped that by landing a force under the heights of Sari Bair we should be able to strangle the Turkish communications to the southwards, whether by land or sea, and so clear the Narrows for the Fleet. Owing to the enemy's superiority, both in numbers and in position; owing to underestimates of the strength of the original entrenchments prepared and sited under German direction; owing to the constant dwindling of the units of my force through wastage; owing also to the intricacy and difficulty of the terrain, these hopes had not hitherto borne fruit. But they were well founded. So much at least had clearly enough been demonstrated by the desperate and costly nature of the Turkish attacks. The Australians and New Zealanders had rooted themselves in very near to the vitals of the enemy. By their tenacity and courage they still held open the doorway from which one strong thrust forward might give us command of the Narrows.

From the naval point of view the auspices were also favourable. Suvla Bay was but one mile further from Mudros than Anzac, and its possession would ensure us a submarine-proof base and a harbour good against gales, excepting those from the south-west. There were, as might be expected, some special difficulties to be overcome. The broken, intricate country – the lack of water – the consequent anxious supply questions. Of these it can only be said that a bad country is better than an entrenched country, and that supply and water problems may be countered by careful preparation.

Before a man of the reinforcements had arrived my mind was made up as to their employment, and by means of a vigorous offensive from Anzac, combined with a surprise landing to the north of it, I meant to try and win through to Maidos, leaving behind me a well-protected line of communications starting from the bay of Suvla.

Another point which had to be fixed in advance was the date. The new troops would gain in fighting value if they could first be given a turn in the trenches. So much was clear. But the relief of the troops already holding those trenches would have been a long and difficult task for the Navy, and time was everything, seeing that everywhere the enemy was digging in as fast as he possibly could dig. Also, where large numbers of troops were to be smuggled into Anzac and another large force was to land by surprise at Suvla, it was essential to eliminate the moon. Unless the plunge could be taken by the second week in August the whole venture must be postponed for a month. The dangers of such delay were clear. To realise them I had only to consider how notably my prospects would have been bettered had these same reinforcements arrived in time to enable me to anticipate the moon of July.

Place and date having shaped themselves, the intervening period had to be filled in with as much fighting as possible. First, to gain ground; secondly, to maintain the moral ascendency which my troops had by this time established; thirdly, to keep the enemy's eyes fixed rather upon Helles than Anzac.

Working out my ammunition allowance, I found I could accumulate just enough high explosive shell to enable me to deliver one serious attack per each period of three weeks. I was thus limited to a single effort on the large scale, plus a prescribed unceasing offensive routine, with bombing, sniping and mining as its methods.

The action of the 12th and 13th of July was meant to be a sequel to the action of the 28th June. That advance had driven back the Turkish right on to their second main system of defence just south of Krithia. But, on my centre and right, the enemy still held their forward system of trenches, and it was my intention on the 12th July to seize the remaining trenches of this foremost system from the sea at the mouth of the Kereves Dere to the main Sedd-el-Bahr–Krithia road, along a front of some 2,000 yards.

On our right the attack was to be entrusted to the French Corps; on the right centre to the 52nd (Lowland) Division. On the 52nd Division's front the operation was planned to take place in two phases: our right was to attack in the morning, our left in the afternoon. Diversions by the 29th Division on the left of the southern section and at Anzac were to take place on the same day, so as to prevent the enemy's reserves from reinforcing the real point of attack.

At 7.35 a.m., after a heavy bombardment, the troops, French and Scottish, dashed out of their trenches and at once captured two lines of enemy trenches. Pushing forward with fine *élan* the 1st Division of the French Corps completed the task assigned to it by carrying the whole of the Turkish forward system of works, namely, the line of trenches skirting the lower part of the Kereves Dere. Further to the left the 2nd French Division and our 155th Brigade maintained the two lines of trenches they had gained. But on the left of the 155th Brigade the 4th Battalion, King's Own Scottish Borderers, pressed on too eagerly. They not only carried the third line of trenches, but charged on up the hill and beyond the third line, then advanced indeed until they came under the "feu de barrage" of the French artillery. Nothing could live under so cruel a cross fire from friend and foe, so the King's Own Scottish Borderers were forced to fall back with heavy losses to the second line of enemy trenches which they had captured in their first rush.

During this fighting telephone wires from forward positions were cut by enemy's shell fire, and here and there in the elaborate network of trenches numbers of Turks were desperately resisting to the last. Thus though the second line of captured trenches continued to be held as a whole, much confused fighting ensued; there were retirements in parts of the line, reserves were rapidly being used up, and generally the situation was anxious and uncertain. But the best way of clearing it up seemed to be to deliver the second phase of the attack by the 157th Brigade just as it had originally been arranged. Accordingly, after a preliminary bombardment, the 157th Brigade rushed forward under heavy machine-gun and rifle fire, and splendidly carried the whole of the enemy trenches allotted as their objective. Here, then, our line had advanced some 400 yards, while the 155th Brigade and the 2nd French Division had advanced between 200 and 300 yards. At 6 p.m. the 52nd Division was ordered to make the line good; it seemed to be fairly in our grasp.

All night long determined counter-attacks, one after another, were repulsed by the French and the 155th Brigade, but about 7.30 a.m. the right of the 157th Brigade gave way before a party of bombers, and our grip upon the enemy began to weaken.

I therefore decided that three battalions of the Royal Naval Division should reinforce a fresh attack to be made that afternoon, 13th July, on such portions of our original objectives as remained in the enemy's hands. This second attack was a success. The 1st French Division pushed their right down to the mouth of the Kereves Dere; the 2nd French Division attacked the trenches they had failed to take on the preceding day; the Nelson Battalion, on the left of the Royal Naval Division attack, valiantly advanced and made good, well supported by the artillery of the French. The Portsmouth Battalion, pressing on too far, fell into precisely the same error at precisely the same spot as did the 4th King's Own Scottish Borderers on the 12th, an over-impetuosity which cost them heavy losses.

The 1/5th Royal Scots Fusiliers, commanded by Lieutenant-Colonel J.B. Pollok-McCall; the 1/7th Royal Scots, commanded by Lieutenant-Colonel W.C. Peebles; the 1/5th King's Own Scottish Borderers, commanded by Lieutenant-Colonel W.J. Millar; and the 1/6th Highland Light Infantry, commanded by Major J. Anderson, are mentioned as having specially distinguished themselves in this engagement.

Generally, the upshot of the attack was this. On our right and on the French left two lines had been captured, but in neither case was the third, or last, line of the system in their hands. Elsewhere a fine feat of arms had been accomplished, and a solid and enduring advance had been achieved, giving us far the best sited line for defence with much the best field for machine-gun and rifle fire we had hitherto obtained upon the peninsula.

A machine-gun and 200 prisoners were captured by the French; the British took a machine-gun and 329 prisoners. The casualties in the French Corps were not heavy, though it is with sorrow that I have to report the mortal wound of General Masnou, commanding the 1st Division. Our own casualties were a little over 3,000; those of the enemy about 5,000.

On 17th July Lieutenant-General Hunter Weston, commanding the 8th Corps, left the peninsula for a few days' rest, and, to my very deep regret, was subsequently invalided home. I have already drawn attention to his invincible self-confidence; untiring energy and trained ability.

As I was anxious to give the Commander of the new troops all the local experience possible I appointed Lieutenant-General Hon. Sir Frederick Stopford, whose own Corps were now assembling at Mudros, temporarily to succeed Lieutenant-General Hunter Weston, but on July 24th, when General Stopford had to set to work with his own Corps, Major-General W. Douglas, General Officer Commanding 42nd Division, took over temporary command of the 8th Corps; while Major-General W.R. Marshall, General Officer Commanding 87th Brigade, assumed temporary command of the 42nd Division.

Only one other action need be mentioned before coming to the big operations of August. On the extreme right of Anzac the flank of a work called Tasmania Post was threatened by the extension of a Turkish trench. The task of capturing this trench was entrusted to the 3rd Australian Brigade. After an artillery bombardment, mines were to be fired, whereupon four columns of 50 men each were to assault and occupy specified lengths of the trench. The regiment supplying the assaulting columns was the 11th Australian Infantry Battalion.

At 10.15 p.m. on 31st July the bombardment was opened. Ten minutes later and the mines were duly fired. The four assaulting parties, dashed forward at once, crossed our own barbed wire on planks, and were into the craters before the whole of the débris had fallen. Total casualties: 11 killed and 74 wounded; Turkish killed, 100.

By the time this action was fought a large proportion of my reinforcements had arrived, and, on the same principle which induced me to put General Stopford in temporary command at Helles, I relieved the war-worn

29th Division at the same place by the 13th Division under Major-General Shaw. The experiences here gained, in looking after themselves, in forgetting the thousand and one details of peace soldiering and in grasping the two or three elementary rules of conduct in war soldiering, were, it turned out, to be of priceless advantage to the 13th Division throughout the heavy fighting of the following month.

And now it was time to determine a date for the great venture. The moon would rise on the morning of the 7th at about 2 a.m. A day or two previously the last reinforcements, the 53rd and 54th Divisions, were due to arrive. The first day of the attack was fixed for the 6th of August. Once the date was decided a certain amount of ingenuity had to be called into play so as to divert the attention of the enemy from my main strategical conception. This – I repeat for the sake of clearness – was:-

(1) To break out with a rush from Anzac and cut off the bulk of the Turkish Army from land communication with Constantinople.

(2) To gain such a command for my artillery as to cut off the bulk of the Turkish Army from sea traffic whether with Constantinople or with Asia.

(3) Incidentally, to secure Suvla Bay as a winter base for Anzac and all the troops operating in the northern theatre.

My schemes for hoodwinking the Turks fell under two heads: First, strategical diversions, meant to draw away enemy reserves not yet committed to the peninsula. Secondly, tactical diversions meant to hold up enemy reserves already on the peninsula. Under the first heading came a surprise landing by a force of 300 men on the northern shore of the Gulf of Xeros; demonstrations by French ships opposite Mitylene along the Syrian coast; concentration at Mitylene; inspections at Mitylene by the Admiral and myself; making to order of a whole set of maps of Asia in Egypt, as well as secret service work, most of which bore fruit. Amongst the tactical diversions were a big containing attack at Helles. Soundings, registration of guns, etc., by Monitors between Gaba Tepe and Kum Tepe. An attack to be carried out by Anzac on Lone Pine trenches, which lay in front of their right wing and as far distant as the local terrain would admit from the scene of the real battle. Thanks entirely to the reality and vigour which the Navy and the troops threw into them, each one of these ruses was, it so turned out, entirely successful, with the result that the Turks, despite their excellent spy system, were caught completely off their guard at dawn on the 7th of August.

Having settled upon the manner and time of the diversions, orders had to be issued for the main operation. And here I must pause a moment to draw your Lordship's attention to the extraordinary complexity of the staff work caused by the unique distribution of my forces. Within the narrow confines of the positions I held on the peninsula it was impossible to concentrate even as much as one third of the fresh troops about to be launched to the attack. Nor could Mudros and Imbros combined absorb the whole of the remainder. The strategic concentration which precedes a normal battle had in my case to be a very wide dispersion. Thus of the forces destined for my offensive, on the day before the battle, part were at Anzac, part at Imbros, part at Mudros, and part at Mitylene. These last three detachments were separated respectively by 14, 60 and 120 miles of sea from the arena into which they were simultaneously to appear. To ensure the punctual arrival of all these masses of inexperienced troops at the right moment and spot, together with their material, munitions, stores, supplies, water, animals and vehicles, was a prodigious undertaking demanding not only competence, but self-confidence; and I will say for my General Staff that I believe the clearness and completeness of their orders for this concentration and landing will hereafter be studied as models in military academies. The need for economy in sea transport, the awkwardness and restriction of open beaches, the impossibility of landing guns, animals or vehicles rapidly – all these made it essential to create a special, separate organ-isation for every single unit taking part in the adventure. A pack mule corps to supply 80,000 men had also to be organised for that specific purpose until such time as other transport could be landed.

As to water, that element of itself was responsible for a whole chapter of preparations. An enormous quantity had to be collected secretly, and as secretly stowed away at Anzac, where a high-level reservoir had to be built, having a holding capacity of 30,000 gallons, and fitted out with a regular system of pipes and distribution tanks. A stationary engine was brought over from Egypt to fill that reservoir. Petroleum tins, with a carrying capacity of 80,000 gallons, were got together, and fixed up with handles, &c., but the collision of the "Moorgate" with another vessel delayed the arrival of large numbers of these just as a breakdown in the stationary engine upset for a while the well-laid plan of the high-level reservoir. But Anzac was ever resourceful in face of misadventures, and when the inevitable accidents arose it was not with folded hands that they were met.

Turning to Suvla Bay, it was believed that good wells and springs existed both in the Biyuk, Anafarta Valley and in Suvla Plain. But nothing so vital could possibly be left to hearsay, and although, as it turned out, our infor-mation was perfectly correct, yet the War Office were asked to despatch with each reinforcing division water receptacles for pack transport at the rate of half a gallon per man.

The sheet-anchor on which hung the whole of these elaborate schemes was the Navy. One tiny flaw in the perfect mutual trust and confidence animating the two services would have wrecked the whole enterprise. Experts at a distance may have guessed as much; it was self-evident to the rawest private on the spot. But with men like Vice-Admiral de Robeck, Commodore Roger Keyes, Rear-Admiral Christian and Captain F.H. Mitchell at our backs, we soldiers were secured against any such risk, and it will be seen how perfect was the precision the sailors put into their job.

The hour was now approaching, and I waited for it with as much confidence as is possible when to the inevitable uncertainties of war are to be added those of the weather. Apart from feints, the first blow was to be dealt in the southern zone.

In that theatre I had my own Poste de Commandement. But upon the 6th of August attacks in the south were only to form a subsidiary part of one great concerted attack. Anzac was to deliver the knock-down blow; Helles and Suvla were complementary operations. Were I to commit myself at the outset to any one of these three theatres I must lose my sense of proportion. Worse, there being no lateral communication between them, as soon as I landed at one I was cut off from present touch with both of the others. At Imbros I was 45 minutes from Helles, 40 minutes from Anzac, and 50 minutes from Suvla. Imbros was the centre of the cable system, and thence I could follow each phase of the triple attack and be ready with my two divisions of reserve to throw in reinforcements where they seemed most to be required. Therefore I decided to follow the opening moves from General Headquarters.

At Helles the attack of the 6th was directed against 1,200 yards of the Turkish front opposite our own right and right centre, and was to be carried out by the 88th Brigade of the 29th Division. Two small Turkish trenches enfilading the main advance had, if possible, to be captured simultaneously, an affair which was entrusted to the 42nd Division.

After bombardment the infantry assaulted at 3.50 p.m. On the left large sections of the enemy's line were carried, but on our centre and right the Turks were encountered in masses, and the attack, pluckily and perseveringly as it was pressed, never had any real success. The 1st Battalion, Essex Regiment, in particular forced their way into the crowded enemy trench opposite them, despite the most determined resistance, but, once in, were subjected to the heaviest musketry fire from both flanks, as well as in reverse, and were shattered by showers of bombs. Two separate resolute attacks were made by the 42nd Division, but both of them recoiled in face of the unexpected volume of fire developed by the Turks.

After dark officer's patrols were sent up to ascertain the exact position of affairs. Heavy Turkish counter-attacks were being pressed against such portions of the line we still retained. Many of our men fought it out where they stood to the last, but by nightfall none of the enemy's line remained in our possession.

Our set-back was in no wise the fault of the troops. That ardour which only dashed itself to pieces against the enemy's strong entrenchments and numerous, stubborn defenders on the 6th of August would, a month earlier, have achieved notable success. Such was the opinion of all. But the *moral*, as well as the strength of the Turks, had had time to rise to great heights since our last serious encounters with them on the 21st and 28th of June and on the 12th of July. On those dates all ranks had felt, as an army feels, instinctively, yet with certitude, that they had fairly got the upper hand of the enemy, and that, given the wherewithal, they could have gone on steadily advancing. Now that self-same, half-beaten enemy were again making as stout a resistance as they had offered us at our original landing!

For this recovery of the Turks there were three reasons: one moral, one material, and one fortuitous.

(1) The news of the enemy's advance on the Eastern front had come to hand and had been advertised to us on posters from the Turkish trenches before we heard about it from home.

(2) Two new divisions had come down south to Helles to replace those we had most severely handled.

(3) The enemy trenches selected for our attack were found to be packed with troops and so were their communication trenches, the reason being, as explained to us by prisoners, that the Turkish Commander had meant to launch from them an attack upon us. We had, in fact, by a coincidence as strange as it was unlucky, anticipated a Turkish offensive by an hour or two at most!

Sure enough, next morning, the enemy in their turn attacked the left of the line from which our own troops had advanced to the assault. A few of them gained a footing in our trenches and were all killed or captured. The remainder were driven back by fire.

As the aim of my action in this southern zone was to advance if I could, but in any case to contain the enemy and prevent him reinforcing to the northwards, I persevered on the 7th with my plans, notwithstanding the counterattack of the Turks which was actually in progress. My objective this time was a double line of Turkish trenches on a front of about 800 yards between the Mal Tepe Dere and the west branch of the Kanli Dere. After a preliminary bombardment the troops of the 125th Brigade on the right and the 129th on the left made the assault at 9.40 a.m. From the outset it was evident that the enemy were full of fight and in great force, and that success would only be gained after a severe struggle. On the right and on the centre the first enemy line was captured, and small parties pushed on to the second line, where they were unable to maintain themselves for long. On the left but little ground was gained, and by 11a.m. what little had been taken had been relinquished. But in the centre a stiff battle raged all day up and down a vineyard some 200 yards long by 100 yards broad on the west of the Krithia road. A large portion of the vineyard had been captured in the first dash, and the East Lancashire men in this part of the field gallantly stood their ground here against a succession of vigorous counter-attacks. The enemy suffered very severely in these counter-attacks, which were launched in strength and at short intervals. Both our Brigades had also lost heavily during the advance and in repelling the fierce onslaughts of the enemy, but, owing to the fine endurance of the 6th and 7th Battalions of the Lancashire Fusiliers, it was found possible to hold the vineyard through the night, and a massive column of the enemy which strove to overwhelm their thinned ranks was shattered to pieces in the attempt. On 8th August Lieutenant-General Sir F.J. Davies took over command of the 8th Army Corps, and Major-General W. Douglas reverted to the command of the 42nd Division. For two more days his troops were called upon to show their qualities of vigilance and power of determined resistance, for the enemy had by no means yet lost hope of wresting from us the ground we had won in the vineyard. This unceasing struggle was a supreme test for battalions already exhausted by 48 hours' desperate fighting and weakened by the loss of so many good leaders and men; but the peculiar grit of the Lancastrians was equal to the strain, and they did not fail. Two specially furious counter-attacks were delivered by the Turks on the 8th August, one at 4.40 a.m. and another at 8.30 p.m., where again our bayonets were too much for them. Throughout the night they made continuous bomb attacks, but the 6th Lancashire Fusiliers and the 4th East Lancashire Regiment stuck gamely to their task at the eastern corner of the vineyard. There was desperate fighting also at the northern corner, where the personal bravery of Lieutenant W.T. Forshaw, 1/9th Manchester Regiment who stuck to his post after his detachment had been relieved (an act for which he has since been awarded the V.C.), was largely instrumental in the repulse of three very determined onslaughts.

By the morning of the 9th August things were quieter, and the sorely tried troops were relieved. On the night of the 12th/13th the enemy made one more sudden, desperate dash for their vineyard – and got it! But, on the 13th, our bombers took the matter in hand. The Turks were finally driven out; the new fire trenches were wired and loopholed, and have since become part of our line.

These two attacks had served their main purpose. If the local successes were not all that had been hoped for, yet a useful advance had been achieved, and not only had they given a fresh, hard fighting enemy more than he had bargained for, but they had actually drawn down Turkish reinforcements to their area. And how can a Commander say enough for the troops who, aware that their task was only a subsidiary one, fought with just as much vim and resolution as if they were storming the battlements of Constantinople.

I will now proceed to tell of the assault on Chunuk Bair by the forces under General Birdwood, and of the landing of the 9th Corps in the neighbourhood of Suvla Bay. The entire details of the operations allotted to the troops to be employed in the Anzac area were formulated by Lieutenant-General Birdwood, subject only to my final approval. So excellently was this vital business worked out on the lines of the instructions issued that I had no modifications to suggest, and all these local preparations were completed by August 6th in a way which reflects the greatest credit, not only on the Corps Commander and his staff, but also upon the troops themselves, who had to toil like slaves to accumulate food, drink and munitions of war. Alone the accommodation for the extra troops to be landed necessitated an immense amount of work in preparing new concealed bivouacs, in making interior communications, and in storing water and supplies, for I was determined to put on shore as many fighting men as our modest holding at Anzac could possibly accommodate or provision. All the work was done by Australian and New Zealand soldiers almost entirely by night, and the uncomplaining efforts of these much-tried troops in preparation are in a sense as much to their credit as their heroism in the battles that followed. Above all, the water problem caused anxiety to the Admiral, to Lieutenant-General Birdwood and to myself. The troops to advance from Suvla Bay across the Anafarta valley might reckon on finding some wells – it was certain, at least, that no water was waiting for us on the crests of the ridges of Sari Bair! Therefore, first, several days' supply had to be stocked into tanks along the beach and thence pumped up into other tanks half-way up the mountains; secondly, a system of mule transport had to be worked out, so that in so far as was humanly possible, thirst should not be allowed to overcome the troops after they had overcome the difficulties of the country and the resistance of the enemy.

On the nights of the 4th, 5th, and 6th August the reinforcing troops were shipped into Anzac very silently at the darkest hours. Then, still silently, they were tucked away from enemy aeroplanes or observatories in their prepared hiding places. The whole sea route lay open to the view of the Turks upon Achi Baba's summit and Battleship Hill. Aeroplanes could count every tent and every ship at Mudros or at Imbros. Within rifle fire of Anzac's open beach hostile riflemen were looking out across the Ægean no more than twenty feet from our opposing lines. Every modern appliance of telescope, telegraph, wireless was at the disposal of the enemy. Yet the instructions worked out at General Headquarters in the minutest detail (the result of conferences with the Royal Navy, which were attended by Brigadier-General Skeen, of General Birdwood's Staff) were such that the scheme was carried through without a hitch. The preparation of the ambush was treated as a simple matter by the services therein engaged, and yet I much doubt whether any more pregnant enterprise than this of landing so large a force under the very eyes of the enemy, and of keeping them concealed there three days, is recorded in the annals of war.

The troops now at the disposal of General Birdwood amounted in round numbers to 37,000 rifles and 72 guns, with naval support from two cruisers, four monitors and two destroyers. Under the scheme these troops were to be divided into two main portions. The task of holding the existing Anzac position, and of making frontal assaults therefrom, was assigned to the Australian Division (plus the 1st and 3rd Light Horse Brigades and two battalions of the 40th Brigade); that of assulting the Chunuk Bair ridge was entrusted to the New Zealand and Australian Division (less the 1st and 3rd Light Horse Brigades), to the 13th Division (less five battalions), and to the 29th Indian Infantry Brigade and to the Indian Mountain Artillery Brigade. The 29th Brigade of the 10th Division (less one battalion) and the 38th Brigade were held in reserve.

The most simple method of developing this complicated series of operations will be first to take the frontal attacks from the existing Anzac position, and afterwards to go on to the assault on the more distant ridges. During the 4th, 5th and 6th of August the works on the enemy's left and centre were subjected to a slow bombardment, and on the afternoon of the 6th August an assault was made upon the formidable Lone Pine entrenchment. Although, in its essence, a diversion to draw the enemy's attention and reserves from the grand attack impending upon his right, yet, in itself, Lone Pine was a distinct step on the way across to Maidos. It commanded one of the main sources of the Turkish water supply, and was a work, or, rather, a series of works, for the safety of which the enemy had always evinced a certain nervousness. The attack was designed to heighten this impression.

The work consisted of a strong *point d'appui* on the south-western end of a plateau, where it confronted, at distances varying from 60 to 120 yards, the salient in the line of our trenches named by us the Pimple. The entrenchment was evidently very strong; it was entangled with wire, and provided with overhead cover, and it was connected by numerous communication trenches with another *point d'appui* known as Johnston's Jolly on the north, as well as with two other works on the east and south. The frontage for attack amounted at most to some 220 yards, and the approaches lay open to heavy enfilade fire, both from the north and from the south.

The detailed scheme of attack was worked out with care and forethought by Major-General H.B. Walker, commanding 1st Australian Division, and his thoroughness contributed, I consider, largely to the success of the enterprise.

The action commenced at 4.30 p.m. with a continuous and heavy bombardment of the Lone Pine and adjacent trenches, H.M.S. "Bacchante" assisting by searching the valleys to the north-east and east, and the Monitors by shelling the enemy's batteries south of Gaba Tepe. The assault had been entrusted to the 1st Australian Brigade (Brigadier-General N.M. Smyth), and punctually at 5.30 p.m. it was carried out by the 2nd, 3rd and 4th Australian Battalions, the 1st Battalion forming the Brigade reserve. Two lines left their trenches simultaneously, and were closely followed up by a third. The rush across the open was a regular race against death, which came in the shape of a hail of shell and rifle bullets from front and from either flank. But the Australians had firmly resolved to reach the enemy's trenches, and in this determination they became for the moment invincible. The barbed wire entanglement was reached and was surmounted. Then came a terrible moment, when it seemed as though it would be physically impossible to penetrate into the trenches. The overhead cover of stout pine beams resisted all individual efforts to move it, and the loopholes continued to spit fire. Groups of our men then bodily lifted up the beams and individual soldiers leaped down into the semi-darkened galleries amongst the Turks. By 5.47 p.m. the 3rd and 4th Battalions were well into the enemy's vitals, and a few minutes later the reserves of the 2nd Battalion advanced over their parados, and driving out, killing or capturing the occupants, made good the whole of the trenches. The reserve companies of the 3rd and 4th Battalions followed, and at 6.20 p.m. the 1st Battalion (in reserve) was launched to consolidate the position.

At once the Turks made it plain, as they have never ceased to do since, that they had no intention of acquiescing in the capture of this capital work. At 7.0 p.m. a determined and violent counter-attack began, both from the north and from the south. Wave upon wave the enemy swept forward with the bayonet. Here and there a well-directed salvo of bombs emptied a section of a trench, but whenever this occurred the gap was quietly filled by the initiative of the officers and the gallantry of the men.

The enemy allowed small respite. At 1.30 that night the battle broke out afresh. Strong parties of Turks swarmed out of the communication trenches, preceded by showers of bombs. For seven hours these counter-attacks continued. All this time consolidation was being attempted, although the presence of so many Turkish prisoners hampered movement and constituted an actual danger. In beating off these desperate counter-attacks very heavy casualties were suffered by the Australians. Part of the 12th Battalion, the reserve of the 3rd Brigade, had therefore to be thrown into the *mêlée*.

Twelve hours later, at 1.30 p.m. on the 7th, another effort was made by the enemy, lasting uninterruptedly at closest quarters till 5 p.m., then being resumed at midnight and proceeding intermittently till dawn. At an early period of this last counter-attack the 4th Battalion were forced by bombs to relinquish portion of a trench, but later on, led by their commanding officer, Lieutenant-Colonel McNaghten, they killed every Turk who had got in.

During the 8th of August advantage was taken of every cessation in the enemy's bombing to consolidate. The 2nd Battalion, which had lost its commanding officer and suffered especially severely, was withdrawn and replaced by the 7th Battalion, the reserve to the 2nd Infantry Brigade.

At 5 a.m. on 9th August the enemy made a sudden attempt to storm from the east and south-east after a feint of fire attack from the north. The 7th Battalion bore the brunt of the shock, and handled the attack so vigorously that by 7.45 a.m. there were clear signs of demoralisation in the enemy's ranks. But, although this marked the end of counter-attacks on the large scale, the bombing and sniping continued, though in less volume, throughout this day and night, and lasted till 12th August, when it at last became manifest that we had gained complete ascendency. During the final grand assault our losses from artillery fire were large, and ever since the work has passed into our hands it has been a favourite daily and nightly mark for heavy shells and bombs.

Thus was Lone Pine taken and held. The Turks were in great force and very full of fight, yet one weak Australian brigade, numbering at the outset but 2,000 rifles, and supported only by two weak battalions, carried the work under the eyes of a whole enemy division, and maintained their grip upon it like a vice during six days' successive counter-attacks. High praise is due to Brigadier-General N.M. Smyth and to his battalion commanders. The irresistible dash and daring of officers and men in the initial charge were a glory to Australia. The stout-heartedness with which they clung to the captured ground in spite of fatigue, severe losses, and the continual strain of shell fire and bomb attacks may seem less striking to the civilian; it is even more admirable to the soldier. From start to finish the artillery support was untiring and vigilant. Owing to the rapid, accurate fire of the 2nd New Zealand Battery, under Major Sykes, several of the Turkish onslaughts were altogether defeated in their attempts to get to grips with the Australians. Not a chance was lost by these gunners, although time and again the enemy's artillery made direct hits on their shields. The hand-to-hand fighting in the semi-obscurity of the trenches was prolonged and very bitterly contested. In one corner eight Turks and six Australians were found lying as they had bayonetted one another. To make room for the fighting men the dead were ranged in rows on either side of the gangway. After the first violence of the counter-attacks had abated, 1,000 corpses – our own and Turkish – were dragged out from the trenches.

For the severity of our own casualties some partial consolation may be found in the facts, first, that those of the enemy were much heavier, our guns and machine-guns having taken toll of them as they advanced in mass formation along the reverse slopes; secondly, that the Lone Pine attack drew all the local enemy reserves towards it, and may be held, more than any other cause, to have been the reason that the Suvla Bay landing was so lightly opposed, and that comparatively few of the enemy were available at first to reinforce against our attack on Sari Bair. Our captures in this feat of arms amounted to 134 prisoners, seven machine-guns, and a large quantity of ammunition and equipment.

Other frontal attacks from the existing Anzac positions were not so fortunate. They fulfilled their object in so far as they prevented the enemy from reinforcing against the attack upon the high ridges, but they failed to make good any ground. Taken in sequence of time, they included an attack upon the work known as German Officer's Trench, on the extreme right of our line, at midnight on August 6–7, also assaults on the Nek and Baby 700 trenches opposite the centre of our line, delivered at 4.30 a.m. on the 7th. The 2nd Australian Brigade did all that men could do; the 8th Light Horse only accepted their repulse after losing three-fourths of that devoted band who so bravely sallied forth from Russell's Top. Some of the works were carried, but in these cases the enemy's concealed machine-guns made it impossible to hold on. But all that day, as the result of these most gallant attacks, Turkish reserves on Battleship Hill were being held back to meet any dangerous development along the front of the old Anzac line, and so were not available to meet our main enterprise, which I will now endeavour to describe.

The first step in the real push – the step which above all others was to count – was the night attack on the summits of the Sari Bair ridge. The crest line of this lofty mountain range runs parallel to the sea, dominating the under-features contained within the Anzac position, although these fortunately defilade the actual landing-place. From the main ridge a series of spurs run down towards the level beach, and are separated from one another by deep, jagged gullies choked up with dense jungle. Two of these leading up to Chunuk Bair are called Chailak Dere and Sazli Beit Dere; another deep ravine runs up to Koja Chemen Tepe (Hill 305), the topmost peak of the whole ridge, and is called the Aghyl Dere.

It was our object to effect a lodgment along the crest of the high main ridge with two columns of troops, but, seeing the nature of the ground and the dispositions of the enemy, the effort had to be made by stages. We were bound, in fact, to undertake a double subsidiary operation before we could hope to launch these attacks with any real prospect of success.

(1) The right covering force was to seize Table Top, as well as all other enemy positions commanding the foothills between the Chailak Dere and the Sazli Beit Dere ravines. If this enterprise succeeded it would open up the ravines for the assaulting columns, whilst at the same time interposing between the right flank of the left covering force and the enemy holding the Sari Bair main ridge.

(2) The left covering force was to march northwards along the beach to seize a hill called Damakjelik Bair, some 1,400 yards north of Table Top. If successful it would be able to hold out a hand to the 9th Corps as it landed south of Nibrunesi Point, whilst at the same time protecting the left flank of the left assaulting column against enemy troops from the Anafarta valley during its climb up the Aghyl Dere ravine.

(3) The right assaulting column was to move up the Chailak Dere and Sazli Beit Dere ravines to the storm of the ridge of Chunuk Bair.

(4) The left assaulting column was to work up the Aghyl Dere and prolong the line of the right assaulting column by storming Hill 305 (Koja Chemen Tepe), the summit of the whole range of hills.

To recapitulate, the two assaulting columns, which were to work up three ravines to the storm of the high ridge, were to be preceded by two covering columns. One of these was to capture the enemy's positions commanding the foothills, first to open the mouths of the ravines, secondly to cover the right flank of another covering force whilst it marched along the beach. The other covering column was to strike far out to the north until, from a hill called Damajelik Bair, it could at the same time facilitate the landing of the 9th Corps at Nibrunesi Point, and guard the left flank of the column assaulting Sari Bair from any forces of the enemy which might be assembled in the Anafarta valley.

The whole of this big attack was placed under the command of Major-General Sir A.J. Godley, General Officer Commanding New Zealand and Australian Division. The two covering and the two assaulting columns were organised as follows:-

Right Covering Column, under Brigadier-General A.H. Russell. – New Zealand Mounted Rifles Brigade, the Otago Mounted Rifles Regiment, the Maori Contingent and New Zealand Field Troop.

Right Assaulting Column, under Brigadier-General F.E. Johnston. – New Zealand Infantry Brigade, Indian Mountain Battery (less one section), one Company New Zealand Engineers. Left covering Column, under Brigadier-General J.H. Travers. – Headquarters 40th Brigade, half the 72nd Field Company, 4th Battalion, South Wales Borderers, and 5th Battalion, Wiltshire Regiment.

Left Assaulting Column, under Brigadier-General (now Major-General) H.V. Cox. – 29th Indian Infantry Brigade, 4th Australian Infantry Brigade, Indian Mountain Battery (less one section), one Company New Zealand Engineers.

Divisional Reserve. – 6th Battalion, South Lancashire Regiment, and 8th Battalion, Welsh Regiment (Pioneers) at Chailak Dere, and the 39th Infantry Brigade and half 72nd Field Company at Aghyl Dere.

The right covering column, it will be remembered, had to gain command of the Sazli Beit Dere and the Aghyl Dere ravines, so as to let the assaulting column arrive intact within striking distance of the Chunuk Bair ridge. To achieve this object it had to clear the Turks off from their right flank positions upon Old No. 3 Post and Table Top.

Old No. 3 Post, connected with Table Top by a razor back, formed the apex of a triangular piece of hill sloping gradually down to our No. 2 and No. 3 outposts. Since its recapture from us by the Turks on 30th May working parties had done their best with unstinted material to convert this commanding point into an impregnable redoubt. Two lines of fire trench, very heavily entangled, protected its southern face – the only one accessible to us – and, with its head cover of solid timber baulks and its strongly revetted outworks, it dominated the approaches of both the Chailak Dere and the Sazli Beit Dere.

Table Top is a steep-sided, flat-topped hill, close on 400 feet above sea level. The sides of the hill are mostly sheer and quite impracticable, but here and there a ravine, choked with scrub, and under fire of enemy trenches, gives precarious foothold up the precipitous cliffs. The small plateau on the summit was honeycombed with trenches, which were connected by a communication alley with that under-feature of Sari Bair, known as Rhododendron Spur.

Amongst other stratagems the Anzac troops, assisted by H.M.S. "Colne," had long and carefully been educating the Turks how they should lose Old No. 3 Post, which could hardly have been rushed by simple force of arms. Every night, exactly at 9 p.m., H.M.S. "Colne" threw the beam of her searchlight on to the redoubt, and opened fire upon it for exactly ten minutes. Then, after a ten minutes' interval, came a second illumination and bombardment, commencing always at 9.20 and ending precisely at 9.30 p.m.

The idea was that, after successive nights of such practice, the enemy would get into the habit of taking the searchlight as a hint to clear out until the shelling was at an end. But on the eventful night of the 6th, the sound of their footsteps drowned by the loud cannonade, unseen as they crept along in that darkest shadow which fringes a searchlight's beam – came the right covering column. At 9.30 the light switched off, and instantly our men poured out of the scrub jungle and into the empty redoubt. By 11 p.m. the whole series of surrounding entrenchments were ours!

Once the capture of Old No. 3 Post was fairly under way, the remainder of the right covering column carried on with their attack upon Bauchop's Hill and the Chailak Dere. By 10 p.m. the northernmost point, with its machine-gun, was captured, and by 1 o'clock in the morning the whole of Bauchop's Hill, a maze of ridge and ravine, everywhere entrenched, was fairly in our hands.

The attack along the Chailak Dere was not so cleanly carried out – made, indeed, just about as ugly a start as any enemy could wish. Pressing eagerly forward through the night, the little column of stormers found themselves held up by a barbed-wire erection of unexampled height, depth and solidity, which completely closed the river bed – that is to say, the only practicable entrance to the ravine. The entanglement was flanked by a strongly-held enemy trench running right across the opening of the Chailak Dere. Here that splendid body of men, the Otago Mounted Rifles, lost some of their bravest and their best, but in the end, when things were beginning to seem desperate, a passage was forced through the stubborn obstacle with most conspicuous and cool courage by Captain Shera and a party of New Zealand Engineers, supported by the Maoris, who showed themselves worthy descendants of the warriors of the Gate Pah. Thus was the mouth of the Chailak Dere opened in time to admit of the unopposed entry of the right assaulting column.

Simultaneously the attack on Table Top had been launched under cover of a heavy bombardment from H.M.S "Colne." No General on peace manoeuvres would ask troops to attempt so break-neck an enterprise. The flanks of Table Top are so steep that the height gives an impression of a mushroom shape – of the summit bulging out over its stem. But just as faith moves mountains, so valour can carry them. The Turks fought bravely. The angle of Table Top's ascent is recognised in our regulations as "impracticable for infantry". But neither Turks nor angles of ascent were destined to stop Russell or his New Zealanders that night. There are moments during battle when life becomes intensified, when men become supermen, when the impossible becomes simple – and this was one of those moments. The scarped heights were scaled, the plateau was carried by midnight. With this brilliant feat the task of the right covering force was at an end. Its attacks had been made with the bayonet and bomb only; magazines were empty by order; hardly a rifle shot had been fired. Some 150 prisoners were captured as well as many rifles and much equipment, ammunition and stores. No words can do justice to the achievement of Brigadier-General Russell and his men. There are exploits which must be seen to be realised.

The right assaulting column had entered the two southerly ravines – Sazli Beit Dere and Chailak Dere – by midnight. At 1.30 a.m. began a hotly-contested fight for the trenches on the lower part of Rhododendron Spur, whilst the Chailak Dere column pressed steadily up the valley against the enemy.

The left covering column, under Brigadier-General Travers, after marching along the beach to No. 3 Outpost, resumed its northerly advance as soon as the attack on Bauchop's Hill had developed. Once the Chailak Dere was cleared the column moved by the mouth of the Aghyl Dere, disregarding the enfilade fire from sections of Bauchop's Hill still uncaptured. The rapid success of this movement was largely due to Lieutenant-Colonel Gillespie, a very fine man, who commanded the advance guard consisting of his own regiment, the 4th South Wales Borderers, a corps worthy of such a leader. Every trench encountered was instantly rushed by the Borderers until, having reached the predetermined spot, the whole column was unhesitatingly launched at Damakjelik Bair. Several Turkish trenches were captured at the bayonet's point, and by 1.30 a.m. the whole of the hill was occupied, thus safeguarding the left rear of the whole of the Anzac attack.

Here was an encouraging sample of what the New Army, under good auspices, could accomplish. Nothing more trying to inexperienced troops can be imagined than a long night march exposed to flanking fire, through a strange country, winding up at the end with a bayonet charge against a height, formless and still in the starlight, garrisoned by those spectres of the imagination, worst enemies of the soldier.

The left assaulting column crossed the Chailak Dere at 12.30 a.m., and entered the Aghyl Dere at the heels of the left covering column. The surprise, on this side, was complete. Two Turkish officers were caught in their pyjamas; enemy arms and ammunition were scattered in every direction.

The grand attack was now in full swing, but the country gave new sensations in cliff climbing even to officers and men who had graduated over the goat tracks of Anzac. The darkness of the night, the density of the scrub, hands and knees progress up the spurs, sheer physical fatigue, exhaustion of the spirit caused by repeated hairbreadth escapes from the hail of random bullets – all these combined to take the edge off the energies of our troops. At last, after advancing some distance up the Aghyl Dere, the column split up into two parts. The 4th Australian Brigade struggled, fighting hard as they went, up to the north of the northern fork of the Aghyl Dere, making for Hill 305 (Koja Chemen Tepe). The 29th Indian Infantry Brigade scrambled up the southern fork of the Aghyl Dere and the spurs north of it to the attack of a portion of the Sari Bair ridge known as Hill Q.

Dawn broke and the crest line was not yet in our hands, although, considering all things, the left assaulting column had made a marvellous advance. The 4th Australian Infantry Brigade was on the line of the Asma Dere (the next ravine north of the Aghyl Dere) and the 29th Indian Infantry Brigade held the ridge west of the Farm below Chunuk Bair and along the spurs to the north-east. The enemy had been flung back from ridge to ridge; an excellent line for the renewal of the attack had been secured, and (except for the exhaustion of the troops) the auspices were propitious.

Turning to the right assaulting column, one battalion, the Canterbury Infantry Battalion, clambered slowly up the Sazli Beit Dere. The remainder of the force, led by the Otago Battalion, wound their way amongst the pitfalls and forced their passage through the scrub of the Chailak Dere, where fierce opposition forced them ere long to deploy. Here, too, the hopeless country was the main hindrance, and it was not until 5.45 a.m. that the bulk of the column joined the Canterbury Battalion on the lower slopes of Rhododendron Spur. The whole force then moved up the spur, gaining touch with the left assaulting column by means of the 10th Gurkhas, in face of very heavy fire and frequent bayonet charges. Eventually they entrenched on the top of Rhododendron Spur, a quarter of a mile short of Chunuk Bair – *i.e.*, of victory.

At seven a.m. the 5th and 6th Gurkhas, belonging to the left assaulting column, had approached the main ridge north-east of Chunuk Bair, whilst, on their left, the 14th Sikhs had got into touch with the 4th Australian Brigade on the southern watershed of the Asma Dere. The 4th Australian Brigade now received orders to leave half a battalion to hold the spur, and, with the rest of its strength, plus the 14th Sikhs, to assault Hill 305 (Koja Chemen Tepe). But by this time the enemy's opposition had hardened, and his reserves were moving up from the direction of Battleship Hill. Artillery support was asked for and given, yet by nine a.m. the attack of the right assaulting column on Chunuk Bair was checked, and any idea of a further advance on Koja Chemen Tepe had to be, for the moment, suspended. The most that could be done was to hold fast to the Asmak Dere watershed whilst attacking the ridge north-east of Chunuk Bair, an attack to be supported by a fresh assault launched against Chunuk Bair itself. At 9.30 a.m. the two assaulting columns pressed forward whilst our guns pounded the enemy moving along the Battleship Hill spurs. But in spite of all their efforts their increasing exhaustion as opposed to the gathering strength of the enemy's fresh troops began to tell – they had shot their bolt. So all day they clung to what they had captured and strove to make ready for the night. At 11 a.m. three battalions of the 39th Infantry Brigade were sent up from the general reserve to be at hand when needed, and, at the same hour, one more battalion of the reserve was dispatched to the

1st Australian Division to meet the drain caused by all the desperate Lone Pine fighting.

By the afternoon the position of the two assaulting columns was unchanged. The right covering force were in occupation of Table Top, Old No. 3 Post and Bauchop Hill, which General Russell had been ordered to maintain with two regiments of Mounted Rifles, so that he might have two other regiments and the Maori Contingent available to move as required. The left covering force held Damakjelik Bair. The forces which had attacked along the front of the original Anzac line were back again in their own trenches. The Lone Pine work was being furiously disputed. All had suffered heavily and all were very tired.

So ended the first phase of the fighting for the Chunuk Bair ridge. Our aims had not fully been attained, and the help we had hoped for from Suvla had not been forthcoming. Yet I fully endorse the words of General Birdwood when he says: "'The troops had performed a feat which is without parallel."

Great kudos is due to Major-Generals Godley and Shaw for their arrangements; to Generals Russell, Johnston, Cox, and Travers for their leading; but most of all, as every one of these officers will gladly admit, to the rank and file for their fighting. Nor may I omit to add that the true destroyer spirit with which H.M.S. "Colne" (Commander Claude Seymour, R.N.) and H.M.S. "Chelmer" (Commander Hugh T. England, R.N.) backed us up will live in the grateful memories of the Army.

In the course of this afternoon (7th August) reconnaissances of Sari Bair were carried out and the troops were got into shape for a fresh advance in three columns, to take place in the early morning.

The columns were composed as follows:-

Right Column, Brigadier-General F.E. Johnston. – 26th Indian Mountain Battery (less one section), Auckland Mounted Rifles, New Zealand Infantry Brigade, two battalions 13th Division, and the Maori Contingent.

Centre and Left Columns. – Major-General H.V. Cox. – 21st Indian Mountain Battery (less one section), 4th Australian Brigade, 39th Infantry Brigade (less one battalion), with 6th Battalion South Lancashire Regiment attached, and the 29th Indian Infantry Brigade.

The right column was to climb up the Chunuk Bair ridge; the left column was to make for the prolongation of the ridge north-east to Koja Chemen Tepe, the topmost peak of the range.

The attack was timed for 4.15 a.m. At the first faint glimmer of dawn observers saw figures moving against the sky-line of Chunuk Bair. Were they our own men, or were they the Turks? Telescopes were anxiously adjusted; the light grew stronger; men were seen climbing up from our side of the ridge; they *were* our own fellows – the topmost summit was ours! On the right General Johnston's column, headed by the Wellington Battalion and supported by the 7th Battalion, Gloucestershire Regiment, the Auckland Mounted Rifles Regiment, the 8th Welsh Pioneers, and the Maori Contingent, the whole most gallantly led by Lieutenant-Colonel W.G. Malone, had raced one another up the steep. Nothing could check them. On they went, until, with a last determined rush, they fixed themselves firmly on the south-western slopes and crest of the main knoll known as the height of Chunuk Bair. With deep regret I have to add that the brave Lieutenant-Colonel Malone fell mortally wounded as he was marking out the line to be held. The 7th Gloucesters suffered terrible losses here. The fire was so hot that they never got a chance to dig their trenches deeper than some six inches, and there they had to withstand attack after attack. In the course of these fights every single officer, company serjeant-major, or company quarter-master-serjeant, was either killed or wounded, and the battalion by mid-day consisted of small groups of men commanded by junior non-commissioned officers or privates. Chapter and verse may be quoted for the view that the rank-and-file of an army cannot long endure the strain of close hand-to-hand fighting unless they are given confidence by the example of good officers. Yet here is at least one instance where a battalion of the New Army fought right on, from midday till sunset, without any officers.

In the centre the 39th Infantry Brigade and the 29th Indian Brigade moved along the gullies leading up to the Sari Bair ridge – the right moving south of the Farm on Chunuk Bair, the left up the spurs to the north-east of the Farm against a portion of the main ridge north-east of Chunuk Bair, and the col to the north of it. So murderous was the enemy's fire that little progress could be made, though some ground was gained on the spurs to the north-east of the farm. On the left the 4th Australian Brigade advanced from the Asmak Dere against the lower slopes of Abdul Rahman Bair (a spur running due north from Koja Chemen Tepe) with the intention of wheeling to its right and advancing up the spur. Cunningly placed Turkish machine-guns and a strong entrenched body of infantry were ready for this move, and the Brigade were unable to get on. At last, on the approach of heavy columns of the enemy, the Australians, virtually surrounded, and having already suffered losses of over 1,000, were withdrawn to their original position. Here they stood at bay, and, though the men were by now half dead with thirst and with fatigue, they bloodily repulsed attack after attack delivered by heavy columns of Turks.

So stood matters at noon. Enough had been done for honour and much ground had everywhere been gained. The expected support from Suvla hung fire, but the capture of Chunuk Bair was a presage of victory; even the troops who had been repulsed were quite undefeated – quite full of fight – and so it was decided to hold hard as we were till nightfall, and then to essay one more grand attack, wherein the footing gained on Chunuk Bair would this time be used as a pivot.

In the afternoon the battle slackened, excepting always at Lone Pine, where the enemy were still coming on in mass, and being mown down by our fire. Elsewhere the troops were busy digging and getting up water and food, no child's play, with their wretched lines of communication running within musketry range of the enemy.

That evening the New Zealand Brigade, with two regiments of New Zealand Mounted Rifles and the Maoris, held Rhododendron Spur and the south-western slopes of the main knoll of Chunuk Bair. The front line was prolonged by the columns of General Cox and General Monash (with the 4th Australian Brigade). Behind the New Zealanders were the 38th Brigade in reserve, and in rear of General Monash two battalions of the 40th Brigade. The inner line was held as before, and the 29th Brigade (less two battalions), had been sent up from the general reserve, and remained still further in rear.

The columns for the renewed attack were composed as follows:-

No. 1 Column, Brigadier-General F.E. Johnston. – 26th Indian Mountain Battery (less one section), the Auckland and Wellington Mounted Rifles Regiments, the New Zealand Infantry Brigade, and two battalions of the 13th Division.

No. 2 Column, Major-General H.V. Cox. – 21st Indian Mountain Battery (less one section), 4th Australian Brigade, 39th Brigade (less the 7th Gloucesters, relieved), with the 6th Battalion South Lancashire Regiment attached, and the Indian Infantry Brigade.

No. 3 Column, Brigadier-General A.H. Baldwin, Commanding 38th Infantry Brigade. – Two battalions each from the 38th and 29th Brigades and one from the 40th Brigade.

No. 1 column was to hold and consolidate the ground gained on the 6th, and, in co-operation with the other columns, to gain the whole of Chunuk Bair, and extend to the south-east. No. 2 column was to attack Hill Q on the Chunuk Bair ridge, and No. 3 column was to move from the Chailak Dere, also on Hill Q. This last column was to make the main attack, and the others were to co-operate with it.

At 4.30 a.m. on August 9th the Chunuk Bair ridge and Hill Q were heavily shelled. The naval guns, all the guns on the left flank, and as many as possible from the right flank (whence the enemy's advance could be enfiladed), took part in this cannonade, which rose to its climax at 5.15 a.m., when the whole ridge seemed a mass of flame and smoke, whence huge clouds of dust drifted slowly upwards in strange patterns on to the sky. At 5.16 a.m. this tremendous bombardment was to be switched off on to the flanks and reverse slopes of the heights. General Baldwin's column had assembled in the Chailak Dere, and was moving up towards General Johnstone's headquarters. Our plan contemplated the massing of this column immediately behind the trenches held by the New Zealand Infantry Brigade. Thence it was intended to launch the battalions in successive lines, keeping them as much as possible on the high ground. Infinite trouble had been taken to ensure that the narrow track should be kept clear, guides also were provided; but in spite of all precautions the darkness, the rough scrub-covered country, its sheer steepness, so delayed the column that they were unable to take full advantage of the configuration of the ground, and, inclining to the left, did not reach the line of the Farm – Chunuk Bair till 5.15 a.m. In plain English, Baldwin, owing to the darkness and the awful country, lost his way – through no fault of his own. The mischance was due to the fact that time did not admit of the detailed careful reconnaissance of routes which is so essential where operations are to be carried out by night.

And now, under that fine leader, Major C.G.L. Allanson, the 6th Gurkhas of the 29th Indian Infantry Brigade pressed up the slopes of Sari Bair, crowned the heights of the col between Chunuk Bair and Hill Q, viewed far beneath them the waters of the Hellespont, viewed the Asiatic shores along which motor transport was bringing supplies to the lighters. Not only did this battalion, as well as some of the 6th South Lancashire Regiment, reach the crest, but they began to attack down the far side of it, firing as they went at the fast retreating enemy. But the fortune of war was against us. At this supreme moment Baldwin's column was still a long way from our trenches on the crest of Chunuk Bair, whence they should even now have been sweeping out towards Q along the whole ridge of the mountain. And instead of Baldwin's support came suddenly a salvo of heavy shell. These falling so unexpectedly among the stormers threw them into terrible confusion. The Turkish commander saw his chance; instantly his troops were rallied and brought back in a counter-charge, and the South Lancashires and Gurkhas, who had seen the promised land and had seemed for a moment to have held victory in their grasp, were forced backwards over the crest and on to the lower slopes whence they had first started.

But where was the main attack – where was Baldwin? When that bold but unlucky commander found he could not possibly reach our trenches on the top of Chunuk Bair in time to take effective part in the fight he deployed for attack where he stood, *i.e.*, at the farm to the left of the New Zealand Brigade's trenches on Rhododendron Spur. Now his men were coming on in fine style and, just as the Turks topped the ridge with shouts of elation, two companies of the 6th East Lancashire Regiment, together with the 10th Hampshire Regiment, charged up our side of the slope with the bayonet. They had gained the high ground immediately below the commanding knoll on Chunuk Bair, and a few minutes earlier would have joined hands with the Gurkhas and South Lancashires and, combined with them, would have carried all before them. But the Turks by this time were lining the whole of the high crest in overwhelming numbers. The New Army troops attacked with a fine audacity, but they were flung back from the height and then pressed still further down the slope, until General Baldwin had to withdraw his command to the vicinity of the Farm, whilst the enemy, much encouraged, turned their attention to the New Zealand troops and the two New Army battalions of No. 1 Column still holding the south-west half of the main knoll of Chunuk Bair. Constant attacks, urged with fanatical persistence, were met here with a sterner resolution, and although, at the end of the day, our troops were greatly exhausted, they still kept their footing on the summit. And if that summit meant much to us, it meant even more to the Turks. For the ridge covered our landing places, it is true, but it covered not only the Turkish beaches at Kilia Leman and Maidos, but also the Narrows themselves and the roads leading northward to Bulair and Constantinople.

That evening our line ran along Rhododendron Spur up to the crest of Chunuk Bair, where about 200 yards were occupied and held by some 800 men. Slight trenches had hastily been dug, but the fatigue of the New Zealanders and the fire of the enemy had prevented solid work being done. The trenches in many places were not more than a few inches deep. They were not protected by wire. Also many officers are of opinion that they had not been well sited in the first instance. On the South African system the main line was withdrawn some twenty-five yards from the crest instead of being actually on the crestline itself, and there were not even look-out posts along the summit. Boer skirmishers would thus have had to show themselves against the skyline before they could annoy. But here we were faced by regulars taught to attack in mass with bayonet or bomb. And the power of collecting overwhelming numbers at very close quarters rested with whichever side held the true skyline in force. From Chunuk Bair the line ran down to the Farm and almost due north to the Asma Dere southern watershed, whence it continued westward to the sea near Asmak Kuyu. On the right the Australian Division was still holding its line and Lone Pine was still being furiously attacked. The 1st Australian Brigade was now reduced from 2,900 to 1,000, and the total casualties up to 8 p.m. on the 9th amounted to about 8,500. But the troops were still in extraordinarily good heart, and nothing could damp their keenness. The only discontent shown was by men who were kept in reserve.

During the night of the 9th–10th, the New Zealand and New Army troops on Chunuk Bair were relieved. For three days and three nights they had been ceaselessly fighting. They were half dead with fatigue. Their lines of communication, started from sea level, ran across trackless ridges and ravines to an altitude of 800 ft., and were exposed all the way to snipers' fire and artillery bombardment. It had become imperative, therefore, to get them enough food, water, and rest; and for this purpose it was imperative also to withdraw them. Chunuk Bair, which they had so magnificently held, was now handed over to two battalions of the 13th Division, which were connected by the 10th Hampshire Regiment with the troops at the farm. General Sir William Birdwood is emphatic on the point that the nature of the ground is such that there was no room on the crest for more than this body of 800 to 1,000 rifles.

The two battalions of the New Army chosen to hold Chunuk Bair were the 6th Loyal North Lancashire Regiment and the 5th Wiltshire Regiment. The first of these arrived in good time and occupied the trenches. Even in the darkness their commanding officer, Lieutenant-Colonel Levinge, recognised how dangerously these trenches were sited, and he began at once to dig observation posts on the actual crest and to strengthen the defences where he could. But he had not time given him to do much. The second battalion, the Wiltshires, were delayed by the intricate country. They did not reach the edge of the entrenchment until 4 a.m., and were then told to lie down in what was believed, erroneously, to be a covered position. At daybreak on Tuesday, 10th August, the Turks delivered a grand attack from the line Chunuk Bair–Hill Q against these two battalions, already weakened in numbers, though not in spirit, by previous fighting. First our men were shelled by every enemy gun, and then, at 5.30 a.m., were assaulted by a huge column, consisting of no less than a full division plus a regiment of three battalions. The North Lancashire men were simply overwhelmed in their shallow trenches by sheer weight of numbers, whilst the Wilts, who were caught out in the open, were literally almost annihilated. The ponderous mass of the enemy swept over the crest, turned the right flank of our line below, swarmed round the Hampshires and General Baldwin's column, which had to give ground, and were only extricated with great difficulty and very heavy losses.

Now it was our turn. The warships and the New Zealand and Australian Artillery, the Indian Mountain Artillery Brigade, and the 69th Brigade Royal Field Artillery were getting the chance of a lifetime. As the successive solid lines of Turks topped the crest of the ridge gaps were torn through their formation, and an iron rain fell on them as they tried to reform in the gullies.

Not here only did the Turks pay dearly for their recapture of the vital crest. Enemy reinforcements continued to move up Battleship Hill under heavy and accurate fire from our guns, and still they kept topping the ridges and pouring down the western slopes of the Chunuk Bair as if determined to regain everything they had lost. But once they were over the crest they became exposed not only to the full blast of the guns, naval and military, but also to a battery of ten machine-guns belonging to the New Zealand Infantry Brigade, which played upon their serried ranks at close range until the barrels were red hot. Enormous losses were inflicted, especially by these ten machine-guns; and, of the swarms which had once fairly crossed the crest line, only the merest handful ever straggled back to their own side of Chunuk Bair.

At this same time strong forces of the enemy (forces which I had reckoned would have been held back to meet our advance from Suvla Bay) were hurled against the Farm and the spurs to the north-east, where there arose a conflict so deadly that it may be considered as the climax of the four days' fighting for the ridge. Portions of our line were pierced, and the troops driven clean down the hill. At the foot of the hill the men were rallied by Staff Captain Street, who was there supervising the transport of food and water. Without a word, unhesitatingly, they followed him back to the Farm, where they plunged again into the midst of that series of struggles in which generals fought in the ranks and men dropped their scientific weapons and caught one another by the throat. So desperate a battle cannot be described. The Turks came on again and again, fighting magnificently, calling upon the name of God. Our men stood to it, and maintained, by many a deed of daring, the old traditions of their race. There was no flinching. They died in the ranks where they stood. Here Generals Cayley, Baldwin, and Cooper and all their gallant men achieved great glory. On this bloody field fell Brigadier-General Baldwin, who earned his first laurels on Caesar's Camp at Ladysmith. There, too, fell Brigadier-General Cooper, badly wounded; and there, too, fell Lieutenant-Colonel M.H. Nunn, commanding the 9th Worcestershire Regiment; Lieutenant-Colonel H.G. Levinge, commanding the 6th Loyal North Lancashire Regiment; and Lieutenant-Colonel J. Carden, commanding the 5th Wiltshire Regiment.

Towards this supreme struggle the absolute last two battalions from the General Reserve were now hurried, but by ten a.m. the effort of the enemy was spent. Soon their shattered remnants began to trickle back, leaving a track of corpses behind them, and by night, except prisoners or wounded, no live Turk was left upon our side of the slope.

That same day, 10th August, two attacks, one in the morning and the other in the afternoon, were delivered on our positions along the Asmak Dere and Damakjelik Bair. Both were repulsed with heavy loss by the 4th Australian Brigade and the 4th South Wales Borderers, the men of the New Army showing all the steadiness of veterans. Sad to say, the Borderers lost their intrepid leader, Lieutenant-Colonel Gillespie, in the course of this affair.

By evening the total casualties of General Birdwood's force had reached 12,000, and included a very large proportion of officers. The 13th Division of the New Army, under Major-General Shaw, had alone lost 6,000 out of a grand total of 10,500. Baldwin was gone and all his staff. Ten commanding officers out of thirteen had disappeared from the fighting effectives. The Warwicks and the Worcesters had lost literally every single officer. The old German notion that no unit would stand a loss of more than 25 per cent. had been completely falsified. The 13th Division and the 29th Brigade of the 10th (Irish) Division had lost more than twice that proportion, and, in spirit, were game for as much more fighting as might be required. But physically, though Birdwood's forces were prepared to hold all they had got, they were now too exhausted to attack – at least until they had rested and reorganised. So far they *had* held on to all they had gained, excepting only the footholds on the ridge between Chunuk Bair and Hill Q, momentarily carried by the Gurkhas, and the salient of Chunuk Bair itself, which they had retained for forty-eight hours. Unfortunately, these two pieces of ground, small and worthless as they seemed, were worth, according to the ethics of war, 10,000 lives, for by their loss or retention they just marked the difference between an important success and a signal victory.

At times I had thought of throwing my reserves into this stubborn central battle, where probably they would have turned the scale. But each time the water troubles made me give up the idea, all ranks at Anzac being reduced to one pint a day. True thirst is a sensation unknown to the dwellers in cool, well-watered England. But at Anzac, when mules with water "pakhals" arrived at the front, the men would rush up to them in swarms, just to lick the moisture that had exuded through the canvas bags. It will be understood, then, that until wells had been discovered under the freshly-won hills, the reinforcing of Anzac by even so much as a brigade was unthinkable.

The grand coup had not come off. The Narrows were still out of sight and beyond field gun range. But this was not the fault of Lieutenant-General Birdwood or any of the officers and men under his command. No mortal can command success; Lieutenant-General Birdwood had done all that mortal man can do to deserve it. The way in which he worked out his instructions into practical arrangements and dispositions upon the terrain reflect high credit upon his military capacity. I also wish to bring to your Lordship's notice the valuable services of Major-General Godley, commanding the New Zealand and Australian Division. He had under him at one time a force amounting to two divisions, which he handled with conspicuous ability. Major-General F.C. Shaw, commanding 13th Division, also rose superior to all the trials and tests of these trying days. His calm and sound judgment proved to be of the greatest value throughout the arduous fighting I have recorded.

As for the troops, the joyous alacrity with which they faced danger, wounds and death, as if they were some new form of exciting recreation, has astonished me – old campaigner as I am. I will say no more, leaving Major-General Godley to speak for what happened under his eyes:- "I cannot close my report," he says, "without placing on record my unbounded admiration of the work performed, and the gallantry displayed, by the troops and their leaders during the severe fighting involved in these operations. Though the Australian, New Zealand, and Indian units had been confined to trench duty in a cramped space for some four months, and though the troops of the New Armies had only just landed from a sea voyage, and many of them had not been previously under fire, I do not believe that any troops in the world could have accomplished more. All ranks vied with one another in the performance of gallant deeds, and more than worthily upheld the best traditions of the British Army." Although the Sari Bair ridge was the key to the whole of my tactical conception, and although the temptation to view this vital Anzac battle at closer quarters was very hard to resist, there was nothing in its course or conduct to call for my personal intervention. The conduct of the operations which were to be based upon Suvla Bay was entrusted to Lieutenant-General The Hon. Sir F. Stopford. At his disposal was placed the 9th Army Corps, less the 13th Division and the 29th Brigade of the 10th Division.

We believed that the Turks were still unsuspicious about Suvla and that their only defences near that part of the coast were a girdle of trenches round Lala Baba and a few unconnected lengths of fire trench on Hill 10 and on the hills forming the northern arm of the bay. There was no wire. Inland a small work had been constructed on Yilghin Burnu (locally known as Chocolate Hills), and a few guns had been placed upon these hills, as well as upon Ismail Oglu Tepe, whence they could be brought into action either against the beaches of Suvla Bay or against any attempt from Anzac to break out north-wards and attack Chunuk Bair. The numbers of the enemy allotted for the defence of the Suvla and Ejelmer areas (including the troops in the Anafarta villages, but exclusive of the general reserves in rear of the Sari Bair) were supposed to be under 4,000. Until the Turkish version of these events is in our hands it is not possible to be certain of the accuracy of this estimate. All that can be said at present is that my Intelligence Department were wonderfully exact in their figures as a rule and that, in the case in question, events, the reports made by prisoners, etc., etc., seem to show that the forecast was correct.

Arrangements for the landing of the 9th Corps at Suvla were worked out in minute detail by my General Headquarters Staff in collaboration with the staff of Vice-Admiral de Robeck, and every precaution was taken to ensure that the destination of the troops was kept secret up to the last moment.

Whilst concentrated at the island of Imbros the spirit and physique of the 11th Division had impressed me very favourably. They were to lead off the landing. From Imbros they were to be ferried over to the Peninsula in destroyers and motor-lighters. Disembarkation was to begin at 10.30 p.m., half an hour later than the attack on the Turkish outposts on the northern flank at Anzac, and I was sanguine enough to hope that the elaborate plan we had worked out would enable three complete brigades of infantry to be set ashore by daylight. Originally it had been intended that all three brigades should land on the beach immediately south of Nibrunesi Point, but in deference to the representations of the Corps Commander I agreed, unfortunately, as it turned out, to one brigade being landed inside the bay.

The first task of the 9th Corps was to seize and hold the Chocolate and Ismail Oglu Hills, together with the high ground on the north and east of Suvla Bay. If the landing went off smoothly, and if my information regarding the strength of the enemy were correct, I hoped that these hills, with their guns, might be well in our possession before daybreak. In that case I hoped, further, that the first division which landed would be strong enough to picket and hold all the important heights within artillery range of the bay, when General Stopford would be able to direct the remainder of his force, as it became available, through the Anafartas to the east of the Sari Bair, where it should soon smash the mainspring of the Turkish opposition to Anzacs.

On the 22nd July I issued secret instructions and tables showing the number of craft available for the 9th Corps commander, their capacity, and the points whereat the troops could be disembarked; also what numbers of troops, animals, vehicles, and stores could be landed simultaneously. The allocation of troops to the ships and boats was left to General Stopford's own discretion, subject only to naval exigencies, otherwise the order of the disembarkation might not have tallied with the order of his operations.

The factors governing the hour of landing were: First, that no craft could quit Kephalos Bay before dark (about 9 p.m.); secondly, that nothing could be done which would attract the attention of the enemy before 10 p.m., the moment when the outposts on the left flank of the Anzac position were to be rushed.

General Stopford next framed his orders on these secret instructions, and after they had received my complete approval he proceeded to expound them to the general officer commanding 11th Division and general officer commanding 10th Division, who came over from Mudros for the purpose.

As in the original landing, the luck of calm weather favoured us, and all the embarkation arrangements at Kephalos were carried out by the Royal Navy in their usual ship-shape style. The 11th Division was to be landed at three places, designated and shown on the map as A, B, and C. Destroyers were told off for these landing-places, each destroyer towing a steam lighter and picket-boat. Every light was to be dowsed, and as they neared the shore the destroyers were to slip their motor-lighters and picket-boats, which would then take the beach and discharge direct on to it. The motor-lighters were new acquisitions since the first landing, and were to prove the greatest possible assistance. They moved five knots an hour under their own engines, and carried 500 men, as well as stores of ammunition and water. After landing their passengers they were to return to the destroyers, and in one trip would empty them also. Ketches with service launches and transport lifeboats were to follow the destroyers and anchor at the entrance of the bay, so that in case of accidents or delays to any one of the motor-lighters a picket-boat could be sent at once to a ketch to pick up a tow of lifeboats and take the place of a disabled motor-lighter. These ketches and tows were afterwards to be used for evacuating the wounded.

H.M.S. "Endymion" and H.M.S. "Theseus," each carrying a thousand men, were also to sail from Imbros after the destroyers, and, lying off the beach, were to discharge their troops directly the motor-lighters – three to each ship – were ready to convey the men to the shore, *i.e.*, after they had finished disembarking their own loads and those of the destroyers. When this was done – *i.e.*, after three trips – the motor lighters would be free to go on transporting guns, stores, mules, etc.

The following crafts brought up the rear:-

(1) Two ketches, each towing four horse-boats carrying four 18-pounder guns and twenty-four horses.
(2) One ketch, towing horse-boats with forty horses.
(3) The sloop "Aster," with 500 men, towing a lighter containing eight mountain guns.
(4) Three ketches, towing horse-boats containing eight 18-pounder guns and seventy-six horses.

Water-lighters, towed by a tank steamer, were also timed to arrive at A beach at daylight. When they had been emptied they were to return at once to Kephalos to refill from the parent water-ship.

A specially fitted-out steamer, the "Prah," with stores (shown by our experience of 25th April to be most necessary) – *i.e.*, water-pumps, hose, tanks, troughs, entrenching tools, and all ordnance stores requisite for the prompt development of wells or springs – was also sent to Suvla.

So much detail I have felt bound, for the sake of clearness, to give in the body of my despatch. The further detail, showing numbers landed, etc., etc., will be found in the appendix and tables attached.

When originally I conceived the idea of these operations, one of the first points to be weighed was that of the water supply in the Biyuk Anafarta valley and the Suvla plain. Experience at Anzac had shown quite clearly that the whole plan must be given up unless a certain amount of water could be counted upon, and, fortunately, the information I received was reassuring. But, in case of accidents, and to be on the safe side, so long ago as June had I begun to take steps to counter the chance that we might, from one cause or another, find difficulty in developing the wells. Having got from the War Office all that they could give me, I addressed myself to India and Egypt, and eventually from these three sources I managed to secure portable receptacles for 100,000 gallons, including petrol tins, milk cans, camel tanks, water bags and pakhals.

Supplementing these were lighters and water-ships, all under naval control. Indeed, by arrangement with the Admiral, the responsibility of the Army was confined to the emptying of the lighters and the distribution of the water to the troops, the Navy undertaking to bring the full lighters to the shore to replace the empty ones, thus providing a continuous supply. Finally 3,700 mules, together with 1,750 water carts, were provided for Anzac and Suvla – this in addition to 950 mules already at Anzac. Representatives of the Director of Supplies and Transport at Suvla and Anzac were sent to allot the transport which was to be used for carrying up whatever was nost needed by units ashore, whether water, food or ammunition. This statement, though necessarily brief, will, I hope, suffice to throw some light upon the complexity of the arrangements thought out beforehand in order, so far as was humanly possible, to combat the disorganisation, the hunger and the thirst which lie in wait for troops landing on a hostile beach.

On the evening of 6th August the 11th Division sailed on its short journey from Imbros (Kephalos) to Suvla Bay and, meeting with no mischance, the landing took place, the brigades of the 11th Division getting ashore practically simultaneously; the 32nd and 33rd Brigades at B and C beaches, the 34th at A beach.

The surprise of the Turks was complete. At B and C the beaches were found to be admirably suited to their purpose, and there was no opposition. The landing at A was more difficult, both because of the shoal water and because there the Turkish pickets and sentries – the normal guardians of the coast – were on the alert and active. Some of the lighters grounded a good way from the shore, and men had to struggle towards the beach in as much as four feet six inches of water. Ropes in several instances were carried from the lighters to the shore to help to sustain the heavily accoutred infantry. To add to the difficulties of the 34th Brigade the lighters came under flanking rifle fire from the Turkish outposts at Lala Baba and Ghazi Baba. The enemy even, knowing every inch of the ground, crept down in the very dark night on to the beach itself, mingling with our troops and getting between our firing line and its supports. Fortunately the number of these enterprising foes was but few, and an end was soon put to their activity on the actual beaches by the sudden storming of Lala Baba from the south. This attack was carried out by the 9th West Yorkshire Regiment and the 6th Yorkshire Regiment, both of the 32nd Brigade, which had landed at B beach and marched up along the coast. The assault succeeded at once and without much loss, but both battalions deserve great credit for the way it was delivered in the inky darkness of the night.

The 32nd Brigade was now pushed on to the support of the 34th Brigade, which was held up by another outpost of the enemy on Hill 10 (117 R and S), and it is feared that some of the losses, incurred here were due to misdirected fire. While this fighting was still in progress the 11th Battalion, Manchester Regiment, of the 34th Brigade was advancing northwards in very fine style, driving the enemy opposed to them back along the ridge of the Karakol Dagh towards the Kiretch Tepe Sirt. Beyond doubt these Lancashire men earned much distinction, fighting with great pluck and grit against an enemy not very numerous perhaps, but having an immense advantage in knowledge of the ground. As they got level with Hill 10 it grew light enough to see, and the enemy began to shell. No one seems to have been present who could take hold of the two brigades, the 32nd and 34th, and launch them in a concerted and cohesive attack. Consequently there was confusion and hesitation, increased by gorse fires lit by hostile shell, but redeemed, I am proud to report, by the conspicuously fine, soldierly conduct of several individual battalions. The whole of the Turks locally available were by now in the field, and they were encouraged to counter-attack by the signs of hesitation, but the 9th Lancashire Fusiliers and the 11th Manchester Regiment took them on with the bayonet, and fairly drove them back in disorder over the flaming Hill 10.

As the infantry were thus making good, the two Highland Mountain batteries and one battery, 59th Brigade, Royal Field Artillery, were landed at B beach. Day was now breaking, and with the dawn sailed into the bay six battalions of the 10th Division, under Brigadier-General Hill, from Mitylene.

Here perhaps I may be allowed to express my gratitude to the Royal Navy for their share in this remarkable achievement, as well as a very natural pride at staff arrangements, which resulted in the infantry of a whole division and three batteries being landed during a single night on a hostile shore, whilst the arrival of the first troops of the supporting division, from another base distant 120 miles, took place at the very psychological moment when support was most needed, namely, at break of dawn.

The intention of the Corps Commander was to keep the 10th Division on the left, and with it to push on as far forward as possible along the Kiretch Tepe Sirt towards the heights above Ejelmer Bay. He wished, therefore, to land these six battalions of the 10th Division at A beach and, seeing Brigadier-General Hill, he told him that as the left of the 34th Brigade was being hard pressed he should get into touch with General Officer Commanding 11th Division, and work in support of his left until the arrival of his own Divisional General. But the Naval authorities, so General Stopford reports, were unwilling, for some reason not specified, to land these troops at A beach, so that they had to be sent in lighters to C beach, whence they marched by Lala Baba to Hill 10, under fire. Hence were caused loss, delay and fatigue. Also the angle of direction from which these fresh troops entered the fight was not nearly so effective. The remainder of the 10th Division, three battalions (from Mudros), and with them the G.O.C. Lieutenant-General Sir B. Mahon, began to arrive, and the Naval authorities having discovered a suitable landing place near Ghazi Baba, these battalions were landed there together with one battalion of the 31st Brigade which had not yet been sent round to "C" beach. By this means it was hoped that both the brigades of the 10th Division would be able to rendezvous about half a mile to the north-west of Hill 10.

After the defeat of the enemy round and about Hill 10, they retreated in an easterly direction towards Sulajik and Kuchuk Anafarta Ova, followed by the 34th and 32nd Brigades of the 11th Division and by the 31st Brigade of the 10th Division, which had entered into the fight, not, as the Corps Commander had intended, on the left of the 11th Division, but between Hill 10 and the Salt Lake. I have failed in my endeavours to get some live human detail about the fighting which followed, but I understand from the Corps Commander that the brunt of it fell upon the 31st Brigade of the 10th (Irish) Division, which consisted of the 6th Royal Inniskilling Fusiliers, the 6th Royal Irish Fusiliers, and the 6th Royal Dublin Fusiliers, the last-named battalion being attached to the 31st Brigade.

By the evening General Hammersley had seized Yilghin Burnu (Chocolate Hills) after a fight for which he specially commends the 6th Lincoln Regiment and the 6th Border Regiment. At the same time he reported that he was unable to make any further progress towards the vital point, Ismail Oglu Tepe. At nightfall his brigade and the 31st Brigade were extended from about Hetman Chair through Chocolate Hills, Sulajik, to near Kuchuk Anafarta Ova.

This same day Sir B. Mahon delivered a spirited attack along the Kiretch Tepe Sirt ridge, in support of the 11th Battalion Manchester Regiment, and, taking some small trenches en route, secured and established himself on a position extending from the sea about 135 p., through the high ground about the p. of Kiretch Tepe Sirt, to about 135 Z. 8. In front of him, on the ridge, he reported the enemy to be strongly entrenched. The 6th Royal Munster Fusiliers have been named as winning special distinction here. The whole advance was well carried out by the Irishmen over difficult ground against an enemy – 500 to 700 Gendarmerie – favoured by the lie of the land.

The weather was very hot, and the new troops suffered much from want of water. Except at the southernmost extremity of the Kiretch Tepe Sirt ridge there was no water in that part of the field, and although it existed in some abundance throughout the area over which the 11th Division was operating, the Corps Commander reports that there was no time to develop its resources. Partly this seems to have been owing to the enemy's fire; partly to a want of that *nous* which stands by as second nature to the old campaigner; partly it was inevitable. Anyway, for as long as such a state of things lasted, the troops became dependent on the lighters and upon the water brought to the beaches in tins, pakhals, etc.

Undoubtedly the distribution of this water to the advancing troops was a matter of great difficulty, and one which required not only well-worked-out schemes from Corps and Divisional Staffs, but also energy and experience on the part of those who had to put them into practice. As it turned out, and judging merely by results, I regret to say that the measures actually taken in regard to the distribution proved to be inadequate, and that suffering and disorganisation ensued. The disembarkation of artillery horses was therefore at once, and rightly, postponed by the Corps Commander, in order that mules might be landed to carry up water. And now General Stopford, recollecting the vast issues which hung upon his success in forestalling the enemy, urged his Divisional commanders to push on. Otherwise, as he saw, all the advantages of the surprise landing must be nullified. But the Divisional Commanders believed themselves, it seems, to be unable to move. Their men, they said, were exhausted by their efforts of the night of the 6th–7th and by the action of the 7th. The want of water had told on the new troops. The distribution from the beaches had not worked smoothly. In some cases the hose had been pierced by individuals wishing to fill their own bottles; in others lighters had grounded so far from the beach that men swam out to fill batches of water-bottles. All this had added to the disorganisation inevitable after a night landing, followed by fights here and there with an enemy scattered over a country to us unknown. These pleas for delay were perfectly well founded. But it seems to have been overlooked that the half-defeated

Turks in front of us were equally exhausted and disorganised, and that an advance was the simplest and swiftest method of solving the water trouble and every other sort of trouble. Be this as it may, the objections overbore the Corps Commander's resolution. He had now got ashore three batteries (two of them mountain batteries), and the great guns of the ships were ready to speak at his request. But it was lack of artillery support which finally decided him to acquiesce in a policy of going slow which, by the time it reached the troops, became translated into a period of inaction. The Divisional Generals were, in fact, informed that, "in view of the inadequate artillery support," General Stopford did not wish them to make frontal attacks on entrenched positions, but desired them, so far as was possible, to try and turn any trenches which were met with. Within the terms of this instruction lies the root of our failure to make use of the priceless daylight hours of the 8th of August.

Normally, it may be correct to say that in modern warfare infantry cannot be expected to advance without artillery preparation. But in a landing on a hostile shore the order has to be inverted. The infantry must advance and seize a suitable position to cover the landing, and to provide artillery positions for the main thrust. The very existence of the force, its water supply, its facilities for munitions and supplies, its power to reinforce, must absolutely depend on the infantry being able instantly to make good sufficient ground without the aid of the artillery other than can be supplied for the purpose by *floating* batteries.

This is not a condition that should take the commander of a covering force by surprise. It is one already foreseen. Driving power was required, and even a certain ruthlessness, to brush aside pleas for a respite for tired troops. The one fatal error was inertia. And inertia prevailed. Late in the evening of the 7th the enemy had withdrawn the few guns which had been in action during the day. Beyond half a dozen shells dropped from very long range into the bay in the early morning of the 8th, no enemy artillery fired that day in the Suvla area. The guns had evidently been moved back, lest they should be captured when we pushed forward. As for the entrenched positions, these, in the ordinary acceptance of the term, were non-existent. The General Staff Officer whom I had sent on to Suvla early in the morning of the 8th reported by telegraph the absence of hostile gun-fire, the small amount of rifle fire, and the enemy's apparent weakness. He also drew attention to the inaction of our own troops, and to the fact that golden opportunities were being missed. Before this message arrived at general headquarters I had made up my mind, from the Corps Commander's own reports, that all was not well at Suvla. There was risk in cutting myself adrift, even temporarily, from touch with the operations at Anzac and Helles; but I did my best to provide against any sudden call by leaving Major-General W.P. Braithwaite, my Chief of the

General Staff, in charge, with instructions to keep me closely informed of events at the other two fronts; and, having done this, I took ship and set out for Suvla.

On arrival at about 5 p.m. I boarded H.M.S. "Jonquil," where I found corps headquarters, and where General Stopford informed me that the General Officer commanding 11th Division was confident of success in an attack he was to make at dawn next morning (the 9th). I felt no such confidence. Beyond a small advance by a part of the 11th Division between the Chocolate Hills and Ismail Oglu Tepe, and some further progress along the Kiretch Tepe Sirt ridge by the 10th Division, the day of the 8th had been lost. The commander of the 11th Division had, it seems, ordered strong patrols to be pushed forward so as to make good all the strong positions in advance which could be occupied without serious fighting; but, as he afterwards reported, "little was done in this respect." Thus a priceless twelve hours had already gone to help the chances of the Turkish reinforcements which were, I knew, both from naval and aerial sources, actually on the march for Suvla. But when I urged that even now, at the eleventh hour, the 11th Division should make a concerted attack upon the hills, I was met by a *non possumus*. The objections of the morning were no longer valid; the men were now well rested, watered, and fed. But the divisional commanders disliked the idea of an advance by night, and General Stopford did not care, it seemed, to force their hands.

So it came about that I was driven to see whether I could not, myself, put concentration of effort and purpose into the direction of the large number of men ashore. The Corps Commander made no objection. He declared himself to be as eager as I could be to advance. The representations made by the Divisional Commanders had seemed to him insuperable. If I could see my way to get over them no one would be more pleased than himself.

Accompanied by Commodore Roger Keyes and Lieutenant-Colonel Aspinall, of the Headquarters General Staff, I landed on the beach, where all seemed quiet and peaceful, and saw the Commander of the 11th Division, Major-General Hammersley. I warned him the sands were running out fast, and that by dawn the high ground to his front might very likely be occupied in force by the enemy. He saw the danger, but declared that it was a physical impossibility, at so late an hour (6 p.m.), to get out orders for a night attack, the troops being very much scattered. There was no other difficulty now, but this was insuperable; he could not recast his orders or get them round to his troops in time. But one brigade, the 32nd, was, so General Hammersley admitted, more or less concentrated and ready to move. The General Staff Officer of the division, Colonel Neil Malcolm, a soldier of experience, on whose opinion I set much value, was consulted. He agreed that the

32nd Brigade was now in a position to act. I, therefore, issued a direct order that, even if it were only with this 32nd Brigade, the advance should begin at the earliest possible moment, so that a portion at least of the 11th Division should anticipate the Turkish reinforcements on the heights and dig themselves in there upon some good tactical point.

In taking upon myself the serious responsibility of thus dealing with a detail of divisional tactics I was careful to limit the scope of the interference. Beyond directing that the one brigade which was reported ready to move at once should try and make good the heights before the enemy got on to them I did nothing, and said not a word calculated to modify or in any way affect the attack already planned for the morning. Out of the thirteen battalions which were to have advanced against the heights at dawn four were now to anticipate that movement by trying to make good the key of the enemy's position at once and under cover of darkness. I have not been able to get a clear and coherent account of the doings of the 32nd Brigade; but I have established the fact that it did not actually commence its advance till 4 a.m. on the 9th of August. The reason given is that the units of the brigade were scattered. In General Stopford's despatch he says that, "'One company of the 6th East Yorks Pioneer Battalion succeeded in getting to the top of the hill north of Anafarta Sagir, but the rest of the battalion and the 32nd Brigade were attacked from both flanks during their advance, and fell back to a line north and south of Sulajik. Very few of the leading company or the Royal Engineers who accompanied it got back, and that evening the strength of the battalion was nine officers and 380 men."

After their retirement from the hill north of Anafarta Sagir (which commanded the whole battlefield) this 32nd Brigade then still marked the high-water level of the advance made at dawn by the rest of the division. When their first retirement was completed they had to fall back further, so as to come into line with the most forward of their comrades. The inference seems clear. Just as the 32nd Brigade in their advance met with markedly less opposition than the troops who attacked an hour and a half later, so, had they themselves started earlier, they would probably have experienced less opposition. Further, it seems reasonable to suppose that had the complete division started at 4 a.m. on the 9th, or, better still, at 10 p.m. on the 8th, they would have made good the whole of the heights in front of them.

That night I stayed at Suvla, preferring to drop direct cable contact with my operations as a whole to losing touch with a corps battle which seemed to be going wrong.

At dawn on the 9th I watched General Hammersley's attack, and very soon realised, by the well-sustained artillery fire of the enemy (so silent the previous day), and by the volume of the musketry, that Turkish reinforcements had arrived; that with the renewed confidence caused by our long delay the guns had been brought back; and that, after all, we were forestalled. This was a bad moment. Our attack failed; our losses were very serious. The enemy's enfilading shrapnel fire seemed to be especially destructive and demoralising, the shell bursting low and all along our line. Time after time it threw back our attack just as it seemed upon the point of making good. The 33rd Brigade at first made most hopeful progress in its attempt to seize Ismail Oglu Tepe. Some of the leading troops gained the summit, and were able to look over on to the other side. Many Turks were killed here. Then the centre seemed to give way. Whether this was the result of the shrapnel fire or whether, as some say, an order to retire came up from the rear, the result was equally fatal to success. As the centre fell back the steady, gallant behaviour of the 6th Battalion, Border Regiment, and the 6th Battalion, Lincoln Regiment, on either flank was especially noteworthy. Scrub fires on Hill 70 did much to harass and hamper our troops. When the 32nd Brigade fell back before attacks from the slopes of the hill north of Anafarta Sagir and from the direction of Abrijka they took up the line north and south through Sulajik. Here their left was protected by two battalions of the 34th Brigade, which came up to their support. The line was later on prolonged by the remainder of the 34th Brigade and two battalions of the 159th Brigade of the 53rd Division. Their right was connected with the Chocolate Hills by the 33rd Brigade on the position to which they had returned after their repulse from the upper slopes of Ismail Oglu Tepe.

Some of the units which took part in this engagement acquitted themselves very bravely. I regret I have not had sufficient detail given me to enable me to mention them by name. The Divisional Commander speaks with appreciation of one freshly-landed battalion of the 53rd Division, a Hereford battalion, presumably the 1/1st Herefordshire, which attacked with impetuosity and courage between Hetman Chair and Kaslar Chair, about Azmak Dere, on the extreme right of his line.

During the night of the 8th/9th and early morning of the 9th the whole of the 53rd (Territorial) Division (my general reserve) had arrived and disembarked. I had ordered it up to Suvla, hoping that by adding its strength to the 9th Corps General Stopford might still be enabled to secure the commanding ground round the bay. The infantry brigades of the 53rd Division (no artillery had accompanied it from England) reinforced the 11th Division.

On August 10th the Corps Commander decided to make another attempt to take the Anafarta ridge. The 11th Division were not sufficiently rested to play a prominent part in the operation, but the 53rd Division, under General Lindley, was to attack, supported by General Hammersley. On the 10th there were one brigade of Royal Field Artillery ashore, with two mountain batteries, and all the ships' guns were available to co-operate. But the attack failed, though the Corps Commander considers that seasoned troops would have succeeded, especially as the enemy were showing signs of being shaken by our artillery fire. General Stopford points out, however, and rightly so, that the attack was delivered over very difficult country, and that it was a high trial for troops who had never been in action before, and with no regulars to set a standard. Many of the battalions fought with great gallantry, and were led forward with much devotion by their officers. At a moment when things were looking dangerous two battalions of the 11th Division (not specified by the Corps Commander) rendered very good service on the left of the Territorials. At the end of the day our troops occupied the line Hill east of Chocolate Hill – Sulajik, whilst the enemy – who had been ably commanded throughout – were still receiving reinforcements, and, apart from their artillery, were three times as strong as they had been on the 7th August.

Orders were issued to the General Officer Commanding 9th Corps to take up and entrench a line across the whole front from near the Azmak Dere, through the knoll east of the Chocolate Hill, to the ground held by the 10th Division about Kiretch Tepe Sirt. General Stopford took advantage of this opportunity to reorganise the divisions, and, as there was a gap in the line between the left of the 53rd Division and the right of the 10th Division, gave orders for the preparation of certain strong points to enable it to be held.

54th Division (infantry only) arrived, and were disembarked on August 11th and placed in reserve. On the following day – August 12th – I proposed that the 54th Division should make a night march in order to attack, at dawn on the 13th, the heights Kavak Tepe–Teke Tepe. The Corps Commander having reason to believe that the enclosed country about Kuchuk Anafarta Ova and the north of it was held by the enemy, ordered one brigade to move forward in advance, and make good Kuchuk Anafarta Ova, so as to ensure an unopposed march for the remainder of the division as far as that place. So that afternoon the 163rd Brigade moved off, and, in spite of serious opposition, established itself about the <u>A.</u> of <u>A</u>nafarta (118m. 4 and 7), in difficult and enclosed country. In the course of the fight, creditable in all respects to the 163rd Brigade, there happened a very mysterious thing. The 1/5th Norfolks were on the right of the line, and found themselves for a moment less strongly opposed than the rest of the brigade. Against the yielding forces of the enemy Colonel Sir H. Beauchamp, a bold, self-confident officer, eagerly pressed forward, followed by the best part of the battalion. The fighting grew hotter, and the ground became more wooded and broken. At this stage many men were wounded or grew exhausted with thirst. These found their way back to camp during the night. But the Colonel, with 16 officers and 250 men, still kept pushing on, driving the enemy before him. Amongst these ardent souls was part of a fine company enlisted from the King's Sandringham estates. Nothing more was ever seen or heard of any of them. They charged into the forest, and were lost to sight or sound. Not one of them ever came back.

The night march and projected attack were now abandoned, owing to the Corps Commander's representations as to the difficulties of keeping the division supplied with food, water, etc., even should they gain the height. General Birdwood had hoped he would soon be able to make a fresh attack on Sari Bair, provided that he might reckon on a corresponding vigorous advance to be made by the 11th and 54th Divisions on Ismail Oglu Tepe. On August 13th I so informed General Stopford. But when it came to business, General Birdwood found he could not yet carry out his new attack on Sari Bair – and, indeed, could only help the 9th Corps with one brigade from Damakjelik Bair. I was obliged, therefore, to abandon this project for the nonce, and directed General Stopford to confine his attention of strengthening his line across his present front. To straighten out the left of this line General Stopford ordered the General Officer Commanding the 10th Division to advance on the following day (15th August), so as to gain possession of the crest of the Kiretch Tepe Sirt, the 54th Division to co-operate.

The 30th and 31st Infantry Brigades of the 10th Irish Division were to attack frontally along the high ridge. The 162nd Infantry Brigade of the 54th Division were to support on the right. The infantry were to be seconded by a machine-gun detachment of the Royal Naval Air Service, by the guns of H.M.S. "Grampus" and H.M.S. "Foxhound" from the Gulf of Saros, by the Argyll Mountain Battery, the 15th Heavy Battery, and the 58th Field Battery. After several hours of indecisive artillery and musketry fighting, the 6th Royal Dublin Fusiliers charged forward with loud cheers, and captured the whole ridge, together with eighteen prisoners. The vigorous support rendered by the naval guns was a feature of this operation. Unfortunately, the point of the ridge was hard to hold, and means for maintaining the forward trenches had not been well thought out. Casualties became very heavy, the 5th Royal Irish Fusiliers having only one officer left, and the 5th Inniskilling Fusiliers also losing heavily in officers. Reinforcements were promised, but before they could arrive the officer left in command decided to evacuate the front trenches. The strength of the Turks opposed to us was steadily rising, and had now reached 20,000.

On the evening of the 15th August General Stopford handed over command of the 9th Corps. The units of the 10th and 11th Divisions had shown their mettle when they leaped into the water to get more quickly to close quarters, or when they stormed Lala Baba in the darkness. They had shown their resolution later when they tackled the Chocolate Hills and drove the enemy from Hill 10 right back out of rifle range from the beaches.

Then had come hesitation. The advantage had not been pressed. The senior Commanders at Suvla had had no personal experience of the new trench warfare; of the Turkish methods; of the paramount importance of time. Strong, clear leadership had not been promptly enough applied. These were the reasons which induced me, with your Lordship's approval, to appoint Major-General H. de B. De Lisle to take over temporary command.

I had already seen General De Lisle on his way from Cape Helles, and my formal instructions – full copy in Appendix – were handed to him by my Chief of the General Staff. Under these he was to make it his most pressing business to get the Corps into fighting trim again, so that as big a proportion of it as possible might be told off for a fresh attack upon Ismail Oglu Tepe and the Anafarta spur. At his disposal were placed the 10th Division (less one brigade), the 11th Division, the 53rd and 54th Divisions – a force imposing enough on paper, but totalling, owing to casualties, under 30,000 rifles.

The fighting strength of ourselves and of our adversaries stood at this time at about the following figures:- Lieutenant-General Birdwood commanded 25,000 rifles, at Anzac; Lieutenant-General Davies, in the southern zone, commanded 23,000 rifles; whilst the French corps alongside of him consisted of some 17,000 rifles. The Turks had been very active in the south, doubtless to prevent us reinforcing Anzac or Suvla; but it is doubtful if there were more than 35,000 of them in that region. The bulk of the enemy were engaged against Anzac or were in reserve in the valleys east and north of Sari Bair. Their strength was estimated at 75,000 rifles.

The Turks then, I reckoned, had 110,000 rifles to our 95,000, and held all the vantages of ground; they had plenty of ammunition, also drafts wherewith to refill ranks depleted in action within two or three days. My hopes that these drafts would be of poor quality had been every time disappointed. After weighing all these points, I sent your Lordship a long cable. In it I urged that if the campaign was to be brought to a quick, victorious decision, large reinforcements must at once be sent out. Autumn, I pointed out, was already upon us, and there was not a moment to be lost. At that time (16th August) my British divisions alone were 45,000 under establishment, and some of my fine battalions had dwindled down so far that I had to withdraw them from the fighting line. Our most vital need was the replenishment of these sadly depleted ranks. When that was done I wanted 50,000 fresh rifles. From what I knew of the Turkish situation, both in its local and general aspects, it seemed, humanly speaking, a certainty that if this help could be sent to me *at once* we could still clear a passage for our fleet to Constantinople.

It may be judged, then, how deep was my disappointment when I learnt that the essential drafts, reinforcements and munitions could not be sent to me, the reason given being one which prevented me from any further insistence. So I resolved to do my very best with the means at my disposal, and forthwith reinforced the northern wing with the 2nd Mounted Division (organised as dismounted troops) from Egypt and the 29th Division from the southern area. These movements, and the work of getting the 9th Corps and attached divisions into battle array took time, and it was not until the 21st that I was ready to renew the attack – an attack to be carried out under very different conditions from those of the 7th and 8th August.

The enemy's positions were now being rapidly entrenched, and, as I could not depend on receiving reinforcing drafts, I was faced with the danger that if I could not drive the Turks back I might lose so many men that I would find myself unable to hold the very extensive new area of ground which had been gained. I therefore decided to mass every available man against Ismail Oglu Tepe, a *sine quâ non* to my plans whether as a first step towards clearing the valley, or, if this proved impossible, towards securing Suvla Bay and Anzac Cove from shell fire.

The scheme for this attack was well planned by General De Lisle. The 53rd and 54th Divisions were to hold the enemy from Sulajik to Kiretch Tepe Sirt while the 29th Division and 11th Division stormed Ismail Oglu Tepe. Two brigades, 10th Division, and the 2nd Mounted Division were retained in Corps Reserve. I arranged that General Birdwood should co-operate by swinging forward his left flank to Susuk Kuyu and Kaiajik Aghala. Naturally I should have liked still further to extend the scope of my attack by ordering an advance of the 9th Corps all along their line, but many of the battalions had been too highly tried, and I felt it was unwise to call upon them for another effort so soon. The attack would only be partial, but it was an essential attack if any real progress was to be made. Also, once the Anafarta ridge was in my hands the enemy would be unable to reinforce through the gap between the two Anafartas, and then, so I believed, my left would find no difficulty in getting on.

My special objective was the hill which forms the south-west corner of the Anafarta Sagir spur. Ismail Oglu Tepe, as it is called, forms a strong natural barrier against an invader from the Ægean who might wish to march direct against the Anafartas. The hill rises 350 feet from the plain, with steep spurs jutting out to the west and south-west, the whole of it covered with dense holly oak scrub, so nearly impenetrable that it breaks up an attack and forces troops to move in single file along goat tracks between the bushes. The comparatively small number of guns landed up to date was a weakness, seeing we had now to storm trenches, but the battleships were there to back us, and as the bombardment was limited, to a narrow front of a mile it was hoped the troops would find themselves able to carry the trenches and that the impetus of the charge would carry them up to the top of the crest. Our chief difficulty lay in the open nature and shallow depth of the ground available for the concentration for attack. The only cover we possessed was the hill Lala Baba, 200 yards from the sea, and Yilghin Burnu, half a mile from the Turkish front, the ground between these two being an exposed plain. The 29th Division, which was to make the attack on the left, occupied the front trenches during the preceding night; the 11th Division, which was to attack on the right, occupied the front trenches on the right of Yilghin Burnu.

By some freak of nature Suvla Bay and plain were wrapped in a strange mist on the afternoon of the 21st of August. This was sheer bad luck, as we had reckoned on the enemy's gunners being blinded by the declining sun and upon the Turkish trenches being shown up by the evening light with singular clearness, as would have been the case on ninety-nine days out of a hundred. Actually we could hardly see the enemy lines this afternoon, whereas out to the westward targets stood out in strong relief against the luminous mist. I wished to postpone the attack, but for various reasons this was not possible, and so, from 2.30 p.m. to 3 p.m. a heavy but none too accurate artillery bombardment from land and sea was directed against the Turkish first line of trenches, whilst twenty-four machine-guns in position on Yilghin Burnu did what they could to lend a hand.

At 3 p.m. an advance was begun by the infantry on the right of the line. The 34th Brigade of the 11th Division rushed the Turkish trenches between Hetman Chair and Aire Klavak, practically without loss, but the 32nd Brigade, directed against Hetman Chair and the communication trench connecting that point with the south-west corner of the Ismail Oglu Tepe spur, failed to make good its point. The brigade had lost direction in the first instance, moving north-east instead of east, and though it attempted to carry the communication trench from the northeast with great bravery and great disregard of life, it never succeeded in rectifying the original mistake. The 33rd Brigade, sent up in haste with orders to capture this communication trench at all costs, fell into precisely the same error, part of it marching north east and part south-east to Susuk Kuyu.

Meanwhile the 29th Division, whose attack had been planned for 3.30 p.m., had attacked Scimitar Hill (Hill 70) with great dash. The 87th Brigade, on the left, carried the trenches on Scimitar Hill, but the 86th Brigade were checked and upset by a raging forest fire across their front. Eventually pressing on, they found themselves unable to advance up the valley between the two spurs owing to the failure of the 32nd Brigade of the 11th Division on their right. The brigade then tried to attack eastwards, but were decimated by a cross fire of shell and musketry from the north and south-east. The leading troops were simply swept off the top of the spur, and had to fall back to a ledge south-west of Scimitar Hill, where they found a little cover. Whilst this fighting was in progress the 2nd Mounted Division moved out from Lala Baba in open formation to take up a position of readiness behind Yilghin Burnu. During this march they came under a remarkably steady and accurate artillery fire. The advance of these English Yeomen was a sight calculated to send a thrill of pride through anyone with a drop of English blood running in their veins. Such superb martial spectacles are rare in modern war. Ordinarily it should always be possible to bring up reserves under some sort of cover from shrapnel fire. Here, for a mile and a half, there was nothing to conceal a mouse, much less some of the most stalwart soldiers England has ever sent from her shores. Despite the critical events in other parts of the field, I could hardly take my glasses from the Yeomen: they moved like men marching on parade. Here and there a shell would take toll of a cluster; there they lay; there was no straggling; the others moved steadily on; not a man was there who hung back or hurried. But such an ordeal must consume some of the battle-winning fighting energy of those subjected to it, and it is lucky indeed for the Turks that the terrain, as well as the lack of trenches, forbade us from letting the 2nd Mounted Division loose at close quarters to the enemy without undergoing this previous too heavy baptism of fire.

Now that the 11th Division had made their effort, and failed, the 2nd South Midland Brigade (commanded by Brigadier-General Earl of Longford) was sent forward from its position of readiness behind Yilghin Burnu, in the hope that they might yet restore the fortunes of the day. This brigade, in action for the first time, encountered both bush fires and musketry without flinching, but the advance had in places to be almost by inches, and the actual close attack by the Yeomen did not take place until night was fast falling. On the left they reached the foremost line of the 29th Division, and on the right also they got as far as the leading battalions. But, as soon as it was dark, one regiment pushed up the valley between Scimitar Hill and Hill 100 (on Ismail Oglu Tepe), and carried the trenches on a small knoll near the centre of this horseshoe. The regiment imagined it had captured Hill 100, which would have been a very notable success, enabling as it would the whole of our line to hang on and dig in. But when the report came in some doubt was felt as to its accuracy, and a reconnaissance by staff officers showed that the knoll was a good way from Hill 100, and that a strongly-held semi-circle of Turkish trenches (the enemy having been heavily reinforced) still denied us access to the top of the hill. As the men were too done, and had lost too heavily to admit of a second immediate assault, and as the knoll actually held would have been swept by fire at daybreak, there was nothing for it but to fall back under cover of darkness to our original line. The losses in this attack fell most heavily on the 29th Division. They were just under 5,000.

I am sorry not to be able to give more detail as to the conduct of individuals and units during this battle. But the 2nd South Midland Brigade has been brought to my notice, and it consisted of the Bucks Yeomanry, the Berks Yeomanry, and the Dorset Yeomanry. The Yeomanry fought very bravely, and on personal, as well as public, grounds I specially deplore the loss of Brigadier-General Earl of Longford, K.P., M.V.O., and Brigadier-General P.A. Kenna, V.C., D.S.O., A.D.C.

The same day, as pre-arranged with General Birdwood, a force consisting of two battalions of New Zealand Mounted Rifles, two battalions of the 29th Irish Brigade, the 4th South Wales Borderers, and 29th Indian Infantry Brigade, the whole under the command of Major-General H.V. Cox, was working independently to support the main attack.

General Cox divided his force into three sections; the left section to press forward and establish a permanent hold on the existing lightly-held outpost line covering the junction of the 11th Division with the Anzac front; the centre section to seize the well at Kabak Kuyu, an asset of utmost value, whether to ourselves or the enemy; the right section to attack and capture the Turkish trenches on the north-east side of the Kaiajik Aghala.

The advance of the left section was a success; after a brisk engagement the well at Kabak Kuyu was seized by the Indian Brigade, and, by 4.30, the right column, under Brigadier-General Russell, under heavy fire, effected a lodgment on the Kaiajik Aghala, where our men entrenched, and began to dig communications across the Kaiajik Dere towards the lines of the 4th Australian Brigade south of the Dere. A pretty stiff bomb fight ensued, in which General Russell's troops held their own through the night against superior force. At 6 a.m. on the morning of the 22nd August, General Russell, reinforced by the newly-arrived 18th Australian Battalion, attacked the summit of the Kaiajik Aghala. The Australians carried 150 yards of the trenches, losing heavily in so doing, and were then forced to fall back again owing to enfilade fire, though in the meantime the New Zealand Mounted Rifles managed, in spite of constant counter-attacks, to make good another 80 yards. A counter-attack in strength launched by the Turks at 10 a.m. was repulsed; the new line from the Kaiajik Aghala to Susuk Kuyu was gradually strengthened, and eventually joined on to the right of the 9th Army Corps, thereby materially improving the whole situation. During this action the 4th Australian Brigade, which remained facing the Turks on the upper part of the Kaiajik Aghala, was able to inflict several hundred casualties on the enemy as they retreated or endeavoured to reinforce.

On the 21st of August we had carried the Turkish entrenchments at several points, but had been unable to hold what we had gained except along the section where Major-General Cox had made a good advance with Anzac and

Indian troops. To be repulsed is not to be defeated, as long as the commander and his troops are game to renew the attack. All were eager for such a renewal of the offensive; but clearly we would have for some time to possess our souls in patience, seeing that reinforcements and munitions were short, that we were already outnumbered by the enemy, and that a serious outbreak of sickness showed how it had become imperative to give a spell of rest to the men who had been fighting so magnificently and so continuously. To calculate on rest, it may be suggested, was to calculate without the enemy. Such an idea has no true bearing on the feelings of the garrison of the peninsula. That the Turks should attack had always been the earnest prayer of all of us, just as much after the 21st August as before it. And now that we had to suspend progress for a bit, work was put in hand upon the line from Suvla to Anzac, a minor offensive routine of sniping and bombing was organised, and, in a word, trench warfare set in on both sides.

On 24th August Lieutenant-General the Hon. J.H.G. Byng, K.C.M.G., C.B., M.V.O., assumed command of the 9th Army Corps.

The last days of the month were illumined by a brilliant affair carried through by the troops under General Birdwood's command. Our object was to complete the capture of Hill 60 north of the Kaiajik Aghala, commenced by Major-General Cox on the 21st August. Hill 60 overlooked the Biyuk Anafarta valley, and was therefore tactically a very important feature.

The conduct of the attack was again entrusted to Major-General Cox, at whose disposal were placed detachments from the 4th and 5th Australian Brigades, the New Zealand Mounted Rifles Brigade, and the 5th Connaught Rangers. The advance was timed to take place at 5 p.m. on the 27th of August, after the heaviest artillery bombardment we could afford. This bombardment seemed effective; but the moment the assailants broke cover they were greeted by an exceeding hot fire from the enemy field guns, rifles, and machine-guns, followed after a brief interval by a shower of heavy shell, some of which, most happily, pitched into the trenches of the Turks. On the right the detachment from the 4th and 5th Australian Brigades could make no headway against a battery of machine-guns which confronted them. In the centre the New Zealanders made a most determined onslaught, and carried one side of the topmost knoll. Hand-to-hand fighting continued here till 9.30 p.m., when it was reported that nine tenths of the summit had been gained. On the left the 250 men of the 5th Connaught Rangers excited the admiration of all beholders by the swiftness and cohesion of their charge. In five minutes they had carried their objective, the northern Turkish communications, when they at once set to and began a lively bomb-fight along the trenches against strong parties which came hurrying up from the enemy supports and afterwards from their reserves. At midnight fresh troops were to have strengthened our grip upon the hill, but before that hour the Irishmen had been out-bombed, and the 9th Australian Light Horse, who had made a most plucky attempt to recapture the lost communication trench, had been repulsed. Luckily, the New Zealand Mounted Rifles refused to recognise that they were worsted. Nothing would shift them. All that night and all next day, through bombing, bayonet charges, musketry, shrapnel, and heavy shell, they hung on to their 150 yards of trench. At 1 a.m. on August 29th the 10th Light Horse made another attack on the lost communication trenches to the left, carried them, and finally held them. This gave us complete command of the underfeature, an outlook over the Anafarta Sagir valley, and safer lateral communications between Anzac and Suvla Bay.

Our casualties in this hotly contested affair amounted to 1,000. The Turks lost out of all proportion more. Their line of retreat was commanded from our Kaiajik Dere trenches, whence our observers were able to direct artillery fire equally upon their fugitives and their reinforcements. The same observers estimated the Turkish casualties as no less than 5,000. Three Turkish machine-guns and forty six prisoners were taken, as well as three trench mortars, 300 Turkish rifles, 60,000 rounds of ammunition, and 500 bombs. Four hundred acres were added to the territories of Anzac. Major-General Cox showed his usual forethought and wisdom. Brigadier-General Russell fought his men splendidly.

My narrative of battle incidents must end here. From this date onwards up to the date of my departure on October 17th the flow of munitions and drafts fell away. Sickness, the legacy of a desperately trying summer, took heavy toll of the survivors of so many arduous conflicts. No longer was there any question of operations on the grand scale, but with such troops it was difficult to be downhearted. All ranks were cheerful; all remained confident that, so long as they stuck to their guns, their country would stick to them, and see them victoriously through the last and greatest of the crusades.

On the 11th October your Lordship cabled asking me for an estimate of the losses which would be involved in an evacuation of the peninsula. On the 12th October I replied in terms showing that such a step was to me unthinkable. On the 16th October I received a cable recalling me to London for the reason, as I was informed by your Lordship on my arrival, that His Majesty's Government desired a fresh, unbiassed opinion, from a responsible Commander, upon the question of early evacuation.

In bringing this dispatch to a close I wish to refer gratefully to the services rendered by certain formations, whose work has so far only been recognised by a sprinkling of individual rewards.

Much might be written on the exploits of the Royal Naval Air Service, but these bold flyers are laconic, and their feats will mostly pass unrecorded. Yet let me here thank them, with their Commander, Colonel F.H. Sykes, of the Royal Marines, for the nonchalance with which they appear to affront danger and death, when and where they can. So doing, they quicken the hearts of their friends on land and sea – an asset of greater military value even than their bombs or aerial reconnaissances, admirable in all respects as these were.

With them I also couple the *Service de l'Aviation* of the *Corps Expeditionnaire d'Orient*, who daily wing their way in and out of the shrapnel under the distinguished leadership of M. le Capitaine Césari.

The Armoured Car Division (Royal Naval Air Service) have never failed to respond to any call which might be made upon them. Their organisation was broken up; their work had to be carried out under strange conditions – from the bows of the "River Clyde," as independent batteries attached to infantry divisions, etc., etc. – and yet they were always cheerful, always ready to lend a hand in any sort of fighting that might give them a chance of settling old scores with the enemy.

Next I come to the Royal Artillery. By their constant vigilance, by their quick grasp of the key to every emergency, by their thundering good shooting, by hundreds of deeds of daring, they have earned the unstinted admiration of all their comrade services. Where all fought so remarkably the junior officers deserve a little niche of their own in the Dardanelles record of fame. Their audacity in reconnaissance, their insouciance under the hottest of fires, stand as a fine example not only to the Army, but to the nation at large.

A feature of every report, narrative or diary I have read has been a tribute to the stretcher bearers. All ranks, from Generals in command to wounded men in hospital, are unanimous in their praise. I have watched a party from the moment when the telephone summoned them from their dug-out to the time when they returned with their wounded. To see them run lightheartedly across fire-swept slopes is to be privileged to witness a superb example of the hero in man. No braver corps exists, and I believe the reason to be that all thought of self is instinctively flung aside when the saving of others is the motive.

The services rendered by Major-General (temporary Lieutenant-General) E.A. Altham, C.B., C.M.G., Inspector-General of Communications, and all the Departments and Services of the Lines of Communication assured us a life-giving flow of drafts, munitions and supplies. The work was carried out under unprecedented conditions, and is deserving, I submit, of handsome recognition.

With General Altham were associated Brigadier-General (temporary Major-General) C.R.R. McGrigor, C.B., at first Commandant of the Base at Alexandria and later Deputy Inspector-General of Communications, and

Colonel T.E. O'Leary, Deputy Adjutant-General, 3rd Echelon. Both of these officers carried out their difficult duties to my entire satisfaction.

My Military Secretary, Lieutenant-Colonel S.H. Pollen, has displayed first-class ability in the conduct of his delicate and responsible duties.

Also I take the opportunity of my last dispatch to mention two of my Aides-de-Camp – Major F.L. Magkill-Crichton-Maitland, Gordon Highlanders, Lieutenant Hon. G. St. J. Brodrick, Surrey Yeomanry.

I have many other names to bring to notice for distinguished and gallant service during the operations under review, and these will form the subject of a separate communication.

And now, before affixing to this dispatch my final signature as Commander-in-Chief of the Mediterranean Expeditionary Force, let me first pay tribute to the everlasting memory of my dear comrades who will return no more. Next, let me thank each and all, Generals, Staff, Regimental Leaders, and rank and file, for their wonderful loyalty, patience, and self-sacrifice. Our progress was constant, and if it was painfully slow – they know the truth. So I bid them all farewell with a special God-speed to the campaigners who have served with me right through from the terrible yet most glorious earlier days – the incomparable 29th Division; the young veterans of the Naval Division; the ever-victorious Australians and New Zealanders; the stout East Lancs, and my own brave fellow-countrymen of the Lowland Division of Scotland.

> I have the honour to be,
> Your Lordship's most obedient servant,
> IAN HAMILTON,
> General, Commander-in-Chief,
> Mediterranean Expeditionary Force.

6

SIR IAN HAMILTON'S
FOURTH GALLIPOLI DESPATCH,
10 MARCH 1916

MONDAY, 27 MARCH, 1916.

War Office, 24th March, 1916.

The following supplementary despatch has been received by the Secretary of State for War from General Sir Ian Hamilton, G.C.B. (The references are to the pages of the Supplement to the London Gazette dated 6th January, 1916, Number 29429):-

MY LORD,-

1, *Hyde Park Gardens, W.*,
March 10th, 1916.

I have the honour to submit herewith a supplement to my despatch of 11th December, 1915. Your Lordship may remember that I was unable to set seriously to work upon this despatch until after my return home at the end of October 1915, and that, when I did so, I was hampered by my separation from my late General Headquarters.

My main difficulty lay in the lack of properly authenticated facts relating to the actions and identities of some of the units which had borne the brunt of the fighting. In the Suvla Bay area especially so many senior commanders had gone under in one way or another that it seemed as if the story must be left half told.

But now, since my despatch has been studied by many who were themselves engaged, fresh light has been thrown upon several episodes hitherto obscure. I have sifted the evidence, and have satisfied myself that full justice has not been done to certain individuals and units. I hope, therefore, these corrigenda and addenda may be permitted to appear:

Page 289. Substitute "127th" for "129th" in line 10 from end of page.

Page 292. Substitute the words "First New Zealand Battery under Major McGilp" for the words "Second New Zealand Battery under Major Sykes."

Page 296. Substitute the words "6th Royal Irish Rifles" for the words "10th Hampshire Regiment." *Page* 300. Brigadier-General Hill's 31st Brigade consisted of the 5th Royal Inniskilling Fusiliers, the 6th Royal Inniskilling Fusiliers, the 5th Royal Irish Fusiliers, and the 6th Royal Irish Fusiliers, plus the 6th Royal Dublin Fusiliers and the 7th Royal Dublin Fusiliers which were temporarily attached thereto. Of these battalions the 5th Royal Inniskilling Fusiliers joined General Mahon, and were, therefore, not present during the fighting at Chocolate Hill. In addition to units already singled out for commendation, the 5th Royal Irish Fusiliers and the 7th Royal Dublin Fusiliers deserve special mention for the energy and boldness which characterised their attack.

Page 302. In the attack on Hill 70, on the 9th August, the 6th Royal Irish Fusiliers and the 6th Royal Dublin Fusiliers of the 31st Brigade (both attached to the 32nd Brigade for this day's operations) rendered distinguished service.

Page 306. The 9th Battalion Sherwood Foresters had constantly maintained stout hearts and a soldierly spirit in despite of the heavy losses they had suffered when carrying out their costly duty of closing the big gap between the left of the Anzac troops and Chocolate Hill from the 8th to 14th August. On the 21st August this same Battalion, together with the 6th Battalion Border Regiment, displayed a vigorous initiative combined with very steady discipline during the attack on Ismail Oglu Tepe.

Since the publication of my despatch of the 11th December the late Commanders of the 11th Division and 9th Corps have drawn my attention to the good work done by the following officers:-

Brigadier-General R.P. Maxwell, commanding the 33rd Brigade. He evinced coolness as well as energy throughout the heavy fighting of August, and stuck to his duty afterwards until, through sickness, he was literally unable to stand.

Brigadier-General H. Haggard, commanding the 32nd Brigade. He was severely wounded on the 7th of August, but not before he had had time to give sure proof of leadership and daring. The following mentions of officers of the Staff of the 29th Brigade and of the 6th Royal Irish Rifles and 10th Hampshire Regiment have only lately come to hand. The original documents seem to have gone entirely astray owing to successive casualties amongst the senior officers to whom they were addressed:-

29TH BRIGADE.
Staff.

Captain A.H. McCleverty, 2nd Rajput Light Infantry, Brigade Major.

10th (Service) Battalion, Hampshire Regiment.

Major (temporary Lieutenant-Colonel) W.D. Bewsher.
Temporary Captain F.M. Hicks.
No. 4410 Serjeant-Major J. Smith.
No. 4291 Company Serjeant-Major W.T. Groves (killed).

6th (Service) Battalion, Royal Irish Rifles.

Lieutenant-Colonel E.C. Bradford.

Captain (temporary Major) W. Eastwood (killed).

Captain (temporary Major) A.L. Wilford, 5th Light Infantry, Indian Army (attached).

Regimental Serjeant-Major P. Mulholland.

11TH DIVISION.
Staff.

Captain J.F.S.D. Coleridge, 8th Gurka Rifles.

32ND BRIGADE.
Staff.

Captain B.W. Shuttleworth, 45th Rattray's Sikhs.

6th (Service) Battalion, York and Lancaster Regiment.

Temporary Captain W.H. Toohey.

Temporary Captain W.P. Baldock (Lieutenant, Reserve of Officers) (killed).

No. 4324 Serjeant A. Ollernshaw.

33RD BRIGADE.
Staff.

Temporary Captain A. Hoade.

6th (Service) Battalion, Lincolnshire Regiment.

Major A.E. Norton, West India Regiment (attached).

*9th (Service) Battalion, Sherwood Foresters
(Nottinghamshire and Derbyshire Regiment).*

Temporary Major A.S. Murray (Captain, Reserve of Officers).

Captain F.F. Loyd.

I have the honour to be.
Your Lordship's most obedient servant,
IAN HAMILTON,
General.
Late Commander-in-Chief Mediterranean
Expeditionary Force.

War Office, 24th March, 1916.

The following corrections are notified in the list of officers and men mentioned in Sir Ian Hamilton's despatch of 11th December, 1915 (London Gazette dated 28th January, 1916):-

STAFF.

The ranks of the undermentioned officers should be as now and not as therein stated:-

Major W. Marriott-Dodington, Oxfordshire and Buckinghamshire Light Infantry.

Major R.M. Wetherell, Duke of Cornwall's Light Infantry.

Major W.J. Ainsworth, D.S.O., Durham Light Infantry.

Major Hon. A.G.A. Hore-Ruthven, V.C., Welsh Guards.

Major B.R. Moberly, D.S.O., 56th Punjabi Rifles.

Major E.C. Anstey, Royal Artillery.

Major D.S. Skelton, Royal Artillery.

Major W.M.B. Sparkes, Royal Army Medical Corps.

Major L.F. Ashburner, M.V.O., D.S.O., Royal Fusiliers.

Major (temporary Lieutenant-Colonel) B.A. Wright, D.S.O., Manchester Regiment (Service Battalion).

Temporary Major A.G. Fitz-R. Day Dorsetshire Regiment (Service Battalion).

In order to avoid the long delay which reference abroad would have involved the Australian portion of the list was published without verification of initials and spelling of names. The list has since been checked with official records, and it is notified that the undermentioned persons should have been described as now instead of as in the London Gazette dated 28th January, 1916:-

AUSTRALIAN TROOPS.
Australian Artillery.

Major O.F. Philips.

No. 805 Corporal E.D. Cook.

No. 2270 Gunner C.G. Carr (killed).

Australian Engineers.

No. 120 Lance-Corporal P.J. Lobb.

No. 73 Lance-Corporal L.J. Jordan.

No. 160 Sapper H.E. Townsend.

No. 100 Driver A.J. Jones.

1st Light Horse Regiment.

No. 566 Corporal B.I. Keys.

6th Light Horse Regiment.
No. 448 Trooper C.S. Paul.

8th Light Horse Regiment.
No. 235 Lance-Corporal J.A. Anderson.
No. 678 Trooper F.L.A. Beckett.

9th Light Horse Regiment.
No. 283 Private C.G. Howell.

AUSTRALIAN INFANTRY.
1st Battalion (New South Wales).
Lieutenant P.S.S. Woodforde.
No. 320 Company Serjeant-Major J.W. Morris.
No. 1369 Private W.J. Kelly.
No. 1509 Private D.F. Allan.
No. 1831 Private R.T. Ramsay.

2nd Battalion (New South Wales).
No. 248 Regimental Serjeant-Major R. Howmans.
No. 1745 Private W. Goudemy.

3rd Battalion (New South Wales).
Major D. McF. McConaghey.
Lieutenant T.D. McLeod.
No. 1113 Serjeant C.O. Clark.
No. 20 Corporal R.L. Graham.
No. 1360 Private G.C. Green.
No. 941 Private T.C. Horan (killed).

4th Battalion (New South Wales).
No. 1115 Serjeant R. Claydon.
No. 787 Private G.W. Hewitt.

7th Battalion (Victoria).
No. 2130 Corporal W. Dunstan, V.C.
No. 1937 Private O. Ellis (killed).

8th Battalion (Victoria).
No. 2257 Private P.J. Young (killed).
No. 1856 Private Thomas Green.
No. 1749 Private F. Hicks (killed).

10th Battalion (South Australia).
No. 1157 Private V.G.R. McDonald.

11*th Battalion (Western Australia)*.
Second Lieutenant C.H. Procter (killed).
Second Lieutenant J.W. Franklyn.
No. 503 Serjeant W. Hallahan.
No. 724 Lance-Corporal L. Taylor.
No. 594 Lance-Corporal S.I. Smith.
No. 388 Private A.R. Retchford.

12*th Battalion (South Australia, Western Australia and Tasmania)*.
No. 1611 Private J. Johnson.

13*th Battalion (New South Wales)*.
No. 371 Private W.S. Doig.

16*th Battalion (South Australia and Western Australia)*.
No. 2065 Private R. Annear.

18*th Battalion (Australian Infantry)*.
No. 215 Corporal R. Dryden.
No. 615 Private R.R. Martin.
No. 707 Private W.G. Collins.

AUSTRALIAN ARMY MEDICAL CORPS.
No. 1599 Private C. Millinger.
No. 119 Private E. Cruickshank.
No. 68 Private H.B. Brighton.
No. 1128 Private A.G. Foster.

7

SIR CHARLES MONRO'S GALLIPOLI DESPATCH, 6 MARCH 1916

FRIDAY, THE 7TH OF APRIL, 1916

War Office, London, S.W., 10*th April*, 1916.

The following despatch has been received by the Secretary of State for War from General Sir C.C. Monro, K.C.B.:-

Headquarters, 1*st Army*,
France,
6*th March*, 1916.

MY LORD,-

I have the honour to submit herewith a brief account of the operations in the Eastern Mediterranean from the 28th October, 1915, on which date I assumed command of the Mediterranean Expeditionary Force, until the 9th January, 1916, when in compliance with your directions, I handed over charge at Cairo to Lieut.-General Sir Archibald Murray, K.C.B., C.V.O., D.S.O.

On the 20th October in London, I received your Lordship's instructions to proceed as soon as possible to the near East and take over the command of the Mediterranean Expeditionary Force.

My duty on arrival was in broad outline:-

(*a*) To report on the military situation on the Gallipoli Peninsula.

(*b*) To express an opinion whether on purely military grounds the Peninsula should be evacuated, or another attempt made to carry it.

(*c*) The number of troops that would be required,

(1) to carry the Peninsula,

(2) to keep the Straits open, and

(3) to take Constantinople.

Two days after my arrival at Imbros, where the headquarters of the M.E.F. was established, I proceeded to the Peninsula to investigate the military situation. The impressions I gathered are summarised very shortly as follows:-

The positions occupied by our troops presented a military situation unique in history. The mere fringe of the coast line had been secured. The beaches and piers upon which they depended for all requirements in personnel and material were exposed to registered and observed Artillery fire. Our entrenchments were dominated almost throughout by the Turks. The possible

Artillery positions were insufficient and defective. The Force, in short, held a line possessing every possible military defect. The position was without depth, the communications were insecure and dependent on the weather. No means existed for the concealment and deployment of fresh troops destined for the offensive – whilst the Turks enjoyed full powers of observation, abundant Artillery positions, and they had been given the time to supplement the natural advantages which the position presented by all the devices at the disposal of the Field Engineer.

Another material factor came prominently before me. The troops on the Peninsula had suffered much from various causes.

(*a*) It was not in the first place possible to withdraw them from the shell-swept area as is done when necessary in France, for every corner on the Peninsula is exposed to hostile fire.

(*b*) They were much enervated from the diseases which are endemic in that part of Europe in the summer.

(*c*) In consequence of the losses which they had suffered in earlier battles, there was a very grave dearth of officers competent to take command of men.

(*d*) In order to maintain the numbers needed to hold the front, the Territorial Divisions had been augmented by the attachment of Yeomanry and Mounted Brigades. Makeshifts of this nature very obviously did not tend to create efficiency.

Other arguments, irrefutable in their conclusions, convinced me that a complete evacuation was the only wise course to pursue.

(*a*) It was obvious that the Turks could hold us in front with a small force and prosecute their designs on Baghdad or Egypt, or both.

(*b*) An advance from the positions we held could not be regarded as a reasonable military operation to expect.

(*c*) Even had we been able to make an advance in the Peninsula, our position would not have been ameliorated to any marked degree, and an advance on Constantinople was quite out of the question.

(*d*) Since we could not hope to achieve any purpose by remaining on the Peninsula, the appalling cost to the nation involved in consequence of embarking on an Overseas Expedition with no base available for the rapid transit of stores, supplies and personnel, made it urgent that we should divert the troops locked up on the Peninsula to a more useful theatre.

Since therefore I could see no military advantage in our continued occupation of positions on the Peninsula, I telegraphed to your Lordship that in my opinion the evacuation of the Peninsula should be taken in hand.

Subsequently I proceeded to Egypt to confer with Colonel Sir H. McMahon, the High Commissioner, and Lieut.-General Sir J. Maxwell, Commanding the Forces in Egypt, over the situation which might be created in Egypt and the Arab world by the evacuation of the Peninsula.

Whilst in Egypt I was ordered by a telegram from the War Office to take command of the troops at Salonika. The purport of this telegram was subsequently cancelled by your Lordship on your arrival at Mudros, and I was then ordered to assume Command of the Forces in the Mediterranean, east of Malta, and exclusive of Egypt.

Consequent on these instructions, I received approval that the two Forces in the Mediterranean should be designated as follows:-

(*a*) The original Mediterranean Expeditionary Force, which comprised the Forces operating on the Gallipoli Peninsula and those employed at Mudros and Imbros as the "Dardanelles Army," under Lieut.-General Sir W. Birdwood, K.C.B., etc., with headquarters at Imbros.

(*b*) The troops destined for Salonika as the "Salonika Army," under Lieut.-General Sir B. Mahon, K.C.B., with headquarters at Salonika.

The Staff of the original M.E.F. was left in part to form the Dardanelles Army, and the remainder were taken to make a General Headquarter Staff for the increased responsibilities now assumed. Other officers doing duty in this theatre with the necessary qualifications were selected, and, with no difficulty or demands on home resources, a thoroughly efficient and adequate Staff was created.

Mudros was selected as being the most suitable site for the establishment of headquarters, as affording an opportunity, in addition to other advantages, of daily consultation with the Inspector General, Line of Communications. The working of the services of the Line of Communications presented difficulties of an unique character, mainly owing to:-

(*a*) the absence of pier and wharfage accommodation at Mudros and the necessity of transferring all Ordnance and Engineer Stores from one ship to another;

(*b*) the submarine danger;

(*c*) the delay caused by rough weather.

Close association with General Altham was therefore most imperative, and by this means many important changes were made which conduced to greater efficiency and more prompt response to the demands of fighting units.

A narrative of the events which occurred in each of the two Armies is now recorded separately for facility of perusal and reference.

SALONIKA ARMY.

Early in October the 10th Division, under Lieut.-General Sir B. Mahon, K.C.B., was transferred from Suvla to Salonika, and fully concentrated there. The dislocation of units caused by the landing on the Peninsula and the subsequent heavy fighting which occurred prevented this Division being despatched intact. The organisation of the Infantry and the Royal Engineers was not disturbed, but the other services had to be improvised from other Divisions as found most accessible.

The arrival of the 10th Division had been preceded by two French Divisions under General Sarrail, whose Force was subsequently augmented by another Division. These three Divisions were then moved into Servia under the understanding arranged between the Allies Governments, which was to the effect that the French Forces were to protect the railway between Krivolak and Veles, and to ensure communication with the Servian Army, whilst the British were to maintain the position from Salonika to Krivolak, and to support the French Right. If communication with the Servian Army could not be opened and maintained, the Allied Forces were to be withdrawn.

With this object, two Battalions of the 10th Division were moved from Salonika on 27th October, and took over the French front from Kosturino to Lake Doiran. The remainder of the Division was sent to Servia on 12th November and following days, and took over the French front eastwards from Kosturino.

The task of moving troops into Servia and maintaining them there presented many difficulties. No road exists from Salonika to Doiran, a few miles of road then obtains, which is followed within a few miles by a track only suitable for pack transport. Sir B. Mahon had therefore to readjust his transport to a pack scale, and was dependent on a railway of uncertain carrying power to convey back his guns and all wheeled traffic in case of a withdrawal, and to supply his troops whilst in Servia.

Very soon afterwards reinforcements commenced to arrive. The disembarkation of these new divisions was an operation which taxed the powers of organisation and resources of the staff at Salonika to the highest degree possible, and it speaks highly for their capacity that they were able to shelter and feed the troops as they arrived.

During November and the early part of December the 10th Division was holding its position in Servia, and the disembarkation of other divisions was proceeding with difficulty.

In order to gain time for the landing of the troops, and their deployment on the positions selected, I represented to General Sarrail and Sir B. Mahon the urgent need of the divisions withdrawing from Servia being utilised as a covering force, and retaining their ground as such until the Forces disembarking were thoroughly in a position to hold their front.

It had been evident for some time that the power of resistance of the Servian Armies was broken, and that the Allied Forces could afford them no material assistance. It was also clear from all information received that the position of our troops was becoming daily more precarious owing to a large German-Bulgarian concentration in the Strumniza Valley. I, therefore, again pressed General Sarrail to proceed with his withdrawal from the positions he was holding. The British Division operating as it was, as the pivot upon which the withdrawal was effected, was compelled to hold its ground until the French Left was brought back.

Before our withdrawal was completed the 10th Division was heavily attacked on the 6th, 7th, and 8th December, by superior Bulgarian Forces. The troops had suffered considerably from the cold in the Highlands of Macedonia, and in the circumstances conducted themselves very creditably in being able to extricate themselves from a difficult position with no great losses. The account of this action was reported by wire to you by General Mahon on the 11th December: no further reference is therefore necessary to this incident.

As soon as I was informed that the 10th Division was being heavily pressed, I directed Sir B. Mahon to send a Brigade up the railway line in support, and to hold another Brigade ready to proceed at short notice. The withdrawal was, however, conducted into Greek territory without further opposition from the Bulgarians.

Meanwhile, the operation of disembarkation at Salonika was being carried out with all possible speed, and the Greek Authorities through their representative from Athens, Colonel Pallis, were informed by me that we intended to proceed to the defensive line selected. This intimation was received in good part by the Greek Generals. They commenced to withdraw their troops further to the East where they did not hamper our plans, and they showed a disposition to meet our demands in a reasonable and friendly spirit.

Whilst dealing with the events above enumerated, I desire to give special prominence to the difficulties to which General Sir B. Mahon was exposed from the time of his landing at Salonika, and the ability which he displayed in overcoming them. The subjoined instances, selected from many which could be given, will illustrate my contention, and the high standard of administrative capacity displayed by the G.O.C. and his Staff:-

(*a*) From the date on which the 10th Division first proceeded into Servia until the date of its withdrawal across the Greek frontier, personnel, guns, supplies and material of all kinds had to be sent up by rail to Doiran, and onwards by march, motor lorries, limbered waggons and pack animals. This railway, moreover, was merely a single track, and had to serve the demands of the local population as well as our needs. The evacuation of the wounded and sick had to be arranged on similar lines, yet the requirements of the troops were fully satisfied.

(*b*) The majority of the Divisions were sent without trains to Salonika, most units without first line transport; in spite of this, part of the Force was converted into a mobile condition with very little delay.

(*c*) The complications presented by the distribution and checking of stores, supplies, ammunition, etc., discharged from ships on to quays, with insufficient accommodation or storehouses, and with crude means of ingress and egress therefrom, and served by a single road which was divided between the French and ourselves, constituted a problem which could only be solved by officers of high administrative powers. I trust, therefore, that full recognition may be given to my recommendation of the officers who rendered such fine service under such arduous conditions.

THE DARDANELLES ARMY.

On my arrival in the Mediterranean theatre a gratifying decline in the high rate of sickness which had prevailed in the Force during the summer months had become apparent. The wastage due to this cause still, however, remained very high.

The Corps Commanders were urged to take all advantage of the improved weather conditions to strengthen their positions by all available means, and to reduce to the last degree possible all animals not actually required for the maintenance of the troops, in order to relieve the strain imposed on the Naval Transport Service.

During the month of November, beyond the execution of very clever and successful minor enterprises carried out by Corps Commanders with a view to maintaining an offensive spirit in their commands, there remains little to record – except that an increased activity of the the Turkish artillery against our front became a noticeable factor.

On the 21st November the Peninsula was visited by a storm said to be nearly unprecedented for the time of the year. The storm was accompanied by torrential rain, which lasted for 24 hours. This was followed by hard frost and a heavy blizzard. In the areas of the 8th Corps and the Anzac Corps the effects were not felt to a very marked degree owing to the protection offered by the surrounding hills. The 9th Corps were less favourably situated, the water courses in this area became converted into surging rivers, which carried all before them. The water rose in many places to the height of the parapets and all means of communications were prevented. The men, drenched as they were by the rain, suffered from the subsequent blizzard most severely. Large numbers collapsed from exposure and exhaustion, and in spite of untiring efforts that were made to mitigate the suffering, I regret to announce that there were 200 deaths from exposure and over 10,000 sick evacuated during the first few days of December.

From reports given by deserters it is probable that the Turks suffered even to a greater degree. In this period our flimsy piers, breakwaters and light shipping became damaged by the storm to a degree which might have involved most serious consequences, and was a very potent indication of the dangers attached to the maintenance and supply of an army operating on a coast line with no harbour, and devoid of all the accessories such as wharves, piers, cranes and derricks for the discharge and distribution of stores, etc.

Towards the latter end of the month, having in view the possibility of an evacuation of the Peninsula being ordered, I directed Lieutenant-General Sir W. Birdwood, Commanding the Dardanelles Army, to prepare a scheme to this end, in order that all details should be ready in case of sanction being given to this operation.

I had in broad outline contemplated soon after my arrival on the Peninsula that an evacuation could best be conducted by a subdivision into three stages.

The first during which all troops, animals and supplies not required for a long campaign should be withdrawn.

The second to comprise the evacuation of all men, guns, animals and stores not required for defence during a period when the conditions of weather might retard the evacuation, or in fact seriously alter the programme contemplated.

The third or final stage, in which the troops on shore should be embarked with all possible speed, leaving behind such guns, animals and stores needed for military reasons at this period.

This problem with which we were confronted was the withdrawal of an army of a considerable size from positions in no cases more than 300 yards from the enemy's trenches, and its embarkation on open beaches, every part of which were within effective range of Turkish guns, and from which in winds from the south or south-west, the withdrawal of troops was not possible.

The attitude which we should adopt from a naval and military point of view in case of withdrawal from the Peninsula being ordered, had given me much anxious thought. According to text-book principles and the lessons to be gathered from history it seemed essential that this operation of evacuation should be immediately preceded by a combined naval and military feint in the vicinity of the Peninsula, with a view to distracting the attention of the Turks from our intention. When endeavouring to work out into concrete fact how such principles could be applied to the situation of our Forces, I came to the conclusion that our chances of success were infinitely more probable if we made no departure of any kind from the normal life which we were following both on sea and on land. A feint which did not fully fulfil its purpose would have been worse than useless, and there was the obvious danger that the suspicion of the Turks would be aroused by our adoption of a course, the real purport of which could not have been long disguised.

On the 8th December, consequent on your Lordship's orders, I directed the General Officer Commanding Dardanelles Army to proceed with the evacuation of Suvla and Anzac at once.

Rapidity of action was imperative, having in view the unsettled weather which might be expected in the Ægean. The success of our operations was entirely dependent on weather conditions. Even a mild wind from the south or south-west was found to raise such a ground swell as to greatly impede communication with the beaches, while anything in the nature of a gale from this direction could not fail to break up the piers, wreck the small craft, and thus definitely prevent any steps being taken towards withdrawal.

We had, moreover, during the gale of the 21st November, learnt how entirely we were at the mercy of the elements with the slender and inadequate means at our disposal by which we had endeavoured to improvise harbours and piers. On that day the harbour at Kephalos was completely wrecked, one of the ships which had been sunk to form a breakwater was broken up, and the whole of the small craft sheltered inside the breakwater were washed ashore. Similar damage was done to our piers, lighters and small craft at Suvla and Anzac.

Lieutenant-General Birdwood proceeded on receipt of his orders with the skill and promptitude which is characteristic of all that he undertakes, and after consultation with Rear-Admiral Wemyss, it was decided, provided the weather was propitious, to complete the evacuation on the night of the 19th–20th December.

Throughout the period 10th to 18th December the withdrawal proceeded under the most auspicious conditions, and the morning of the 18th December found the positions both at Anzac and Suvla reduced to the numbers deter-mined, while the evacuation of guns, animals, stores and supplies had con-tinued most satisfactorily.

The arrangements for the final withdrawal made by Corps Commanders were as follows:-

It was imperative, of course, that the front line trenches should be held, however lightly, until the very last moment and that the withdrawal from these trenches should be simultaneous throughout the line. To ensure this being done, Lieutenant-General Sir W. Birdwood arranged that the with-drawal of the inner flanks of corps should be conducted to a common embark-ing area under the orders of the G.O.C., 9th Corps.

In the rear of the front line trenches at Suvla the General Officer Com-manding 9th Corps broke up his area into two sections divided roughly by the Salt Lake. In the Southern Section a defensive line had been prepared from the Salt Lake to the Sea and Lala Baba had been prepared for defence, on the left the second line ran from Kara Kol Dagh through Hill 10 to the Salt Lake. These lines were only to be held in case of emergency – the principle govern-ing the withdrawal being that the troops should proceed direct from the trenches to the distributing centres near the Beach, and that no intermediate positions should be occupied except in case of necessity.

At Anzac, owing to the proximity of the trenches to the Beach, no second position was prepared except at Anzac Cove, where a small keep was arranged to cover the withdrawal of the rearmost parties in case of necessity.

The good fortune which had attended the evacuation continued during the night of the 19th–20th. The night was perfectly calm with a slight haze over the moon, an additional stroke of good luck, as there was a full moon on that night.

Soon after dark the covering ships were all in position, and the final withdrawal began. At 1.30 a.m. the withdrawal of the rear parties commenced from the front trenches at Suvla and the left of Anzac. Those on the right of Anzac who were nearer the Beach remained in position until 2 a.m. By 5.30 a.m. the last man had quitted the trenches.

At Anzac, 4 18-pounder guns, 2 5-inch howitzers, one 4.7 Naval gun, 1 anti-aircraft, and 2 3-pounder Hotchkiss guns were left, but they were destroyed before the troops finally embarked. In addition, 56 mules, a certain number of carts, mostly stripped of their wheels, and some supplies which were set on fire, were also abandoned.

At Suvla every gun, vehicle and animal was embarked, and all that remained was a small stock of supplies which were burnt.

Early in December orders had been issued for the withdrawal of the French troops on Helles, other than their artillery, and a portion of the line held by French Creoles had already been taken over by the Royal Naval Division on the 12th December. On the 21st December, having strengthened the 8th Corps with the 86th Brigade, the number of the French garrison doing duty on the Peninsula was reduced to 4,000 men. These it was hoped to relieve early in January, but before doing so it was necessary to give some respite from trench work to the 42nd Division, which was badly in need of a rest. My intention, therefore, was first to relieve the 42nd Division by the 88th Brigade, then to bring up the 13th Division, which was resting at Imbros since the evacuation of Suvla, in place of the 29th Division, and finally to bring up the 11th Division in relief of the French. The Helles would then be held by the 52nd, 11th and 13th Divisions, with the Royal Naval Division and the 42nd Division in reserve on adjacent islands.

On the 24th December, General Sir W. Birdwood was directed to make all preliminary preparations for immediate evacuation, in the event of orders to this effect being received.

On 28th December your Lordship's telegram ordering the evacuation of Helles was received, whereupon, in view of the possibility of bad weather intervening, I instructed the General Officer Commanding Dardanelles Army to complete the operation as rapidly as possible. He was reminded that every effort conditional on not exposing the personnel to undue risk should be made to save all 60-pounder and 18-pounder guns, 6-inch and 4.5 howitzers, with their ammunition and other accessories, such as mules and A.T. carts, limbered waggons, etc. In addition, I expressed my wish that the final evacuation should be completed in one night, and that the troops should withdraw direct from the front trenches to the beaches, and not occupy any intermediate position unless seriously molested. At a meeting which was attended by the Vice-Admiral and the General Officer Commanding Dardanelles Army, I explained the course which I thought we should adopt to again deceive the Turks as to our intentions.

The situation on the Peninsula had not materially changed owing to our withdrawal from Suvla and Anzac, except that there was a marked increased activity in aerial reconnaissance over our positions, and the islands of Mudros and Imbros, and that hostile patrolling of our trenches was more frequent and daring. The most apparent factor was that the number of heavy guns on the European and Asiatic shores had been considerably augmented, and that these guns were more liberally supplied with German ammunition, the result of which was that our beaches were continuously shelled, especially from the Asiatic shore. I gave it as my opinion that in my judgment I did not regard a feint as an operation offering any prospect of success. Time, the uncertainty of weather conditions in the Ægean, the absence of a suitable locality, and the withdrawal of small craft from the main issue for such an operation were some of the reasons which influenced me in the decision at which I arrived. With the concurrence of the Vice-Admiral, therefore, it was decided the Navy should do their utmost to pursue a course of retaliation against the Turkish Batteries, but to refrain from any unusually aggressive attitude should the Turkish guns remain quiescent.

General Sir W. Birdwood had, in anticipation of being ordered to evacuate Helles, made such complete and far-seeing arrangements that he was able to proceed without delay to the issue of the comprehensive orders which the consummation of such a delicate operation in war requires.

He primarily arranged with General Brulard, who commanded the French Forces on the Peninsula, that in order to escape the disadvantages of divided command in the final stage, the French Infantry should be relieved as early as possible, but that their artillery should pass under the orders of the General Officer Commanding 8th Corps, and be withdrawn concurrently with the British guns at the opportune moment.

On the 30th December, in consequence of the instructions I had received from the Chief of the General Staff to hand over my command at Alexandria to Lieutenant-General Sir A. Murray, who, it was stated, was to leave England on the 28th December, I broke up my Headquarters at Mudros and proceeded with a small staff, comprising representatives of the General Staff, the Quartermaster-General and Adjutant-General branches, on H.M.S. "Cornwallis" to Alexandria. The rest of the Staff were sent on in front so as to have offices in working order when my successor should arrive.

In the meantime the evacuation, following the same system as was practised at Suvla and Anzac, proceeded without delay. The French Infantry remaining on the Peninsula were relieved on the night of the 1st–2nd January, and were embarked by the French Navy on the following nights. Progress, however, was slower than had been hoped, owing to delays caused by accident and the weather. One of our largest horse ships was sunk by a French battleship, whereby the withdrawal was considerably retarded, and at the same time strong winds sprang up which interfered materially with work on the beaches. The character of the weather now setting in offered so little hope of a calm period of any duration, that General Sir W. Birdwood arranged with Admiral Sir J. de Robeck for the assistance of some Destroyers in order to accelerate the progress of re-embarkation. They then determined to fix the final stage of the evacuation for the 8th January, or for the first fine night after that date.

Meanwhile the 8th Corps had maintained the offensive spirit in bombing and minor operations with which they had established the moral superiority they enjoyed over the enemy. On the 29th December the 52nd Division completed the excellent work which they had been carrying out for so long by capturing a considerable portion of the Turkish trenches, and by successfully holding these in the face of repeated counter-attacks. The shelling of our trenches and beaches, however, increased in frequency and intensity, and the average daily casualties continued to increase.

The method of evacuation adopted by Lieutenant-General Sir F.J. Davies, K.C.B., Commanding 8th Corps, followed in general outline that which had proved successful in the Northern Zone. As the removal of the whole of the heavy guns capable of replying to the enemy's artillery would have indicated our intentions to the enemy, it was decided to retain, but eventually destroy, one 6-inch British gun and six French heavy guns of old pattern which it would be impossible to remove on the last night. General Brulard himself suggested the destruction of these French guns.

The first step taken as regards the withdrawal of the troops was the formation of a strong Embarkation Staff and the preparation of positions covering the landings, in which small garrisons could maintain themselves against attack for a short time should the enemy become aware of our intention and follow up the movement.

Major-General the Hon. H.A. Lawrence, commanding the 52nd Division, was selected to take charge of all embarkation operations. At the same time the services of various staff officers were placed at the disposal of the General Officer Commanding, 8th Corps, and they rendered very valuable assistance.

The General Officer Commanding, 13th Division, selected and prepared a position covering Gully Beach. Other lines were selected and entrenched, covering the remainder of the beaches from the sea north of Sedd-el-Bahr to "X" Beach inclusive. Garrisons were detailed for these defences, those at Gully Beach being under the General Officer Commanding, 13th Division, and those covering the remainder of the beaches being placed under the command of a selected Officer, whose headquarters were established at an early date, together with those of the General Officer Commanding Embarkation, at Corps Headquarters.

As the withdrawing troops passed within the line of these defences they came under the orders of the General Officer Commanding, Embarkation, which were conveyed to them by his staff officers at each beach.

In addition to these beach defences four lines of defence were arranged, three being already in existence and strongly wired. The fourth was a line of posts extending from De Tott's Battery on the east to the position covering Gully Beach on the west.

The time fixed for the last parties to leave the front trenches was 11.45 p.m., in order to permit the majority of the troops being already embarked before the front line was vacated. It was calculated that it would take between two and three hours for them to reach the beaches, at the conclusion of which time the craft to embark them would be ready.

The Naval arrangements for embarkation were placed in the hands of Captain C.M. Staveley, R.N., assisted by a staff of Naval officers at each place of embarkation.

On the 7th January the enemy developed heavy artillery fire on the trenches held by the 13th Division, while the Asiatic guns shelled those occupied by the Royal Naval Division. The bombardment, which was reported to be the heaviest experienced since we landed in April, lasted from noon until 5 p.m., and was intensive between 3 p.m. and 3.30. Considerable damage was done to our parapets and communication trenches, and telephone communications were interrupted. At 3.30 p.m. two Turkish mines were sprung near Fusilier Bluff, and the Turkish trenches were seen to be full of men whom their officers appeared to be urging to the assault. No attack, however, was developed except against Fusilier Bluff, where a half-hearted assault was quickly repulsed. Our shortage of artillery at this time was amply compensated for by the support received from fire of the supporting squadron under Captain D.L. Dent, R.N. Our casualties amounted to 2 officers and 56 other ranks killed, and 4 officers and 102 other ranks wounded.

The 8th January was a bright, calm day, with a light breeze from the south. There was every indication of the continuance of favourable conditions, and, in the opinion of the Meteorological Officer, no important change was to be expected for at least 24 hours. The Turkish artillery were unusually inactive. All preparations for the execution of the final stage were complete.

The embarkation was fixed at such an hour that the troops detailed for the first trip might be able to leave their positions after dark. The second trip was timed so that at least a greater portion of the troops for this trip would, if all went well, be embarked before the final parties had left the front trenches. The numbers to be embarked at the first trip were fixed by the maximum that could be carried by the craft available, those of the second trip being reduced in order to provide for the possibility of casualties occurring amongst the craft required to carry them.

The numbers for the third trip consisted only of the parties left to hold front trenches to the last, together with the garrisons of the beach defences, the Naval and Military beach personnel and such R.E. personnel as might be required to effect the necessary repairs to any piers or harbour works that might be damaged.

About 7 p.m. the breeze freshened considerably from the south-west, the most unfavourable quarter, but the first trip, timed for 8 p.m., was despatched without difficulty. The wind, however, continued to rise until, by 11 p.m., the connecting pier between the hulks and the shore at "W" Beach was washed away by heavy seas, and further embarkation into destroyers from these hulks became impracticable. In spite of these difficulties the second trips, which commenced at 11.30 p.m., were carried out well up to time, and the embarkation of guns continued uninterruptedly. Early in the evening reports had been received from the right flank that a hostile submarine was believed to be moving down the Straits, and about midnight H.M.S. "Prince George," which had embarked 2,000 men, and was sailing for Mudros, reported she was struck by a torpedo which failed to explode. The indications of the presence of a submarine added considerably to the anxiety for the safety of the troop carriers, and made it necessary for the Vice-Admiral to modify the arrangements made for the subsequent bombardment of the evacuated positions.

At 1.50 a.m., Gully Beach reported that the embarkation at that beach was complete, and that the lighters were about to push off, but at 2.10 a.m. a telephone message was received that one of the lighters was aground and could not be refloated. The N.T.O. at once took all possible steps to have another lighter sent in to Gully Beach, and this was, as a matter of fact, done within an hour, but in the meantime at 2.30 a.m. it was decided to move the 160 men, who had been relanded from the grounded lighter, to "W" Beach and embark them there.

From 2.40 a.m. the steadily increasing swell caused the N.T.O. the greatest anxiety as to the possibility of embarking the remainder of the troops if their arrival was much deferred.

At 3.30 a.m. the evacuation was complete, and abandoned heaps of stores and supplies were successfully set on fire by time fuzes after the last man had embarked. Two magazines of ammunition and explosives were also successfully blown up at 4 a.m. These conflagrations were apparently the first intimation received by the Turks that we had withdrawn. Red lights were immediately discharged from the enemy's trenches, and heavy artillery fire opened on our trenches and beaches. This shelling was maintained until about 6.30 a.m.

Apart from four unserviceable fifteen pounders which had been destroyed earlier in the month, 10 worn-out fifteen-pounders, 1 six inch Mark VII. gun, and 6 old heavy French guns, all of which were previously blown up, were left on the Peninsula. In addition to the above, 508 animals, most of which were destroyed, and a number of vehicles and considerable quantities of stores, material, and supplies, all of which were destroyed by burning, had to be abandoned.

It would have been possible, of course, by extending the period during which the process of evacuation proceeded to have reduced the quantity of stores and material that was left behind on the Peninsula, but not to the degree that may seem apparent at first sight. Our chances of enjoying a continuity of fine weather in the Ægean were very slender in the month of January; it was indeed a contingency that had to be reckoned with that we might very probably be visited by a spell of bad weather which would cut us off completely from the Peninsula for a fortnight or perhaps for even longer.

Supplies, ammunition and material to a certain degree had therefore to be left to the last moment for fear of the isolation of the garrison at any moment when the evacuation might be in progress. I decided therefore that our aim should be primarily the withdrawal of the bulk of the personnel, artillery and ammunition in the intermediate period, and that no risks should be taken in prolonging the withdrawal of personnel at the final stage with a view to reducing the quantity of stores left.

The entire evacuation of the Peninsula had now been completed. It demanded for its successful realisation two important military essentials, viz., good luck and skilled disciplined organisation, and they were both forthcoming to a marked degree at the hour needed. Our luck was in the ascendant by the marvellous spell of calm weather which prevailed. But we were able to turn to the fullest advantage these accidents of fortune.

Lieutenant-General Sir W. Birdwood and his Corps Commanders elaborated and prepared the orders in reference to the evacuation with a skill, competence and courage which could not have been surpassed, and we had a further stroke of good fortune in being associated with Vice-Admiral Sir J. de Robeck, K.C.B., Vice-Admiral Wemyss, and a body of Naval Officers whose work remained throughout this anxious period at that standard of accuracy and professional ability which is beyond the power of criticism or cavil.

The Line of Communication Staff, both Naval and Military, represented respectively by Lieutenant-General E.A. Altham, C.B., C.M.G., Commodore M.S. FitzMaurice, R.N., principal Naval Transport Officer, and Captain H.V. Simpson, R.N., Superintending Transport Officer, contributed to the success of the operation by their untiring zeal and conspicuous ability.

The members of the Headquarters Staff showed themselves, without exception, to be officers with whom it was a privilege to be associated; their competence, zeal and devotion to duty were uniform and unbroken. Amongst such a highly trained body of officers it is difficult to select and discriminate. I confine myself, therefore, to placing on record the fine services rendered by-

Colonel (temporary Major-General) Arthur Lynden Lynden-Bell, C.B., C.M.G., Chief of General Staff, G.H.Q.;

Colonel (temporary Major-General) Walter Campbell, C.B., D.S.O., Deputy Quartermaster-General, G.H.Q., M.E.F.;

Lieutenant-Colonel (temporary Brigadier-General) W. Gillman, C.M.G., D.S.O., Brigadier-General, General Staff;

Brevet Major (temporary Lieutenant-Colonel) G.P. Dawnay, D.S.O., M.V.O., General Staff;

and whilst bringing to notice the names of these officers to whom I am so much indebted, I trust I may be permitted to represent the loyal, cordial, and unswerving assistance rendered by General J.M.J.A. Brulard, Commanding the French Troops in the Peninsula.

Before concluding this inadequate account of the events which happened during my tenure of command of the Forces in the Eastern Mediterranean, I desire to give a brief explanation of the work which was carried out on the

Line of Communications, and to place on record my appreciation of the admirable work rendered by the officers responsible for this important service.

On the Dardanelles Peninsula it may be said that the whole of the machinery by which the text-books contemplate the maintenance and supply of an army was non-existent. The zone commanded by the enemy's guns extended not only to the landing places on the Peninsula, but even over the sea in the vicinity.

The beaches were the advanced depôts and refilling points at which the services of supply had to be carried out under artillery fire. The landing of stores as well as of troops was only possible under cover of darkness.

The sea, the ships, lighters and tugs took, in fact, the place of railways and roads, with their railway trains, mechanical transport, etc., but with this difference, that the use of the latter is subject only to the intervention of the enemy, while that of the former was dependent on the weather.

Between the beaches and the Base at Alexandria, 800 miles to the south, the Line of Communications had but two harbours, Kephalos Bay on the island of Imbros, 15 miles roughly from the beaches, and Mudros Bay, at a distance of 60 miles. In neither were there any piers, breakwaters, wharves or store houses of any description before the advent of the troops. On the shores of these two bays there were no roads of any military value, or buildings fit for military usage. The water supply at these islands was, until developed, totally inadequate for our needs.

The Peninsula landing places were open beaches. Kephalos Bay is without protection from the north, and swept by a high sea in northerly gales. In Mudros Harbour, trans-shipments and disembarkations were often seriously impeded with a wind from the north or south. These difficulties were accentuated by the advent of submarines in the Ægean Sea, on account of which the Vice-Admiral deemed it necessary to prohibit any transport or store ship exceeding 1,500 tons proceeding north of Mudros, and although this rule was relaxed in the case of supply ships proceeding within the netted area of Suvla, it necessitated the trans-shipment of practically all reinforcements, stores and supplies – other than those for Suvla – into small ships in Mudros Harbour.

At Suvla and Anzac, disembarkation could only be effected by lighters and tugs, thus for all personnel and material there was at least one trans-shipment, and for the greater portion of both two trans-shipments.

Yet notwithstanding the difficulties which have been set forth above, the Army was well maintained in equipment and ammunition. It was well fed, it received its full supply of winter clothing at the beginning of December. The evacuation of the sick and wounded was carried out with the minimum of inconvenience, and the provision of hospital accommodation for them on the

Dardanelles Line of Communication and elsewhere in the Mediterranean met all requirements.

The above is a very brief exposition of the extreme difficulties with which the officers responsible were confronted in dealing with a problem of peculiar complexity. They were fortunate in being associated in their onerous and anxious task with a most competent and highly trained Naval Staff. The members of the two Staffs worked throughout in perfect harmony and cordiality, and it was owing to their joint efforts that the requirements of the troops were so well responded to.

In accordance with the instructions received from your Lordship by telegram on 10/1/16, I had the honour of telegraphing the names of the undermentioned Officers who rendered most valuable and distinguished service in connection with the evacuation of Gallipoli, to be specially submitted for His Majesty's gracious consideration for promotion and reward, viz.:-

Colonel (temporary Major-General) Arthur Lynden Lynden-Bell, C.B., C.M.G., Chief of General Staff, G.H.Q., M.E.F.

Colonel (temporary Major-General) Walter Campbell, C.B., D.S.O., Deputy Quartermaster-General, G.H.Q., M.E.F.

Lieutenant-General Sir William Riddell Birdwood, K.C.S.I., K.C.M.G., C.B., C.I.E., D.S.O., Commander, Dardanelles Army.

Major-General (temporary Lieutenant-General) Edward Altham Altham, C.B., C.M.G., Inspector-General of Communications, M.E.F.

Major-General (temporary Lieutenant-General) Hon. Sir Julian Hedworth George Byng, K.C.M.G., C.B., M.V.O., Commander, 9th Army Corps.

Major-General (temporary Lieutenant-General) Sir Alexander John Godley, K.C.M.G., C.B., Commander, A. and N.Z. Army Corps.

Major-General (temporary Lieutenant-General) Sir Francis John Davies, K.C.B., Commander, 8th Army Corps.

Brevet Colonel (temporary Brigadier-General) George Fletcher MacMunn, D.S.O., R.A., D.A. and Q.M.G., Dardanelles Army.

Lieutenant-Colonel (temporary Brigadier-General) Hamilton Lyster Reed, V.C. C.M.G., R.A., Brigadier-General, General Staff, 9th Army Corps.

Lieutenant-Colonel (temporary Brigadier-General) Cyril Brudenel Bingham White, R.A., D.S.O., Brigadier-General, General Staff, Anzac.

Colonel (temporary Brigadier-General) Robert John Tudway, C.B., D.S.O., D.A. and Q.M.G., 8th Army Corps.

Brevet Colonel (temporary Brigadier-General) Harold Edward Street, R.A., Brigadier-General, General Staff, 8th Army Corps.

Major (temporary Brigadier-General) Arthur George Preston McNalty, A.S.C., Acting D.A. and Q.M.G., 9th Army Corps.

Major (temporary Lieutenant-Colonel) Cecil Faber Aspinall, Royal Munster Fusiliers, Acting Brigadier-General, General Staff, Dardanelles Army.

ROYAL NAVY.

Captain F.H. Mitchell, D.S.O., R.N., Naval Adviser at G.H.Q., M.E.F.

Captain Edwin Unwin, R.N., V.C., attached to Headquarters, Dardanelles Army.

FRENCH ARMY.

J.M.J.A. Brulard, Général de Division, Grand Officier de la Legion d'Honneur.

In the course of a few days I propose to forward recommendations for gallant and distinguished conduct performed by officers and men in the period under reference.

I have the honour to be,
Your Lordship's most obedient Servant,
C.C. MONRO,
General.

8

SIR JOHN DE ROBECK'S
EVACUATION DESPATCH,
22 DECEMBER 1915

WEDNESDAY, 11 APRIL, 1917.

Admiralty, 11th April, 1917.

The following despatches from Vice-Admiral Sir John M. de Robeck, K.C.B., late Vice-Admiral Commanding the Eastern Mediterranean Squadron, and Vice-Admiral Sir Rosslyn E. Wemyss, K.C.B., K.C.M.G., M.V.O., late Senior Naval Officer, Mudros, describe the naval operations in connection with the withdrawal of the Army from the Gallipoli Peninsula:-

SIR,-

"Lord Nelson" at Mudros,
22nd December, 1915.

Be pleased to lay before the Lords Commissioners of the Admiralty the following report on the operations connected with the evacuation of the positions at Suvla and Anzac.

The evacuation was carried out in three stages, as follows:-

(*a*) A *Preliminary Stage.*
During this stage all personnel, animals, and vehicles not necessary for a winter campaign were removed. This necessitated no special arrangements, and was completed by the date on which definite orders to evacuate Suvla and Anzac were received.

(*b*) An *Intermediate Stage.*
During this stage all personnel, guns, and animals which were not absolutely necessary for the defence of the positions in the event of an enemy attack at the last moment were removed. This also was carried out without special arrangements beyond the withdrawal of increased amounts of material each night.

(*c*) *Final Stage.*
Special and detailed orders were necessary for the operations of this stage, which had to be completed in thirty-six hours, and which included the embarkation of all personnel remaining, and of all guns and animals not previously withdrawn.

The principle decided upon for all three stages was secrecy and the attempt to take the enemy entirely by surprise. It was hoped that he would ascribe any unusual activity, if observed, to the preparation for an attack. Every effort was therefore made during the whole of the operations to maintain the beaches, offing, etc., in their usual appearance, and all embarkations were carried out during the dark hours. The increase in the number of motor lighters, boats, etc., in use at the beaches was hidden as far as possible during the daytime.

The preliminary stage was completed satisfactorily by the 10th December, when the definite orders to evacuate were received.

It had been computed that ten nights would be required for the intermediate stage, on each of which three thousand personnel and a proportion of guns and animals would be embarked from each beach. This estimate was eventually reduced, special efforts being made in order to take advantage of the fine weather, the duration of which could not be relied on at this season.

The intermediate stage was completed on the night of the 17th/18th December, and, from the absence of any unusual shelling of the beaches during these nights, it was apparent that the enemy had no idea of the movement in progress.

Some forty-four thousand personnel, nearly 200 guns, numerous wagons, and 3,000 animals, were evacuated during this period, together with a large amount of stores and ammunition.

The final stage commenced on the night of the 18th/19th December, and was completed on the night of the 19th/20th December. The fixing of the date for this stage had been a question of some discussion. On the one hand, it was deemed most advisable that the operation should be carried on with the utmost despatch and without loss of time for fear of the weather breaking; on the other hand, the moon on the 18th was very near its full. It was considered, however, that this fact might not altogether be a disadvantage, as the benefit accruing to us would probably counteract any advantage gained by the enemy. The weather conditions, however, proved to be ideal. An absolutely smooth sea, no wind, and a cloudy sky caused grey nights which were of the utmost benefit to the work on the beaches, and were apparently not sufficiently light to enable the enemy to get an idea of what was taking place.

On each of the two nights of the final stage it was necessary to evacuate rather more than ten thousand personnel from each beach, and for this special arrangement were necessary. The chief possible difficulties to contend with were two:- Firstly, the bad weather to be expected at this season; secondly, interference by the enemy.

After some heavy winds, fine weather set in with December, and, except for a strong north-easterly wind on the 15th, continued until 24 hours after the completion of the evacuation. This prolonged period of fine weather alone made possible the success which attended the operation. It enabled light piers, and improvements of a temporary nature to existing piers, to be carried out. A southerly wind of even moderate force at any time during this period must have wrecked piers, and have caused very considerable losses among the small craft assembled for the operations, and would have necessitated the embarkation being carried out from the open beaches. Such loss of small craft would have made anything in the nature of rapid evacuation an impossibility, and would have enormously increased the difficulties. To cope with such an eventuality a reserve of small craft up to 50 per cent, would not have been too great; actually the reserve maintained had to be very much smaller.

Interference by the enemy would have been most serious, as the beaches were fully exposed to shell fire, and the damage inflicted to personnel, small craft, piers, &c., might have been most serious, as he would have had no inducement to husband his ammunition.

Under such conditions it was most improbable that anything beyond personnel could have been evacuated. Casualties would also have been heavy, and removal of wounded out of the question. To meet the latter possibility, arrangements were made to leave the hospital clearing stations intact, with a proportion of medical staff in attendance, and thus ensure that our wounded would not suffer from want of attention, which the enemy, with all the good will in the world, might have been unable to supply. It was also arranged that in such circumstances an attempt would have been made to negotiate an armistice on the morning after the evacuation to collect and, if possible, bring off our wounded. Fortunately neither of these two dangers matured, but the probability of either or both doing so made this stage of the operations most anxious for all concerned.

The final concentration of the ships and craft required at Kephalo was completed on the 17th December, and in order to prevent enemy's aircraft observing the unusual quantity of shipping, a constant air patrol was maintained to keep these at a distance.

Reports of the presence of enemy submarines were also received during these two days: patrols were strengthened, but no attacks by these craft were made.

The evacuation was carried out in accordance with orders. No delays occurred, and there were no accidents to ships or boats.

On the night of the 18th/19th December, when I embarked in H.M.S. "Arno," accompanied by General Sir William Birdwood, the embarkation was finished at Suvla by 3 a.m., and at Anzac by 5.30 a.m., and by daylight the beaches and anchorages at these places had resumed their normal aspect.

The second night's operations, as far as the Navy was concerned, differed in no wise from the first; precisely the same routine being adhered to. The weather conditions were similar and could not have suited our purpose better.

On this night I hoisted my flag in H.M.S. "Chatham," and was accompanied by General Sir William Birdwood and members of our two Staffs.

The last troops left the front trenches at 1.30 a.m., and I received the signal that the evacuation was complete at 4.15 a.m. at Anzac and 5.39 a.m. at Suvla.

A large mine was exploded at about 3.15 a.m. by the Australians, and at Suvla all perishable stores which had not been taken off and which were heaped up in large mounds with petrol poured over them, were fired at 4 a.m., making a vast bonfire which lighted everything round for a very long distance.

In spite of all this, the enemy seemed perfectly unaware of what had taken place. As day dawned, soon after 6.30, the anchorages of both places were clear of all craft, except the covering Squadrons, which had been ordered up during the night, and when the sun had sufficiently risen for objects to be made out, the bombardment of the beaches commenced with the object of destroying everything that remained. At Suvla this consisted only of some water tanks and four motor lighters, which, I regret to say, had been washed ashore in the gale of 28th of November and had never been recovered, owing principally to lack of time. At Anzac it had been deemed inadvisable to set a light to the stores which had been found impossible to embark, so that here the bombardment was more severe and large fires were started by the bursting shell.

A curious spectacle now presented itself, certain areas absolutely clear of troops being subjected to a heavy shell fire from our own and the enemy's guns.

It seems incredible that all this work had taken place without the enemy becoming aware of our object, for although the utmost care was taken to preserve the beaches and offing as near as possible normal, yet it proved quite impracticable to get up boats and troop carriers in sufficient time to carry out the night's work, and yet for them not to have been visible from some parts of the Peninsula.

The morning bombardment lasted but a very short time, for I felt that the use of much ammunition would merely be a waste; moreover the risk of submarines appearing on the scene of action had never been absent from my mind at any time during the whole operation. Consequently at 7.25 a.m., I ordered the Squadron to return to Kephalo, leaving two specially protected cruisers to watch the area. These subsequently reported that they had caused a good deal of damage amongst the enemy when they eventually swarmed down to take possession of the loot, the realisation of which, I trust, was a great disappointment to them.

All the arrangements were most admirably carried out, and the time table previously laid down was adhered to exactly.

Before closing this despatch, I would like to emphasise the fact that what made this operation so successful, apart from the kindness of the weather and of the enemy, was the hearty co-operation of both services. The evacuation forms an excellent example of the cordial manner in which the Navy and Army have worked together during these last eight months.

For the Army the evacuation was an operation of great probable danger, shared by the naval beach personnel; it was also, specially for the former, one of considerable sadness. Throughout the whole proceedings nothing could have exceeded the courtesy of Generals Sir William Birdwood, Sir Julian Byng, and Sir Alexander Godley, and their respective Staffs, and this attitude was typical of the whole Army. The traditions of the Navy were fully maintained, the seamanship and resource displayed reaching a very high standard. From the Commanding Officers of men-of-war, transports, and large supply ships, to the Midshipmen in charge of steamboats and pulling boats off the beaches, all did well.

> I am, Sir,
> Your obedient Servant,
> R.E. WEMYSS.

"Lord Nelson,"
SIR,- *26th January*, 1916.
I have the honour to forward the following despatch dealing with the withdrawal of the Army from the Gallipoli Peninsula.

In considering the evacuation of the Helles position it was laid down by Sir Charles Monro, for the guidance of the Army, that-

(*a*) The withdrawal should be conducted with the utmost rapidity, the final stage being limited to one night.

(*b*) Every effort should be made to improve embarkation facilities at as many points on the coast as could be used, other than W and V beaches.

(*c*) Every endeavour should be made to evacuate as many as possible of the following:-

British:
18-pdr. guns.
4.5-inch howitzers.
60-pdr. guns.
6-inch guns.

French:
75 mm. guns.
Heavy guns.

Also artillery ammunition and such small-arm ammunition as could safely be withdrawn before the final stage.

(*d*) The period of time which must elapse before the final stage could be undertaken would be determined by the time required to collect necessary shipping and to make essential preparations ashore (work on beaches, pathways, &c.) taken in conjunction with the necessity for evacuating the superfluous personnel and as much as possible of the material mentioned in (c).
(*e*) During the "intermediate stage" the duration of which would be determined by the foregoing considerations, such other animals, material, stores and supplies as could be embarked without prolonging this period would also be evacuated.

Forty-eight hours before the evacuation was completed the number of men remaining on the peninsula was to be cut down to 22,000.

Of these 7,000 were to embark on the last night but one, leaving 15,000 for the final night; at the request of the military the latter number was increased to 17,000.

As few guns as possible were to be left to the final night and arrangements were made to destroy any of these which it might be found impossible to remove or which, by reason of their condition, were considered not worth removing.

The original intention was to use Gully, "X," "W" and "V" beaches for the embarkation of troops on the final night; this was deemed advisable in consequence of the very accurate and heavy fire which the enemy could bring to bear on "W" and "V" beaches, on to both of which their guns were carefully registered.

The decision not to use "X" beach and to use Gully beach only to embark the last 700 men was arrived at on the 6th January.

This alteration of plan was recommended by General Sir Francis Davies, commanding the 8th Corps; he based his objections to the use of "X" and Gully beaches to:-

(*a*) The probability of bad weather. Embarkation from these beaches, even in a moderately strong northerly blow, was impossible.
(*b*) "X" and Gully beaches had not been used for a considerable time as landing places; and should the movements of ships and boats off the beaches be observed by the enemy, it might awaken their suspicions as to what was taking place.

The essence of the operation being secrecy, the second of these reasons decided me to concur in this change of plan almost at the eleventh hour.

The preliminary stage commenced on the night of the 30th/31st December and terminated on the night of the 7th/8th January.

During this stage all personnel except 17,000 were removed, as well as the majority of the guns and a great quantity of animals, stores, &c.

The amount of stores remaining, on shore after the preliminary stage was greater than was anticipated or intended; this was almost entirely due to the unfavourable weather conditions and, as men were evacuated, to a shortage in working parties.

On 1st January the weather showed signs of breaking; on the 2nd and 3rd strong north-easterly winds blew all day; the morning of the 4th was calm, but the weather broke at 7 p.m. and by 11 p.m. it was blowing a gale from the N.E., which, however, moderated on the evening of the 5th; on the 6th and 7th the weather conditions were favourable.

Fortunately the wind remained in the north to north-east which permitted work to continue on "V" and "W" beaches. The transfer of guns, animals and stores, &c., from motor lighters to transports and supply ships lying off the beaches was a matter of great difficulty under such conditions of weather.

During the whole of this period "V" and "W" beaches were subjected to a heavy and accurate shell fire from the enemy's batteries mounted on the Asiatic shore and also from guns firing from positions to north of Achi Baba.

All these guns were accurately registered on to the beaches, and the shelling continued day and night at frequent and uncertain intervals; that the actual loss of life from this fire was very small borders on the miraculous; the beach parties were completely exposed, and piers and foreshore constantly hit by shells while officers and men were working on them; even when resting in the dug-outs security from enemy's fire could not be assured, and several casualties occurred under these conditions.

The work on the beaches was practically continuous; during the day time motor lighters, &c., were loaded up with stores, &c., to be transferred to store ships at night; by night the work was most strenuous.

During the whole time there remained the paramount necessity of preventing the enemy gaining intelligence of what was in progress; this added greatly to the difficulties of work during daylight. Enemy aircraft paid frequent visits to the peninsula; on these occasions, whilst the "Taube" was in evidence, animals and transports approaching the beaches were turned and marched in the opposite direction, and stores and horses already in lighters were even unloaded on to the beaches to give the appearance of a disembarkation.

On the afternoon of the 7th the enemy delivered a very heavy artillery attack against certain portions of our advanced position, probably the most intense bombardment our trenches in the Helles area have ever been subjected to.

Attempts were made by the enemy to follow up this bombardment by an infantry attack, but the few Turks who could be persuaded to quit their trenches were instantly shot down, and the infantry advance was a complete failure.

This bombardment and attack most fortunately took place at a time when our forward position was fully manned and when there were still about sixty guns in position on the peninsula, with a very large supply of ammunition.

The ships supporting the left flank opened a heavy fire on the Turkish position. H.M.S. "Grafton" (Captain Henry E. Grace), H.M.S. "Raglan" (Captain Cecil D.S. Raikes), and H.M. Destroyer "Wolverine" (Lieutenant-Commander Adrian St. V. Keyes), were on duty in position to support the army, which they did most ably, undoubtedly inflicting heavy loss on the enemy. They were reinforced by H.M.S. "Russell," H.M.S. "Havelock," and H.M. Destroyer "Scorpion."

Arrangements were also made to reinforce Helles with one brigade of infantry from Imbros, should such a step become necessary.

The principal reasons the enemy did not discover that the evacuation was taking place were, I consider: -

(a) The excellent arrangements made by the military and the beach parties to prevent the enemy noticing any change in the landscape or any undue activity on the beaches.

(b) The probable unexpected force encountered in their attack on the 7th. It appears reasonable to suppose that the enemy, having thus convinced himself that the peninsula was still held in force by us, was satisfied that no evacuation would take place for some days.

(c) The fact that on the 8th the wind was in the south and blowing on to "W" and "V" beaches, and that by 9 p.m. it had freshened so considerably as to render any evacuation a most difficult and hazardous proceeding.

The enemy were certainly deceived as to the date of our final departure from his shores, and his artillery fire on the final night of the evacuation was negligible.

The decision arrived at on the 6th to evacuate practically all the personnel of the final night from "W" and "V" beaches necessitated some rearrangement of plans, as some 5,000 additional troops had to be embarked from these beaches.

To use motor lighters from the already crowded piers would have lengthened the operation very considerably, and it was therefore decided to employ destroyers to embark 5,200 men from the blockships, which were fitted with stagings and connected to the shore; thus existing arrangements would be interfered with as little as possible. The result was excellent. The destroyers which were laid alongside the blockships, in spite of a nasty sea, being handled with great skill by their commanding officers, once more showing their powers of adaptability.

The necessary amendments to orders were issued on the morning of the 7th, and, in spite of the short notice given, the naval operations on the night of the 8th/9th were carried out without confusion or delay, a fact which reflects great credit on all concerned, especially on the beach personnel, who were chiefly affected by the change of plan.

On the 8th January the weather was favourable except that the wind was from the south; this showed no signs of freshening at 5 p.m., and orders were given to carry out the final stage.

The actual embarkation on the 8th commenced at 8 p.m., and the last section were to commence embarking at 6.30 a.m.

By 9 p.m. the wind had freshened considerably, still blowing from the south; a slight sea got up, and caused much inconvenience on the beaches.

A floating bridge at "W" beach commenced to break up, necessitating arrangements being made to ferry the last section of the personnel to the waiting destroyers.

At Gully beach matters were worse, and, after a portion of the 700 troops had been embarked in motor lighters and sent off to H.M.S. "Talbot," it was found impossible to continue using this beach (one motor lighter was already badly on shore – she was subsequently destroyed by gunfire), and orders were given for the remainder of the Gully beach party to embark from "W" beach; this was done without confusion, special steps having been taken by the beachmaster to cope with such an eventuality.

After a temporary lull the wind again increased, and by 3 a.m. a very nasty sea was running into "W" beach.

It was only by the great skill and determination displayed by the beach personnel that the embarkation was brought to a successful conclusion, and all the small craft except one steamboat (damaged in collision) got away in safety.

The last troops were leaving at 3.45 a.m., after which the beach personnel embarked.

Great difficulty was experienced in getting the last motor lighters away, owing to the heavy seas running into the harbour.

This was unfortunate, as the piles of stores which it had been found impossible to take off, and which were prepared for burning, were lit perhaps rather sooner than was necessary, as were also the fuses leading to the magazine.

The latter blew up before all the boats were clear, and, I regret to report, caused the death of one of the crew of the hospital barge, which was amongst the last boats to leave.

It was fortunate that more casualties were not caused by the explosion, debris from which fell over and around a great many boats.

The success of the operations was due principally to-

(a) Excellent staff work.

(b) The untiring energy and skill displayed by officers and men, both Army and Navy, comprising the beach parties.

(c) The good seamanship and zeal of the officers and crews of the various craft employed in the evacuation of the troops.

(d) The excellent punctuality of the Army in the arrival of the troops for embarkation at the different beaches.

The Navy has especially to thank Generals Sir William Birdwood and Sir Francis Davies for their forethought and hearty co-operation in all matters.

The staff work was above reproach, and I hope I may be permitted to mention some of those military officers who rendered special assistance to the Navy. They are:-

Major-General the Hon. H.A. Lawrence,
Brigadier-General H.E. Street, and
Colonel A.B. Carey, R.E.

the latter of whom performed work of inestimable value in the last few days by improving piers and preparing means of rapid embarkation from the block-ships.

The programme and plans as regards the naval portion of the operations were due to the work of my chief of staff, Commodore Roger J.B. Keyes, to whom too great credit cannot be given; to Captain Francis H. Mitchell, R.N., attached to General Headquarters; Major William W. Godfrey, R.M.L.I., of my staff; Captain Cecil M Staveley (principal beach master at Cape Helles); Captain Henry F.G. Talbot, in charge of the vessels taking part; and Acting Commander George F.A. Mulock (chief assistant to Captain Staveley).

The organisation of the communications, on which so much depended, was very ably carried out by my Fleet Wireless Officer (Commander James F. Somerville) and my Signal Officer (Lieutenant Hugh S. Bowlby). The arrangement by which H.M.S. "Triad" (on board of which was the General Officer commanding Helles Army) was anchored close in under Cape Tekeh, and connected with the shore telephone system by two cables, thus leaving her wireless installation free for communicating with the ships of covering squadron, &c., was especially good.

The naval covering squadron was under the command of Rear-Admiral Sydney R. Fremantle in H.M.S. "Hibernia," who had a most able colleague in

Captain Douglas L. Dent, of H.M.S. "Edgar," whose ability had done so much to improve the naval gun support to the Helles Army.

The work of this squadron was conducted with great energy, and was in every way satisfactory. It controlled to a great extent the enemy's guns firing on to the beaches. Whenever the enemy opened fire, whether by day or night, there were always ships in position to reply, a result which reflects much credit on the officers named.

The Army Headquarters gave us again the invaluable assistance and experience of Lieutenant-Colonel C.F. Aspinall in arranging details, and I cannot help laying special stress on this officer's excellent co-operation with my staff on all occasions.

I now have the pleasure of bringing to your notice the loyal support and assistance we received, now, as always, from our French friends.

Contre Admiral de Bon was responsible for the French naval programme of evacuation, and on its completion he rendered us every assistance with his beach parties, who were under the immediate command of a most able and gallant officer – Capitaine de Frégate Bréart de Boisanger – an officer whom I have already brought to your Lordships' notice in a previous despatch.

There are many officers and men who have performed meritorious service in connection with this evacuation; their names will be forwarded in due course in a separate letter.

I have the honour to be,
Sir,
Your obedient Servant,
J.M. DE ROBECK,
Vice-Admiral.

Admiralty, 11th April, 1917.

In addition to the honours notified in the Supplements to the London Gazette dated 14th March, 15th May (3rd Supplement), and 31st May, 1916 (3rd Supplement), The KING has been graciously pleased to give orders for the following appointment to the Distinguished Service Order and for the award of the Distinguished Service Cross to the undermentioned officers, in recognition of their services in the Eastern Mediterranean up to the 30th June, 1916:-

To be Companion of the Distinguished Service Order.
Captain Alexander V. Campbell, M.V.O., R.N.
Performed meritorious service whilst in command of H.M.S. "Prince George," which took part in the actions of 25th February and 18th March, 1915. "Prince George" supported the Army from inside the Straits

between 25th April and 10th May, 1915, and also at Suvla for several weeks continuously under fire. Captain Campbell also did good service during the evacuation.

To receive the Distinguished Service Cross.

Lieutenant Kenneth Edwards, R.N.

Performed good service at the landing and at the evacuation of Helles. Set a fine example to his men whilst assisting at salvage operations on Monitor M.30 under fire from enemy's guns.

Lieutenant Charles Leonard Fawell, R.N.V.R.

For consistent good service, often under heavy fire, whilst in command of motor gunboat in the Smyrna inner patrol.

The following awards have also been made:-

To receive the Distinguished Service Medal.

Chief Petty Officer Arthur James, O.N. 142389 (Po.).

Petty Officer Walter Alger, O.N. 162321 (Ch.).

Leading Seaman Harry T. Coleman, O.N. 231247 (Ch.).

Chief E.R.A. Samuel Fletcher, O.N. 269985 (Ch.).

Armourer's Mate Charles H. Hazel, O.N. M.4491 (Dev.).

First Writer Walter J.V. Keeble, O.N. 231499 (Dev.).

Ship's Steward William H. Bromidge, O.N. 345206 (Dev.).

Chief Motor Mechanic T. Thurburn, O.N., M.B.369.

Sergeant Albert V. Proctor, No. R.M.A./5508.

The following officers and men have been mentioned in despatches:-

Captain Michael H. Hodges, M.V.O., R.N.

Captain Francis Clifton Brown, R.N.

Captain Edmund C. Carver, R.N.

Commander Morton Smart, R.N.V.R.

Lieutenant-Commander (now Commander) Basil H. Piercy, R.N.

Lieutenant-Commander Claude P. Champion de Crespigny, R.N.

Lieutenant Commander Henry C. Summers, R.N.V.R.

Mr. Hugh F. Bevan, Gunner, R.N.

Mr. Charles E.A.W. Cox, Gunner (now Mate), R.N.

Mr. Leonard W. Brock, Gunner, R.N.

Mr. Philip J. Jones, Signal Boatswain.

Petty Officer Thomas Hoban, O.N. 192417 (Po.).

Petty Officer James Mather, O.N. 213655 (Ch.).

Petty Officer Lawrence V. Parsons, O.N. 191341 (Po.).

Leading Seaman Thomas G. Maylor, O.N. 238210 (Dev.).

Yeoman of Signals Samuel R.J. Hillier, O.N. 224951 (Ch.).
Chief E.R.A., 2nd Class, David Thompson, O.N. 272337 (Ch.).
Chief Stoker James W. French, O.N. 282587 (Ch.).
Chief Writer H.J.W. Gains, O.N. 343680 (Ch.).
Private John Gollop, R.M.L.I., No. Ply./12330.

Index

(1) Index of Persons

(2) Index of Military and Naval Units

Honour your First World War ancestors – at findmypast.co.uk

While many of us are aware that an ancestor fought in the First World War, all too often we know few details of their story – a date of death, a rumour that they fought in the Somme, photographs, letters and medals. Yet, even if they died on the battlefields of the Western Front, we can still piece together what their wartime lives were like, and learn how the fallen spent their final days.

Using records to piece together a soldier's career can be a complex process, but you'll find it easier if you make full use of all available public records. The best way to do so is to search them online. At *www.findmypast.co.uk* you'll find millions of digitised records to help you discover your heritage or flesh out the stories behind your family tree.

Britain's leading family history website covers a large range of military records, as well as everything from the census to parish registers, occupational records to institution registers. Simple to search and with original documents available on screen in seconds, it is both the ideal starting point for researchers and a brilliant resource to help more experienced genealogists uncover new information.

- Use a soldier's service record to pin-point the battles he fought in. Retrace his journey across the battlefields of the Western Front and beyond.

- Not all servicemen fought in the trenches. Follow the careers of relatives who joined the navy or the air force or were posted further afield through the records. Find records of Military Nurses.

- Did your ancestor win an award for an act of bravery? Medal recipients are well documented, and easy to uncover.

- If you're struggling to locate a soldier, then you may still find him in more unusual First World War records on findmypast.co.uk. Search biographies of veterans in The National Roll of the Great War; records of prisoners of war; or servicemen who received pioneering plastic surgery.

Read all about them!

Newspapers can act as an excellent source of background material for First World War research. They often reported detailed accounts of events on the home front and overseas; individual acts of bravery; and obituaries of servicemen. You can easily access scans of original news reports through a simple online search. Findmypast.co.uk is working with the British Library to digitise its collection of local British newspapers and already has over 6.5 million pages from 1710 to 1963 online. You can search these by using the names of ancestors, dates, locations and key words. Search the newspapers at **www.findmypast.co.uk/ search/newspapers**

Find out more about available records and pricing at
www.findmypast.co.uk